POLITICAL PROTEST
AND CULTURAL
REVOLUTION

POLITICAL PROTEST AND CULTURAL REVOLUTION

*Nonviolent
Direct Action
in the 1970s
and 1980s*

BARBARA EPSTEIN

UNIVERSITY OF CALIFORNIA PRESS
BERKELEY   LOS ANGELES   LONDON

University of California Press
Berkeley and Los Angeles, California

University of California Press, Ltd.
London, England

© 1991 by
The Regents of the University of California

First Paperback Printing 1993

Library of Congress Cataloging-in-Publication Data

Epstein, Barbara.
    Political protest and cultural revolution : nonviolent
direct action in the 1970s and 1980s / Barbara Epstein.
        p.   cm.
    Includes bibliographical references and index.
    ISBN 0-520-08433-0
    1. Radicalism—United States—Case studies.   2. Social
movements—United States—Case studies.   3. Direct
action—Case studies.   4. Nonviolence—Case studies.
I. Title.   HN90.R3E67   1991   90-44230
303.6′1—dc20   CIP

Printed in the United States of America

1 2 3 4 5 6 7 8 9

For Claudia

Contents

Abbreviations

Abalone	Abalone Alliance
AFSC	American Friends Service Committee
ACDC	Antinuclear Civil Disobedience Community
CDAS	Clams for Direct Action at Seabrook
Clamshell	Clamshell Alliance
Sane	Committee for a Sane Nuclear Policy
CNVA	Committee for Nonviolent Action
CORE	Congress of Racial Equality
DSOC	Democratic Socialist Organizing Committee
LNS	Liberation News Service
LAG	Livermore Action Group
NAANW	Nonviolent Action Against Nuclear Weapons
AQAG	A Quaker Action Group
SNCC	Student Nonviolent Co-ordinating Committee
SDS	Students for a Democratic Society

Acknowledgments

This book was made possible by all the people who shared their memories of the direct action movement with me, many of whom also put me up, fed me, and entrusted me with their collections of materials from the movement. For giving me access to such materials I would like to thank the staff of the Abalone Alliance, Nancy Alach, Aikos Barton, Murray Bookchin, Laura Booth, Guy Chichester, Fred Cook, Marcy Darnovsky, Crystal Gray, Anna Gyorgy, Harvey Halpern, Sharon Helsel, Susan Lawrence, Mary Moore, Jim Rice, Vicki Rovere, Noël Sturgeon, Susan Swift, and Cathy Wolff. I am grateful for the openness with which many movement participants discussed their experiences and views with me, in spite of differences among them and, in some cases, differences with me.

My greatest intellectual debt is to Jeffrey Escoffier, who worked with me as an editor while I was writing this manuscript, but in fact was more mentor than editor. He encouraged me to develop the theoretical implications of my account and pointed me toward relevant literatures. He helped me structure the book, define its themes, and formulate its arguments. Jeffrey's influence is pervasive; in places even the words are his. This would have been a very different, and much less interesting, book without his involvement. He is of course not responsible for its weaknesses.

I would like to thank Peter Dale Scott, who encouraged me to write this book in the first place. The book benefited from the comments and criticisms of many people (none of whom are likely to be entirely satisfied by the final version). Claudia Carr, Barbara Haber, Donna Haraway, Richard Healey, Michael Klare, David

Kotz, John Lofland, Margit Mayer, Osha Neumann, Jim O'Connor, Robbie Osman, Frances Fox Piven, Alan Steinbach, and Kay Trimberger all gave me helpful comments and criticisms at various stages. Larry Casalino gave the entire manuscript a thoughtful reading in its last stages. Richard Flacks, who read the manuscript for the University of California Press, was a helpful critic and editor. My understanding of the direct action movement was influenced by Marcy Danovsky's work on the relationship between direct action and the media and by Noël Sturgeon's work on the political philosophy of the direct action movement.

It is impossible to list all the people who contributed to this book indirectly, but I could not have written it without the support and stimulation of a number of linked political/intellectual communities. Friendships begun in the Livermore Action Group have continued in smaller networks of support and collective actions. My work benefited greatly from the encouraging and challenging atmosphere of the History of Consciousness Board at the University of California, Santa Cruz; from the interest that friends inside and outside the university took in the issues this book addresses; and from friendships that sustained me through this project. Many of the people listed above, who commented on the manuscript, were also important to me in these ways as well. I would especially like to thank Kay Trimberger for her sustained friendship, empathy, and ability to make constructive criticisms. Claudia Carr's friendship and support have been crucial. Osha Neumann and Anna de Leon have been both friends and comrades through this process. David Kotz gave me steady encouragement and support, as he has for the past twenty-five years or so; Elinor Gollay, as she has since we were both three. Michael Goldhaber's friendship helped sustain me through years of research and writing, as did my Santa Cruz household of Donna Haraway, Rusten Hogness, and Jaye Miller. I would also like to thank Mina and Tom Caulfield, Jim Clifford, Mike Davis, Paul and Andy Epstein, Candace Falk, Ilene Feinman, Marge Frantz, Billie Harris, Sharon Helsel, JJ and Gesundheit, Suzanne Jonas, Steven Joseph, Teresa di Lauretis, Gary Lease, Carollee Peterson, Carol Stack, Rich Weiner and the Mariposa community, Hayden White, Leon Wofsy, and Eli Zaretsky. I would like to thank Daniel Wenger for help with computer problems. The Research Committee of the University of California, Santa Cruz, Academic Senate provided financial support for the project. Finally, I was very lucky to have been able to work with Alain Hénon at the University of California Press.

Introduction

This book is about nonviolent direct action, a movement or perhaps more accurately a node linking a number of movements in the United States in the late 1970s and the 1980s. In each of these movements there has been a radical wing made up of people who believe in nonviolence, engage in political action through affinity groups, practice decision making by consensus, and employ the tactic of mass civil disobedience. The politics of direct action addresses a series of issues. Formulated first in the protest against nuclear power, it has spread to the peace movement, the ecology movement, the women's and gay and lesbian movements, the anti-intervention movement. The direct action wings of these movements have been loosely held together by a shared ideology that combines feminism, ecology, a form of anarchism that rests on grass roots democracy, and a leaning toward spirituality. In each of the issue-based movements in which it has appeared, nonviolent direct action has involved building community and trying to realize radically egalitarian values within the movement itself. Because direct action is as much about a particular social vision (and the practice of community building) as it is about the particular issues it has taken on, it has influenced the thinking of activists throughout the movements of the 1970s and 1980s.

I became involved in the direct action movement in 1983, after it was well under way. In June of that year I found myself in jail along with roughly a thousand other people who had blocked the road in front of the Lawrence Livermore Laboratory, the University of California's nuclear weapons research facility, about fifty

1

miles southeast of Oakland. The blockade had been organized by the Livermore Action Group (LAG), a San Francisco Bay Area organization with affiliated groups throughout Northern California dedicated to closing down Livermore and challenging the arms race through nonviolent direct action. I had also been among 1,300 people arrested at a previous LAG action the year before, but that time I did not go to jail; that time demonstrators were given the choice between signing police citations and receiving a fine or going to jail for a couple of nights, without further prosecution.

At the 1983 action I intended to go to jail rather than "cite out," but I expected that the experience would be similar to that of the year before and that I would be out of jail in two days at the most. This time, however, the judge decided to try to break the movement by keeping us in jail as long as possible. For the first three days no one was allowed to bail out except for medical reasons. We were then told that we could come to arraignment and receive sentences of two years' probation, restraining our participation in further civil disobedience. Most of us opted to stay in jail, holding out for eleven days, until we won an agreement that there would be no probation.

Mass jail experiences can be terrible or wonderful. Either people cannot get along with one another and agree about how to behave or what demands to make, and tensions escalate, or they work well together and an atmosphere of militant community builds. The jail experience of 1983 was of the latter sort. A spirit of solidarity emerged that sustained everyone through eleven days of uncertainty and difficult conditions: terrible food, sleep disturbed by lights and the guards' constant talk, cold nights without enough blankets. In the already overflowing Santa Rita Prison, circus tents were set up for us on the prison grounds, the women's tents by the freeway, the men's tents perhaps a quarter of a mile farther back. Because we had not yet been arraigned, we had access to telephones, a right that is lost after one has been arraigned and sentenced to a period in jail. Two banks of pay telephones, one on the women's side, one on the men's, allowed us to arrive at common strategies and to communicate with the outside world.

Anyone who planned to be arrested was required to take part in nonviolence training, a day-long workshop introducing participants to the movement's consensus decision-making process and teaching nonviolent responses to potential provocations. The workshops gave inexperienced members a short course in the movement's methods and language and a means of becoming part of an affinity group of ten to fifteen people, the movement's basic unit. Membership in an affinity group was a prerequisite for taking part in the blockade; most of the affinity groups that participated had existed for some time in this and the earlier antinuclear movement. Members of established affinity groups were already likely to know each other well; newly formed groups got to know one another quickly in jail. The affinity groups provided a context for talking issues through; they also served as a brake on disruptive impulses that might have emerged if we had gone through the jail experience as individuals rather than members of small groups of people responsible to one another.

In jail, affinity groups were organized by clusters. The clusters were not necessarily huge, because most affinity groups formed outside jail included men and women, and not everyone in a group participated in every action. Thus many groups had only a few members present in the jail. Whenever a decision had to be made (often several times a day) the clusters would meet to work out their views and arrive at consensus. Anyone who disagreed strongly with a collective decision had the right to block it, although it was understood that this power should not be used unless a fundamental moral issue was at stake. Each cluster sent a "spokes" to a "spokescouncil" that met with the clusters; runners were sent between clusters and spokescouncil, bringing questions to be addressed to the clusters and conveying the decisions to the spokescouncil. Spokes were rotated daily, so as to discourage the emergence of a leading group. But although there was no formal leadership, there was an informal group of people who were in fact looked to for leadership and who spent a good deal of time meeting among themselves and with others, trying to avoid problems and facilitate the operation of what we were coming to call the peace camp in the tents. When we were not meeting in our clusters or affinity groups, there were workshops and seminars on everything from how to fold paper cranes to the history of the Cold War. Some people spent a good deal of their time sunbathing. In the evenings, there were talent shows; on Emma Goldman's birthday, we held a party. First there were presentations about Emma Goldman's life and the history of anarchism, and then we danced to drum music improvised on empty aluminum storage cans.

But the authorities never left us to our own devices for very long. Twice a day the guards would round us up and herd us into one of the tents, where we would sit with our clusters in case quick decisions were needed. The sheriff would then appear at the front of the tent and announce through a bullhorn that the court was open and the judge was waiting for us to present ourselves for arraignment. Each time several women would leave the tent to board the bus for the court; our spokeswoman would then go to the front of the tent and present the refusal of the rest of us, pointing out that we had not yet been offered a satisfactory sentence. The same scene was played out simultaneously on the men's side.

The first time, as the women who had decided to leave boarded the bus, the rest of us, relieved that there were so few of them, rose and sang "Solidarity Forever." In the brief general meeting that followed, one woman expressed her dismay. To sing "Solidarity Forever" while women were leaving was, she pointed out, to exclude them from that solidarity; it was an implicit criticism of their action. A committee was formed to try to find some way of affirming our solidarity without implying that those who decided to leave were breaking it. The next day, when we were again invited to arraignment, women in pairs began to form a bridge with their outstretched arms; the bridge lengthened to include everyone who was not leaving. As the women who were leaving walked under this human bridge, the women who made up the bridge sang a song to them: "Listen, listen, listen, to our heart song, we will never forget you, we will never forsake you." Those who were part of the bridge were able to hug and kiss the departing women as they left. Only after the buses left did the rest of us sing "Solidarity Forever."

I do not believe that I had ever before seen a movement that actually went out of its way to affirm its solidarity with those who had decided to leave an action or in some other way separate themselves from the main course that the movement was taking. In the Old Left and the antiwar movement, both of which I had been part of, pressures to conform to the prevailing line had been routine. It often seemed that a collective sense of the movement's fragility brought about a particularly relentless policing of boundaries, and that the movement became a terrain for the exercise of an authoritarianism very much like what we protested in the society at large. Especially in the late sixties and early seventies, I became accustomed to being told by self-designated left and feminist authorities where the line lay between correct and incorrect ideas and behavior. It had seemed to me that unwillingness to accept individual differences, in views and in degree of commitment, and the sense of entitlement leaders exhibited in demanding sacrifices from participants, had been reasons for that movement's disintegration. The fact that the nonviolent direct action movement was able to treat internal difference with respect made me want to learn more about it. I had known very few of the women in the tents before finding myself in jail with them: there were few academics among them, and hardly anyone from the Bay Area intellectual/left/feminist circles with which I am familiar, and which tend to lay claim to the legacy of sixties activism.

The women in jail with me ranged in age from eighteen to eighty, though a majority were in their late twenties and thirties. (There was, in addition, one sixteen-year-old who had managed to disguise her age when she was arrested; she hid in one of the privies when the authorities tried to find her in order to release her.) There were large numbers of women who worked in health care, elementary and high school teaching, social work, or therapy of various kinds. The counterculture was well represented, and there were a substantial number of women who worked in health food stores or lived in rural communes. Lesbians claimed to make up about a third of the camp; they knew their own community well enough to provide a reliable estimate of their strength. The camp also contained many older women, some of them longtime peace activists, but also women from the suburbs who had never before been involved in protest but found the issues of war and disarmament compelling enough to induce them to go to jail.

Religious differences in the camp, like the generational differences, were more complementary than divisive. There were a number of Christian affinity groups, some made up of members of Bay Area congregations; one, involving younger women, from the radical Christian community outside the organized churches. There was also an affinity group of witches and a broader grouping of women who considered themselves Pagans. There were also many Jewish women, but we tended to be secular and, in a community that resonated with a variety of strong religious overtones, relatively silent. Feminism, pacifism, and ecology were all part of the ethos of the camp. Though there were many women who would have said, if asked, that they were in favor of socialism, anarchism provided the vocabulary for political discussion. If any one group brought all these tendencies together and set a common tone, it was the witches and the Pagans, whose rituals were open to anyone who cared to participate.

The extraordinary sense of community I witnessed in Santa Rita in 1983 was not limited to the women's tents. The experience of a roughly equal number of men (about five hundred women and five hundred men had been arrested) confined to tents perhaps a quarter of a mile away was parallel. Like the women, the men were organized into affinity groups and clusters of affinity groups; the men also appointed rotating spokes to a spokescouncil. The same decision-making procedure was followed, with the same flurry of meetings following every invitation by the sheriff to come to court and be arraigned. The bank of telephones made it possible to pass information quickly: each side knew what was being discussed on the other side and what decisions had been made. Information was also carried by the collective of movement lawyers who spent most of their time, while we were in jail, when they were not negotiating with the court, going from one side to the other, giving us information and asking for instructions. A quieter role was played by a woman doctor, a movement sympathizer and personal friend of many among both the women and the men, who managed to get herself appointed head of the medical team for the camp. In addition to treating minor ailments (and bringing in books, warm clothing, and other such items) she conveyed messages from one side to the other.

The many channels of communication between the two camps no doubt helped to establish the sense that we were all part of one camp, but it was nevertheless remarkable how similar was the experience in the men's and the women's tents. Men who went through this experience describe collective swings of mood that synchronized with those that took place on the women's side. The beginning of the second week of incarceration was a low point on both sides; pulling through it without losing many to arraignment gave both sides a sense of achievement that sustained solidarity until an agreement with the judge was arrived at. The men, like the women, were mostly white, mostly of at least middle-class background, but quite diverse in age and in culture. As on the women's side, countercultural core LAG activists coexisted easily with straighter, often older men, for many of whom this was the first arrest. As on the women's side, a "liberation school" was set up in one of the men's tents. Here the classes included one by Dan Ellsberg on U.S. national security policy. Many of the similarities between the two camps were a result of months of planning for the jail experience by a LAG collective. On both sides, there was a sizable core of people who had been through a number of mass jail experiences before: after the occupation of the Diablo Canyon nuclear plant in 1981 (under the aegis of the Abalone Alliance, the predecessor to LAG), the 1982 blockade of the Lawrence Livermore National Laboratory, and the blockade of the Vandenberg Air Force Base earlier in 1983. Through these experiences, a shared understanding had been constructed about how to handle the jail experience, how to organize the camp, how to confront the authorities, how to sustain morale and build solidarity so that the movement as a whole would be strengthened by the experience. In this regard the "solidarity ritual" of collectively honoring those who left the camp was an innovation of the 1983 jail experience. Designed by the women, it was quickly adopted by the men, though in a slightly altered form. The men, who were herded into a courtyard for the invitation to arraignment, stood back while those who were leaving stepped into the center. The men who were remaining clapped and cheered; some stepped into the center to embrace departing friends.

The often euphoric sense of community and solidarity was as strong on the men's side as it was on the women's. One of the women in the camp, whose husband was on the men's side, was a little taken aback when her husband told her in a telephone conversation that for the first time he felt that he had a family. Other men, recalling the experience, have described it as a high point of the sense of community in their experience in the movement. Osha Neumann, a core LAG activist who had been involved in the planning that went into the jail experience, suggested that part of the reason it went so well was that people felt good about being in jail. "It was sort of like Thoreau," he said. "It was a feeling of, why are you on the outside, not why are we here. It was precisely the right place to be." The jail experience was a high point for the movement, Osha argued, because it provided a rare opportunity to realize the movement's fundamental values, at least in a limited way.

The basis of LAG philosophy was an attempt to eliminate centers of power, to create a version of participation that was as complete as people could imagine; not to reproduce the errors of the earlier movement [of the sixties]. The experience confirmed some of what we believed, that people crave a certain kind of community. A community that is formed in the process of struggle is a very precious thing, and fulfills a lot of needs that are not met in daily life. That's a great strength for a movement, something that should be nourished. On the one hand people feel part of an intentional community, with a sense of genuine participation, support, love; on the other hand, the face of power shows itself. These can be key events. What was set up was a place where each person was confronted with a decision: whether to step over the line and get arrested or not. Making that decision was an important moment in people's lives. When people made the decision to step over the line and get arrested, they found that they also made the decision to step into a community that felt fulfilling and liberating.[1]

Robbie Osman, also a core LAG activist, described the jail experience as having been infused with a collective creativity and sense of humor that in ordinary circumstances finds little outlet. He recalled that often, for no apparent reason, the guards would begin herding the men from one place to another. During one such operation someone began mooing like a cow; soon everyone was mooing. "It was a way of making fun of the guards and making the situation ours that was nonhostile, nonaggressive," Robbie said.

There are some very rare times when you feel there's a real movement, you have the sense of people being out at the limits of their creativity and cooperation. You have a sense of the opportunities of community that have been denied us, so deeply denied that we almost forget that it's possible. Experiences like that create an incredible momentum for involving us with each other and committing ourselves to a common program. It just isn't created by analysis, even the best analysis. No analysis is enough unless you can get that chemistry going. And that was the potential that the jail experience held.[2]

It seemed to me that the movement that I had stumbled upon in jail was something new and vital. It presented a sharp contrast with the organized left with which I was familiar, the democratic-socialist and Marxist-Leninist organizations that remained from the movements of the sixties and that by 1983 seemed dated and all but lifeless. My sense was that LAG was beginning to construct a political language and style that was more appropriate to the issues that have become prominent in the eighties, such as nuclear war and the survival of the environment and of the human race, which so immediately involve fundamental values. The direct action movement seemed to have at least part of the answer to the question of how to break through the isolation of the left and speak to broader audiences. This persuaded me to continue to participate in the movement after I got out of jail and also to study the larger nonviolent direct action movement on which LAG was modeled.

Because it has been relatively invisible to people outside activist circles (except during mass actions, when thousands of people blockade or occupy a site and go to jail), it seems worthwhile to give a brief description of the main organizations within the direct action movement. It must be kept in mind, however, that the basic unit of the direct action movement is the affinity group. A description of the large direct action organizations, which have been centered in New England and California, leaves out all of the affinity groups in other parts of the country. Although the large organizations have held the most highly publicized actions, the movement also has included countless numbers of affinity groups, working singly or together, in other areas of the country.

The model for the structure and philosophy of the nonviolent direct action movement was the Clamshell Alliance. The Clamshell Alliance was founded in 1976 in New Hampshire after the Public Service Corporation announced its intention to go ahead with plans to build a nuclear power plant on the New Hampshire coast, in the town of Seabrook. The people who came together to form the Clamshell Alliance (which took its name from the clams threatened by the plant) included local environmental activists who had attempted to block the construction of the plant through elections and had decided that it was time to turn to direct action, former antiwar activists who had moved to rural northern New England in the early seventies, and two women from the American Friends Service Committee (AFSC) who saw the potential for a movement that would share the Quaker values of nonviolence and community. The Clamshell Alliance adopted the principle of nonviolence, agreed to make all decisions in small groups by consensus, and held a series of occupations of the Seabrook nuclear site. Many residents of Seabrook and other nearby towns were sympathetic to the Clamshell; many offered material support, and some became part of the movement themselves. But the base of the Clamshell was the radical ecological counterculture activists who had moved to the northern New England countryside when the antiwar movement waned. Clamshell actions also drew large numbers of young people from the cities, especially Boston.

After two small occupations in the summer of 1976 efforts were directed toward organizing a mass occupation, which was held in late April of the following year; roughly 24,000 people occupied the site, and 1,401, after being told to leave by Governor Thompson, remained to be arrested. Protesters were taken to seven armories throughout New Hampshire, where most remained for two weeks. The mass occupation of the site and the stay in the armories brought the Clamshell and the issue of nuclear power a great deal of publicity. In the armories, where decisions were made by consensus within and among affinity groups, and officials were forced to negotiate with a "leaderless" movement that put forward different representatives every day, a powerful spirit of community was created. After the 1977 occupation the Clamshell grew rapidly. A year later it was destroyed by a bitter internal split, but in the meantime it had trained many thousands of activists in the use of consensus process and massive nonviolent direct action, and it inspired the formation of dozens of other alliances against nuclear power and other environmental threats elsewhere in the country.

The largest of these was the Abalone Alliance, also organized in 1976, in Northern California. The target of the Abalone was the Diablo Canyon nuclear plant near San Luis Obispo on the central California coast, which Pacific Gas and Electric (PG & E) had been preparing for some time to put on-line. Mothers for Peace, a San Luis Obispo group that had formed in opposition to the war in Vietnam, had fought against the plant. Leading peace activists in Northern California, as in New England including members of the AFSC, saw nuclear power as an opportunity to build a nonviolent movement that might, in time, take on the issue of nuclear weapons, and perhaps move on to the broad aim of nonviolent revolution. The Abalone Alliance modeled itself on the Clamshell Alliance: organization based on local groups, the use of consensus decision making, and a strict adherence to nonviolence. Like the Clamshell, the Abalone brought together two constituencies: people in and near San Luis Obispo who wanted to get rid of the plant, and radical ecologically oriented activists, mostly from Northern California, many of them part of the substantial counterculture that remained from the sixties and early seventies.

Like the Clamshell, the Abalone held an escalating series of occupations at the Diablo plant. The Abalone decided to refrain from calling a massive occupation until the license to operate the plant was granted. Meanwhile public awareness of the dangers of nuclear power increased enormously after the accident at Three Mile Island, March 28, 1979. In September of 1981 the Diablo Canyon plant was licensed and the Abalone called for a massive occupation; over a two-week period, waves of protesters entered the plant site; in all there were more than 1,900 arrests. On the day that the occupation was ended, a PG & E engineer announced that he had found a crucial error in the plant's blueprints, requiring that the plant be closed down indefinitely for major repairs. Protesters believed that the questions they raised about nuclear power might have encouraged the engineer to check the blueprints, and that the occupation created an atmosphere in which he could make such an announcement. Whether or not this was true, the occupation of Diablo helped turn public opinion against nuclear power. It also created a small army of activists trained in the philosophy and process of nonviolent direct action.

The Abalone had avoided the internal battles that had torn the Clamshell apart, because the Abalone was in California, where movement activists in general are less eager to join internal ideological battles than their counterparts on the East Coast. Abalone members also watched what happened to the Clamshell and tried to build greater flexibility into their own organization. By the early eighties, the nuclear industry was clearly in decline, partly because protest had been effective, partly because of its own technical and economic difficulties. Activists began to turn to other issues, and the Abalone, while formally remaining in existence, ceased to be a center of political activity. Some affinity groups disbanded; others turned to new issues, disarmament in particular.

The next major focus of the direct action movement was nuclear weapons. While Diablo protesters were in jail, those interested in applying the philosophy and tactics of nonviolent direct action to the Livermore Laboratory were invited to sign a list. The result of this effort was the Livermore Action Group (LAG), which had its office in Berkeley and was strongest in the Bay Area, but inherited affinity groups from all over California that had participated in the Abalone Alliance. LAG quickly became the militant cutting edge of the disarmament movement in the Bay Area, holding a series of blockades of the Livermore Laboratory that drew large numbers of people and considerable media attention. LAG attracted a more diverse constituency than the Abalone (or for that matter the Clamshell). Especially in the context of the Reagan administration's belligerent anti-Soviet rhetoric, the arms race drove many people to protest who had never done so before. Many religious people, and many middle-aged, middle-class people, especially women, saw civil disobedience as the only effective way to register their opinions. Though the radical counterculture was the source of most of LAG's day-to-day activists, mass actions included large numbers of older and more established people, some of whom maintained their affinity groups outside jail and continued to participate in LAG activities and in the peace movement more broadly.

From the formation of the Clamshell on, the direct action movement has identified strongly with feminism. The terms "consensus" and "feminist process" have been generally used interchangeably; the movement has seen itself as developing a feminist way of doing politics. At the same time that the movement was turning toward the issue of peace, lesbians were entering the movement in large numbers (the timing having to do with the fact that the lesbian community was secure enough for lesbians to feel comfortable entering mixed movements). Many women, lesbian and straight, believed that the basis for a women's peace movement existed. The feminist orientation of the direct action movement as a whole was strengthened by the appearance of a specifically feminist wing of the movement around the issue of disarmament, through the organization of a number of women's peace actions and peace camps. In LAG, a women's caucus was organized that held its own actions.

After several years of protests that were very effective in raising public awareness around the arms race, LAG declined in much the same way that the Abalone had before it; affinity groups disbanded or turned their attention to new issues. The extreme belligerence of the Reagan administration toward the Soviet Union met so much public opposition, in the United States and Western Europe, that it had been forced to back down at least to some degree. By Reagan's second term in office the focus of his international efforts was the assertion of U.S. power in the Third World, especially in Central America. Anti-intervention became the emphasis of the direct action movement. Affinity groups that had come together in LAG now concentrated on protesting aid to the Contras and arms shipments to El Salvador. The religious community (mostly Christian denominations, with some religious Jews) played a particularly prominent role in nonviolent direct action against intervention—the Christians largely because of their identification with liberation theology and the Jews because of parallels with the Holocaust. The direct action wing of the anti-intervention movement has not revolved around any one organization, but Pledge of Resistance and Witness for Peace, both "faith-based," have been important centers for nonviolent civil disobedience, and both have employed consensus process.

The Clamshell, the Abalone, LAG, and other direct action organizations have each been part of two distinct movements (or perhaps more accurately, two distinct arenas within the movement for social change). Each has been part of the nonviolent direct action movement, which includes all these groups and more.

Each has also been a center of radical politics in an issue-oriented movement that includes organizations with a variety of methods and perspectives. In each of these issue-oriented movements, the direct action element is smaller than the more conventional, electorally oriented element. In the environmental movement as a whole, mainstream organizations such as the Sierra Club have played a larger role in discouraging the further development of nuclear power than the Clamshell and the Abalone. The Nuclear Freeze did more than LAG (and other direct action groups) to shift the Reagan administration away from its confrontational stance toward the Soviet Union. By taking a more militant approach than other organizations, direct action groups have provided a cutting edge. Mass civil disobedience has drawn public attention to the dangers of nuclear power, the arms race, and other issues and inspired others to take some action themselves, even if it does not involve the same level of risk.

This book is not a study of the nonviolent direct action movement as a whole, but of a relatively tightly linked set of organizations within a larger field, one that stretches back in time as well as includes groups contemporaneous with those examined here. Since the 1930s at least the American peace movement has included groups that were pacifist in philosophy and willing to risk arrest on behalf of their beliefs. In the late forties and fifties radical pacifism was a major part of the peace movement, but that movement as a whole was quite small. The early civil rights movement (which had important links to the radical pacifist movement, and was also influenced by Gandhian nonviolence) was the first example, in the United States, of a mass movement committed to nonviolent direct action. The civil rights movement was a major source of inspiration for the organizations that I have looked at.

The civil rights movement also inspired the growing peace and student movements of the late fifties and early sixties, and helped to bring ideas of nonviolent direct action to the early New Left. As the relatively gentle early New Left turned into a larger and angrier antiwar movement, nonviolent direct action was largely supplanted by more strident approaches but never entirely lost. It was maintained by the pacifist wing of the movement, especially by Quakers and other radical Christians. In the early 1970s the influence of nonviolent direct action grew: the massive May Day blockade of the Pentagon in 1971 largely came out of the efforts of the nonviolent movement and followed its precepts. On the West Coast, the Institute for the Study of Nonviolence in Palo Alto provided support for mass actions employing nonviolent direct action against the war in a number of cities. Nonviolence was not restricted to white middle-class activists. The largely Chicano United Farm Workers adhered to the philosophy of nonviolence in its campaign for farm workers' rights, employing direct action along with other tactics.

The direct action organizations at which I have looked emerged when interest in nonviolence was growing in some sectors of the broader movement for social change. These organizations brought nonviolent direct action to issues of nuclear energy, nuclear arms, and U.S. intervention in the Third World, making this philosophy and method the basis for mass actions, for organizations that at times took on mass proportions, and for the creation of a political culture that has had wide-ranging influence. The direct action movement's approach to politics has been fresh and appealing, in contrast to a certain staleness elsewhere on the left, and has enabled the movement to draw upon constituencies that have been leery of more traditional left politics. Mass civil disobedience has given a voice to those who despaired of making themselves heard through conventional channels. The movement has drawn on what is evidently a widely felt desire to create community and collectively to affirm values of nonviolence and equality, which, in the late twentieth century, have often been in short supply.

I wrote this book partly to persuade activists who espouse a more conventional style of protest that the direct action movement should be taken seriously and that there are lessons to be learned from it. The leaders of electorally oriented organizations for social change have tended to see direct action groups as unwelcome competition. In the mass membership organizations of the peace movement, for instance, although ideas of consensus and nonviolent direct action pervaded local groups, national leadership often regarded these as incorrect views that must be fought. But the ideas of the direct action movement have spread through the activist bases of the social movements of the eighties and have profoundly affected the thinking of a new generation

of activists, as well as many older people who are new to political
activism. These ideas are likely to remain an important influence
within the social movements of the late twentieth-century United
States. It would be a pity to repeat the mistakes of the early sixties, when veterans of the Old Left denounced the emerging New
Left as incorrect and misguided.

The main purpose of this book, however, is not to defend the
direct action movement, but to explore the questions raised by
the prefigurative, utopian approach to politics the movement has
represented. The direct action movement has been about cultural
revolution, its aim not only to transform political and economic
structures but to bring to social relations as a whole the values of
egalitarianism and nonviolence. In particular I wanted to look at
the question of whether a movement that holds such a vision and
tries to express its values in its own structure and actions can
sustain itself over time and be effective in helping to change society. In each of the major organizations of the direct action
movement, some people have been most interested in the immediate objectives (preventing the operation of a particular nuclear
plant, for instance, or, on a broader scale, building a movement
capable of stopping nuclear power altogether) and have seen direct action as a means to that end. But in each case the great
majority of participants have seen the specific objectives of the
movement as inseparable from a vision of an ecologically balanced, nonviolent, egalitarian society. To most movement activists, a vision of the future is meaningful only if it is acted upon
in the present, even if doing so disrupts daily life and produces
organizations that often do not function smoothly within a political structure based on different values.

The impulse toward a transformation of society that goes beyond political and economic structures to a broad redefinition of
social values has been a current throughout the history of the
American left, sometimes relatively prominent, sometimes submerged. Conceptions of equality have always been part of the
impulse toward cultural revolution, but they have not always taken
the same form. In the direct action movement, "cultural revolution" has been framed in terms of what I call utopian democracy:
a decentralized society based on communities governed by mutual participation of equals, communities in which violence is not

used and neither special privilege nor hierarchies of power exist. Many social movements define themselves in relation to particular aims and judge their success by their ability to accomplish those aims: organizing workers and gaining rights for labor, winning equal rights for particular groups, protecting the environment. The visionary core of the direct action movement has been expressed only partially in each of the movement's specific issues. Because the movement's vision has been most fully expressed in its organizational structure and practice—consensus and nonviolent direct action—these have been the main components of its identity. When the requirements of effective action have collided with these principles, the principles have generally won out. Over time there has been some redefinition of consensus process, and at times tactics other than direct action have been used, but most movement participants have seen changes that might undercut these commitments as threatening the movement itself.

It has been commonly assumed, on the American left at least, that cultural revolution has an internal logic that would be distorted if it were harnessed by a strategy or linked to a project, a particular social vision. If egalitarianism means that everyone's views have equal merit, then adopting a particular project and strategy (and rejecting or subordinating others) seems to go against the movement's values. There is a broad consensus within the direct action movement about what kind of society people want, but there is also a widespread reluctance even to consider the question of strategy. Some of the Christians in the movement see discussion of strategy as a form of blasphemy: one simply acts on one's conscience and the results are in the hands of God. This view intersects with the tendency of many others to see political action as consisting of acting out one's vision and hoping that others will join in or at least begin to see things differently. To interject strategic considerations into what might be called the politics of imagination or of experience seems to many to dilute its power. The anarchist, antiauthoritarian impulse that runs through the direct action movement, and through the larger tendency toward cultural revolution, is offended by the idea of bringing spontaneity under the discipline of strategy.

The politics of imagination has often given movements for social change a special power. Civil rights activists forced the American public to confront the reality of racism by acting as if blacks had equal rights. The sight of blacks being beaten and arrested for walking down a public road in plain daylight aroused a level of public fury that could not have been tapped by a speech or a political program. Occupying a nuclear plant site or blockading an arms-producing laboratory is a little different in that it involves breaking the law rather than demonstrating the unjust application of the law, but is based on the same idea of awakening public concern by acting on one's conscience. The problem with a movement that defines itself through direct action rather than seeing action as part of a strategy is that it can dissolve into a series of tableaux with no particular direction.

This book is intended not only as a contribution to discussions among activists but also as part of a debate with left and feminist intellectuals of my generation. The direct action movement's rejection of strategy is an expression of a much broader political and intellectual current. The attraction to cultural revolution, and the idea that culture is a substitute for strategy, has been an important current in the movements of the sixties and beyond; it has become dominant among left and feminist intellectuals. In the late seventies and eighties the great majority of critical intellectuals have been drawn to cultural studies. Especially under the influence of postmodernism, an intellectual movement that calls for exposing and questioning the assumptions behind all accepted ideas, the critique of culture has come to be seen as in itself political practice.

Separating cultural criticism from strategy means substituting the process of cultural transformation for consciously directed cultural revolution. Traditionally, the Marxist left at least paid little attention to the cultural arena. In the twenties and thirties Antonio Gramsci, the Italian Communist leader and Marxist theorist, argued that developed, consumer capitalism required the loyalty of the population to function smoothly and through mass education and other vehicles had found ways of developing such loyalty. The left, Gramsci argued, could not hope to defeat capitalism until it won the adherence of the working class and other sections of the population to a different social order. Thus mass culture and ideology had become a crucial terrain of struggle. The left must put forward a hegemonic project. It must challenge the existing organization of society with its alternative conception and it must wage a battle for the legitimacy of its values and worldview. It was through Gramsci that culture came to be understood as a legitimate object of concern on the left.

Gramsci linked the critique of culture with a project and a strategy. In the seventies and eighties the dominant trend among American left intellectuals (and to some degree Western Europeans as well) was to detach the critique of culture from the concept of a hegemonic project. In Gramsci's conception, the struggle for hegemony, or cultural revolution, involves a worldview consciously constructed by particular agents. During the same period the dominant trend among American critical intellectuals (and to some degree among Europeans as well) was to break the link between culture and strategy. The postmodernist conception puts forward instead a random process of cultural transformation, in which there is no conscious direction and no conception of agency. Ernesto Laclau and Chantal Mouffe, for instance, in their book *Hegemony and Socialist Strategy*,[3] take the radical democracy of the new social movements as a model in their search for an answer to the problems of Marxism. They argue for a decentered politics involving tenuous, shifting alliances among social agents whose own identities are always in question, and an avoidance of any attempt to find a unifying project. This model becomes not just a recognition of diversity but a celebration of fragmentation. It implies endorsing the chaos of late capitalism, renouncing any effort to take control over it or consciously to try to create something better. The postmodernist spirit, which has become dominant among intellectuals on the left, involves an appreciation of many of the qualities of the direct action movement, especially its spontaneity and imagination. But it reinforces the movement's most crippling weaknesses, its avoidance of strategy and its disdain for lasting organizational structure.

A note on method: because the direct action movement is politically and culturally unconventional, conventional methods of studying it would not have worked very well. In combining the roles of participant and observer, I have abandoned any effort at neutrality (though not at accuracy, or at some degree of critical distance, both of which I have tried to achieve). I believe that in a movement such as this, active engagement is the most reliable path to understanding. This movement has few if any texts. It would not be possible to base a study of the movement on its documents, because they are not of central importance. The various occupation handbooks are useful sources, but they do not provide a key to understanding the movement in the way that, for instance, the Port Huron Statement does in relation to SDS. There is no point in basing an account of the movement on its theory, because there is relatively little of it; it is mostly implicit in the movement's practice. In this arena, actions and speech count for more than the written word. Because the movement has developed its own language, interviews would be confusing if taken out of the context of the movement's practice. In order to be understood in any depth the worldview of the movement, the meaning of its actions, needs to be seen from the inside. I believe that in general one can learn more about a movement from the inside than from the outside, and that a position of engagement and critical identification tends to be more fruitful than objectivity achieved by maintaining a distance. It is not possible to study all movements this way: this method obviously cannot be applied to movements of the past or to those one does not sincerely support. But where it is possible, this method can have great advantages.

Chapter One

Protest in
the 1960s and 1980s

The Blocked Cultural Revolution

Cultural revolution, the transformation not just of economic or political structures but of the ideas that govern social life as a whole, has been a continuing theme in protest politics in the United States, sometimes prominent, sometimes submerged. Cultural revolution flowered in the movements of the 1960s. It gave those movements their distinctive character, distinguished the New Left from the Old, and held out the promise of a politics appropriate to the postwar era. But cultural revolution was a widely felt impulse rather than a coherent political direction. By the end of the decade it was being undermined, first by the revival of more traditional left politics within the antiwar movement and then, in the early seventies, by the beginnings of a national shift to the right in politics and culture. In the late seventies and early eighties, the direct action movement took up the task of cultural revolution and tried to give it greater coherence, to articulate it as a philosophy of political protest, and to draw out its implications for forms of organization and styles of political action.

The importance of this movement does not lie in its size, which was relatively small, especially in the United States, but in the fact that its ideas about revolution and revolutionary practice influenced activists in many of the movements of the late seventies and eighties. The direct action movement achieved this influence by drawing upon and developing the egalitarianism, feminism, and ecology that were all important strands within earlier movements. By the early 1970s these elements were becoming intertwined within a diffuse countercultural left, but had yet to be brought together and given clear political expression. The main accomplishment of the direct action movement is that it has taken the first step toward articulating a politics of cultural revolution that unites these currents with the philosophy of nonviolence.

Understanding the direct action movement of the late seventies requires understanding the efforts toward cultural revolution of the sixties and how they were derailed. Because movements confront different tasks at different times, there is no timeless model of correct revolutionary theory or practice; they must continually reconstruct their conceptions of revolutionary politics if they are to remain vital. In the United States, movements of different eras have tended to condemn one another: New Left activists charged the movements of the thirties with having failed to press for revolution; veterans of the thirties accused the movements of the sixties of having abandoned the working class. In the eighties, many activists whose formative experience was in the sixties looked at the direct action movement with skepticism, if not hostility, and argued that it was taking cultural revolution too far. The history of the left in the United States has been cyclical: periods of flourishing activism have been followed by periods in which protest activity is almost invisible. The tendency of each generation to cling to the perspective developed during its formative years has made it difficult for generations to communicate and for movements to place their own experiences in a historical perspective. The tendency of each movement to understand only its own present has stood in the way of developing a flexible revolutionary politics, which requires not only a commitment to bringing about change but an understanding of historical context.[1]

The movements of the thirties can be seen as a baseline for the politics of the postwar era: they established the importance of class, especially of the organization of the working class. The experience of the thirties also brought the relationship between protest movements and the state into focus: it was the pressure of the organized working class and its allies that led to the creation of the welfare state. Both the centrality of the working class and the orientation toward the state have become problematic for postwar movements. In the sixties some activists abandoned the conception of class and turned to race or gender instead; others argued for redefining the working class. In the late seventies and eighties, the direct action movement has tried to move away from a focus on the state, both by placing the transformation of culture at the center of political activity and by envisioning a revolution that does not entail seizing state power.

Because the experience of the 1930s has been the ground for various alternative conceptions of revolutionary politics in the postwar period, I start this chapter with a reminder that the politics of the thirties were in many ways appropriate for their times and that some aspects of those politics continue to be valid. The main argument of the chapter is that in the postwar era broad social changes made cultural revolution even more urgent than it had been in the thirties. I argue that the movements of the 1960s began to respond to this need but that by the end of the decade cultural revolution had been stalled, largely by internal problems. In making this argument I am disagreeing with a leading interpretation of why the movements of the sixties failed, namely, that they turned toward revolution at all. In the early sixties, that argument goes, student activists in the North and civil rights workers in the South were on the right track in demanding only that the United States live up to its democratic aspirations. In the later sixties, frustrated by repeated failures, many activists decided that the changes they wanted could not be accomplished within the existing system but required revolution. The turn toward revolution was a mistake, in this account, because it lacked support and because it was a turn toward violence that deepened the existing divisions between the radical movements and the rest of the American public.

I believe, however, that revolution was an appropriate goal, even though it was vaguely conceived and even if there was little chance of its being accomplished in the near future. The movements of the early sixties were small; only in the late sixties, under the rubrics of both opposition to the war and revolutionary politics, did the movement expand to encompass almost a whole generation of young people. The widely felt desire for revolution was a response to the facts that society was changing rapidly and

that many people, especially the young, were torn by contradictory pressures and alienated from a social order that seemed unable to satisfy their most fundamental needs. That most of these
people had a clearer idea of what they did not like about the
existing society than of what kind of society they wanted, that the
conception of revolution remained amorphous, did not mean that
the demand was meaningless or mistaken. Old conceptions of
revolution were no longer adequate, but the movement had not
yet found the words for a new conception. What was called for
was a theory of revolution that was cultural as well as economic
and that pointed to the need for revolution without raising the
expectation that it would happen quickly. Activists of the early
sixties hesitated to talk about revolution in part because they
understood that in the United States, in the late twentieth century, the idea needed a different definition from that used in
other times and places. The activists of the late sixties often for-
got this fact and looked for solutions in traditional, largely economic conceptions of change, imagining that revolution was on
the horizon. They reached for the models most readily available,
which were mostly either outdated or based on foreign experience. The conditions for imminent revolution were not present
in the United States in the late sixties. It was a mistake to take
widespread opposition to the war in Vietnam as an indication of
popular desire for revolutionary change; the desire was in fact
limited to a sector of young people. Attempts to impose an inappropriate conception of revolution were bound to fail and, to the
extent that the movement was fueled by the expectation of imminent revolution, to destroy the movement.

The Class Politics of the Thirties

The movements of the 1930s were propelled by the Depression.
Their tasks were shaped by the inadequacy of state structures to
control its effects and the resulting opportunities for the industrial working class to organize and for the labor movement and
its largely first- and second-generation immigrant constituency to
gain some degree of acceptance. In the late twenties and the early
thirties, the Communist Party imagined that a socialist revolution
could take place in the United States. The policies of the so-called

Third Period (based on the 1928 Communist International's prediction that the international capitalist system would soon enter a crisis that would be the context for worldwide socialist revolution) called for building revolutionary organizations and denouncing and refusing to cooperate with liberals and Socialists. At first the depth of the crisis caused by the Depression seemed to give these policies some legitimacy. Militant politics helped the Party to build organizations of the unemployed and to attract blacks and intellectuals. In establishing unions outside the framework of the American Federation of Labor (AFL), Communists gained experience in organizing industrial unions among the workers the AFL shunned—the unskilled and semiskilled, many of them immigrants.

Roosevelt's New Deal policies, however, proved enormously successful, at least in their ability to generate confidence in the system. Whatever revolutionary prospects might have existed in the early years of the Depression were undermined, and socialism faded from the agenda of the American left, which the Communist Party had come to dominate. The failure of attempts at socialist revolution elsewhere as well, especially in Germany, and the growth of fascism persuaded the Comintern to abandon the policies of the Third Period, which threatened to isolate Communists from the mass movements that surrounded them. Instead, the Communist movement adopted the policies of the Popular Front, which put the revolution off into the future and focused on winning a series of democratic reforms. In the United States, this tactic meant organizing basic industry through the creation of the Congress of Industrial Organizations (CIO) and winning a place for the labor movement in the political process, constructing a welfare system, and gaining legitimacy for the industrial working class in American life.[2]

The Communist Party and the left, by feeding ideas to the labor movement and the New Deal, helped to make American society more democratic by giving more of its members some social standing and by winning greater acceptance for a definition of American culture as multiethnic and multiracial. But these changes did not challenge capitalism or the hierarchical assumptions underlying political and social life in the United States. The Party could not sustain the revolutionary quality of its politics in the early thirties because it was caught up in nonrevolutionary social processes and also because, as one of the leading forces in a democratic but nonrevolutionary transformation of American society, it became a vehicle for upward mobility and Americanization. For many young immigrants from the ghettos, the Communist Party was the route to involvement in politics or in intellectual or artistic circles.[3] Through the thirties and the early forties, it was at the center of an arena in which one did not have to choose between left politics and career aspirations: they went together. This fact no doubt helped to pave the way for the bitter anti-Communism of many who left the Party in the late forties and fifties. With the advent of McCarthyism, membership in the Party suddenly ceased to be a way of finding a place in society and instead became a threat to one's career and to one's acceptance as an American.[4]

The move to abandon the left after the thirties and early forties was not confined to former Party members who wished to dissociate themselves from Stalinism or were afraid that their earlier associations would throw their respectability into question. Postwar Cold War policies abroad seemed linked with prosperity at home, and most of the labor movement was willing to exchange its radicalism for higher wages, better working conditions, and improved status. Because the left of the thirties had not seriously challenged the hierarchical culture of American society, the legitimacy of the rules governing the exercise of power, it was bound to collapse when many constituent groups and individuals were incorporated into the mainstream. The successful organization of the CIO, its emergence as a major political force in the thirties and later, and the prosperity of the years immediately after World War Two made it possible for formerly marginal immigrants and children of immigrants to enter the central institutions of American society—political parties, higher education, entertainment and the arts, even the business world. In the conservative, patriotic atmosphere of the postwar years, many came to believe that it was necessary to leave radicalism behind to be an American.

In asserting the rights of labor and the legitimacy of a variety of cultures within American society, the Communist Party and the broader left of the thirties drew upon important strands in the legacy of American protest, but they set aside other elements within the same tradition. The protest movements of the late nineteenth and early twentieth centuries had been built on native-born Americans and relatively recent immigrants; these groups brought quite different histories and worldviews to the left.[5] Native-born American radicals tended to be farmers, skilled workers, or the self-employed; they shaped the politics and culture of Populism, the Knights of Labor, feminism and the larger women's movement, and a wide range of reform movements often infused with a Christian sensibility that shaded into utopianism.

The radicalism that shaped the movements of the emerging industrial working class, made up mostly of recent immigrants, had a quite different sensibility: oriented to questions of class, more politically pragmatic, grounded in Marxism and related intellectual traditions of socialism, it was in some ways less experimental than native-born radicalism, less open to feminism, spirituality, and utopianism. The division between the two cultures of the left, around the turn of the century, was not hard and fast. The two tendencies coexisted as separate organized elements within the Socialist Party. On the West Coast, where immigrants and native-born Americans worked and lived together, the Industrial Workers of the World (IWW) organized both and constructed a radical culture combining class focus and socialist thought with a utopian radicalism in which there was even room for feminism.[6] In New York, the Women's Trade Union League succeeded for a few years in creating a political space in which immigrant women trade unionists and their native-born allies came together around the issues of feminism and the organization of working women.[7] But especially in the cities of the East Coast and the Midwest, where the working class was overwhelmingly a product of recent immigration, the tension between the two sides of the American left tradition remained. The movements of the 1930s drew upon the traditional emphasis on class and the language of Marxism, because organizing the working class provided most of the momentum for the growth of the left as a whole. Meanwhile, issues of gender were put aside, and the spiritually oriented and utopian side of American radicalism receded.

Cultural radicalism reappeared in the American left in the radical pacifist current that became prominent in the peace movement during and after World War Two. The peace movement had been large in the early thirties but dwindled as the threat of fascism grew in Europe and increasing numbers of Americans were persuaded that the United States' entry into the war was necessary to save democracy. In view of popular enthusiasm for the war, sustaining pacifism more or less required a certain kind of obstinacy, a willingness to disregard popular opinion and follow one's conscience with little confidence that one's views would prevail, that was more common among radical pacifists than elsewhere in the peace movement. During the war and through the fifties the peace organizations that survived drew radical pacifists who were not only opposed to war but critical of the social structure and culture that sustained it. Many were determined to act on their beliefs by constructing egalitarian and self-sufficient communities that did not contribute to a military-dominated economy. Other radical pacifists saw these communities as too limited in their impact, but worked to build movements for disarmament and racial equality on the same values. The radical egalitarianism of the peace and social justice movements of the late fifties and early sixties was largely inspired by the radical pacifists, as was the direct action movement two decades later.

During World War Two, radical pacifism was centered less in the peace organizations themselves than in the Civilian Public Service camps and the jails, where men who refused to go to war confronted harsh authorities, and found a strong sense of community. A generation of radical pacifists emerged from the war experience ready to challenge the cautious older leadership of the existing peace movement. The most important organizations were the religiously inclined Fellowship of Reconciliation and its secular offshoot, the War Resister's League. Though there were radical pacifists in both organizations (A. J. Muste, for instance, the leading spokesman for radical pacifism, was prominent in both), many were reluctant to support militant pacifist actions. Veterans of the jails and the camps demanded a politics of nonviolent direct action. To avoid participating in a military economy, some went further and formed self-sufficient rural communities. The radical pacifist impulse led to the formation of the short-lived Conference on Non-Violent Revolutionary Socialism, dedicated to socialism, anarchism, and pacifism. Peacemakers, formed in

1948, was dedicated to civil disobedience and "cells" devoted to simple living and the practice of nonviolent values. The founders of Peacemakers hoped that these cells would be bases for peace action, but in fact they turned inward and played little role in the development of an activist peace movement.

Other radical pacifists meanwhile worked to build organizations they hoped would become the basis for mass nonviolence, ultimately for nonviolent revolution. In 1941, radical pacifists played a major role in the formation of the Congress of Racial Equality (CORE), an interracial organization dedicated to applying Gandhian ideas of nonviolent direct action to racial discrimination. In 1947 CORE sponsored a "Journey of Conciliation," in which CORE members traveled through the South to test a Supreme Court ruling against state laws requiring segregated seating in interstate travel. CORE maintained a close relationship with the Fellowship of Reconciliation. These organizations fostered a network of radical pacifists who were concerned with both racial justice and peace and hoped to build a nonviolent, ultimately revolutionary, movement. When a mass civil rights movement began to build among southern blacks, with the Montgomery bus boycott of 1956, nonviolent direct action was adopted virtually without debate. Martin Luther King was already familiar with the thinking of Gandhi, and the black churches, the social basis of the movement, were open to militant nonviolent radicalism. The network of radical pacifists around CORE and the Fellowship of Reconciliation easily became part of the civil rights movement; Bayard Rustin in particular played an important role. In the otherwise discouraging political atmosphere of Cold War America, the radical pacifists were greatly encouraged by the emergence of the civil rights movement. Radical nonviolence achieved its greatest influence with the wave of student sit-ins at lunch counters in 1960 and the subsequent formation of the Student Nonviolent Co-ordinating Committee (SNCC). The genius of SNCC was its nonviolent but militant defense of the right of blacks to exercise fundamental constitutional rights. Nonviolent resistance to violence from police and other whites and the policy of dramatizing protest by refusing bail conferred enormous moral authority and made SNCC the militant cutting edge of the civil rights movement.

In the bleak landscape of the American left of the late fifties, radical pacifism provided the strongest intellectual basis for a new politics. The journal *Liberation,* founded by Muste, Rustin, and others in 1956, served as the focus for the radical pacifist network; it applauded the civil rights movement and tried to foster the development of a movement for peace and disarmament. There were other efforts to stimulate new thinking on the left in the late fifties, the formation of the journal *Dissent* being the most important. But *Dissent* remained more distant from activism than *Liberation,* and it also tended to support Cold War foreign policies and anti-Communism, both of which *Liberation* rejected. The radical pacifists connected with *Liberation* recognized that for the time being at least a mass peace movement would require cooperation with liberals and traditional pacifists who were not willing to engage in direct action. A meeting of peace activists in 1957, including liberals and traditional pacifists oriented toward electoral activity and education and radical pacifists who stressed the role of nonviolent civil disobedience, produced an agreement that a strong peace movement required a division of labor among mutually supportive organizations. Two organizations resulted: the Committee for a Sane Nuclear Policy (Sane) and Nonviolent Action Against Nuclear Weapons (NAANW), later renamed the Committee for Nonviolent Action (CNVA). Radical pacifism was seen as providing the leading edge for what it was hoped would be an expanding peace movement.

The two major sources of inspiration for the radical pacifism of the fifties were various forms of Christian nonresistance, especially (but by no means exclusively) the Society of Friends, and the example of Gandhi and his philosophy of nonviolent resistance. The Society of Friends encompassed political views from conservatism to radicalism; since World War One the American Friends Service Committee had attracted Quakers who understood their religion as requiring social activism. While the AFSC was itself politically neutral and included many members who were drawn simply by the opportunity for social service, it also provided a base for radical Quakers. Partly because of their institutional base and their access to resources, partly because they represented a long-established philosophy of pacifism and a well worked out process of consensus decision making, AFSC members played an important role in the peace and civil rights movements of the late fifties and early sixties. Two decades later AFSC members brought the same resources to the formation of the Clamshell Alliance and the organizations that followed it. Here the Quaker influence was felt through the involvement not only of AFSC members but also of the Movement for a Nonviolent Society, formed by Quakers and ex-Quakers to promote the philosophy and techniques of nonviolent revolution in organizations with the potential to build a mass movement.

Gandhi's mass movement did a great deal to reinforce Christian radical pacifism in the United States. The peace movement of the thirties, especially its Christian section, was influenced by Gandhi's example; many of the radical pacifists of the fifties were inspired by Gandhi and his writings. Gandhi's understanding of nonviolence was in fact different in important respects from leading variants of Christian pacifism, and his philosophy tended to suffer in translation, even (sometimes especially) in the hands of his greatest admirers, who often liked to portray him as a latter-day Christ. Gandhi distinguished his concept of satyagraha, or truthforce, from passive resistance. Satyagraha, or nonviolent direct action, was, he argued, an effective instrument of struggle, not merely a renunciation of violence on moral or religious principle.[8] Some radical Christian pacifists in the United States, such as A. J. Muste, who were concerned with building a mass movement, understood satyagraha in this way. But many Christian pacifists with humanitarian or liberal, rather than radical, perspectives (such as John Haynes Holmes, a founder of the Fellowship of Reconciliation) understood satyagraha primarily as a model of religious or moral conduct and used Gandhi's example to reinforce an understanding of nonviolence as abstention from conflict.[9]

Both ways of understanding nonviolence have continued as currents within the nonviolent movement. The early civil rights movement was strongly influenced by Gandhi's concept of nonviolence. Perhaps because the civil rights movement emerged in a setting in which conflict was an unavoidable part of daily life, nonviolence was understood as a way of bringing conflict under control, using it to achieve the ends of social justice, rather than in any way standing aside from it. In the nonviolent direct action movement of the seventies and eighties, especially in LAG and the disarmament phase of the movement generally, the understanding of nonviolence has been shaped by a suspicion of conflict, a vision of a conflict-free society, and a desire to minimize conflict within the movement.

From the end of World War Two through the mid-fifties, the peace movement in the United States was confined to committed pacifists, radical or otherwise. Toward 1960, the movement began to grow rapidly and to draw people who did not themselves adhere to a philosophy of nonviolence. That growth was largely due to public concern over nuclear testing, even then known to pose serious health hazards. In 1958, NAANW sponsored an attempt by four Quakers to sail into the Pacific nuclear test site on the ketch *Golden Rule*. The crew was arrested in Honolulu, but anthropologist Earle Reynolds and his family, who happened to be in port at the same time, attended the trial of the *Golden Rule*'s crew and decided to continue the journey in their place. The Reynolds successfully sailed into the test site on their yacht, the *Phoenix of Hiroshima*, before being arrested. The voyages of the *Golden Rule* and the *Phoenix* brought considerable public sympathy and support. The images of four Quakers, and a family, willing to face arrest and physical danger for what were obviously deeply held convictions, appealed to many in the United States and elsewhere.

In spite of the success of this action and others (in particular the defeat of the New York civil defense program in the late fifties by a coalition of radical pacifists and high school students through civil disobedience), radical pacifism did not become the basis of a lasting mass peace movement at this time. Other NAANW/CNVA actions proved to have less public appeal than the voyage of the *Golden Rule*, and the alliance between radical pacifists and the more cautious elements of the peace movement began to break down. A vigil combined with civil disobedience at the Nevada site of a nuclear test provoked criticism from other sections of the peace movement. Some argued that by their willingness to take risks and their deep religiosity the radical pacifists were setting themselves apart from the American public, making peace appear the concern of an inaccessible few. A demonstration involving civil disobedience at an ICBM base in Omaha, Nebraska, and a series of boardings of submarines bearing nuclear weapons near New London, Connecticut, brought the same complaints. Many liberals and traditional pacifists also argued that the peace movement should refrain from addressing the production of nuclear weapons and restrict itself to the more acceptable issue of testing. The most serious rupture of unity within the peace movement came in 1960, when Norman Cousins, the chair of Sane, acceded to a demand from senator Thomas Dodd that he help purge Sane of Communists. Many left the organization when national and local leaders were asked to sign a non-Communist loyalty oath. Student Sane, the organization's youth wing, fought the demand for two years and was expelled as a result. *Liberation* published a sharp critique of Sane's willingness to compromise with Cold War mentality.[10]

Cultural Transformation
in the Postwar Era

The civil rights and peace struggles of the late 1950s and early 1960s provided the framework for the emergence of the student New Left. Northern students were inspired by the heroism of the civil rights movements in the South. The struggle for civil rights also pointed out the gap between American claims of democracy and social reality. The peace movement opened up the question of whether the Cold War and the arms race were necessary or consistent with democratic ideals. The Students for a Democratic Society (SDS), formed in 1960, was strongly influenced by the spirit of radical pacifism and the example of SNCC. Many regarded themselves as part of a nonviolent anarchist or quasi-anarchist tradition. But SDS and other organizations of the New Left distanced themselves from the organizations that had preceded them—in part because of simple ignorance. Growing up in McCarthyite America, they had learned little of the tradition of protest, even in its most recent manifestations. They wanted also to see themselves as creating an entirely new movement having nothing to do with the sectarian squabbles that consumed the remnants of the Old Left and finally destroyed the peace movement of the late fifties and early sixties as well. The anti-ideological bent of the early student movement was an element in its openness to radical pacifism, which was seen as a welcome relief from the left ideologies of the past, but it also contributed to the failure of radical pacifism to take hold. Early SDS avoided focusing its attention on any theory, ideology, or worldview that might exclude others. The result was that particular approaches to politics such as nonviolence were discarded easily. Enthusiasm for nonviolence began to wane in the northern student movement as the war in Vietnam expanded. Meanwhile, SNCC was beginning to abandon the ideal as well; in 1964 a debate began over nonviolence that led ultimately to the rejection of that principle. The radical pacifist organizations continued their work, but in the student and youth movement as a whole violence was increasingly glorified.

The New Left of the early 1960s distanced itself quite deliberately from the tradition of the Old Left, its chief historical antecedent. The Old Left meant mainly the Communist Party, the dominant left organization of the thirties, but included the social democratic and Trotskyist anti-Communists who remained on the left. The activists of the sixties had grown up in the McCarthyite fifties and were reluctant to associate themselves with a discredited movement. The movement's anti-Communism was also a reaction to Stalinism and the sectarian battles that by the late fifties were all that was visible of the Old Left.[11] Most important, the activists of the sixties confronted different issues from those that had dominated the thirties, and they brought a different sensibility to political activity. Though many of them were the children of the second-generation immigrants who had been swept up in the movements of the thirties and supported the New Deal, most had grown up thoroughly middle-class, secure in the American identity that had been so problematic for their parents and grandparents.[12]

It is axiomatic that World War Two profoundly transformed American society. Massive economic growth, technological innovation, and unprecedented migrations more or less destroyed twentieth-century remnants of traditional communities and undermined the already fragile autonomy of the host of particular cultures that made up American society. The experience of the war and the celebration of prosperity that followed it were all that united the country. The war dramatically accelerated the transformation of family and personal life that had been under way since at least the turn of the century by bringing enormous numbers of women into the workplace, a change that became permanent as increasing numbers of families found it difficult to live on one income. World War Two also undermined the rationale for racism: the role of blacks in the war highlighted the absurdity of their second-class status in peacetime, and the massive migration of blacks to the northern cities, with the shift of loyalty to the Democratic party as a result of the New Deal, made it much more difficult for the Democrats to ignore blacks' demands. The integration of the South's economic and political life into that of the nation, greatly accelerated by the war, made the feudal organization of the South finally untenable.[13]

These profound social changes led to deep tensions between experience and long-accepted ideas about social relations. These tensions in turn opened up new possibilities of cultural transformation. Social changes were felt by all, but the generation that reached middle age in the 1960s had formed its social and political commitments in the heat of the New Deal and World War Two and was in general not ready to adopt a new worldview. It was the young people who entered their twenties in the 1960s who pointed out the contradictions between ideology and reality and could see the opportunities for creating something new.

The emergence of any new social movement is generally related to a widespread perception of a gap between experience and the ideas that govern society, and a belief that things could be organized differently. It is notable that in the postwar years, when fundamental changes were taking place simultaneously in many different areas, at least within the white middle class accepted ideas about social relations only became more rigid. The most profound and most widely experienced changes were those affecting gender, family, and personal life. The young women of the middle and upper middle classes who attended college in the mid-sixties (and who found themselves drawn to feminism) had no models for their futures that made sense: they were preparing for work outside the home; jobs were available; contraceptives made it possible to put off having children without forgoing sexual relations. Yet old ideas about femininity and relations between men and women, modeled on female domestic dependence, continued to hold sway. These issues were not explicitly addressed until the late sixties, when feminists forced the rest of the movements of the period to confront them. Changing relations between men and women, however, were the basis for the culture of the sixties, the sense that there was an enormous gap between reality and outmoded rules, and the hope that in that gap something new and liberatory could be created.[14]

A parallel, though less dramatic, process of change was taking place in relation to issues of work. The first and second generations of immigrant men aspired to enter business and the professions and pursued success through hard work. Sons of the third generation who attended college in the sixties were the first to have the option to enter those arenas easily; they were expected to be grateful and to pursue their opportunities avidly. But many found their fathers' examples uninspiring and saw other alternatives in an economy rapidly being transformed by technological innovation. The economic expansion of the fifties and early sixties suggested that prosperity would last forever and that technological advances could break the connection between success and long hours of tedious work. The accepted boundaries between work and leisure were thrown into question; suddenly it seemed possible to live more creatively. The New Left, the anti-war movement, and the left counterculture offered ways to put these ideas into practice: one could forget about professional training or getting an ordinary job and instead construct an identity around political activity, art, a craft, while living simply and communally.

The revolt against traditional definitions of work was largely masculine. Whereas men found a sense of liberation in abandoning traditional work roles, for women, the opportunity to pursue careers was liberating.[15] In the end it was the revolt against traditional feminine roles that was sustained. Feminism appeared in the movement later than other issues, but it gained momentum in the late sixties and seventies and remains a major social force. The revolt against traditional definitions of work was articulated early in the New Left but diminished with the economic decline of the seventies.

Race relations were also transformed in the postwar era. The civil rights movement that inaugurated the movements of the sixties was based on the growth of black higher education in the

South in the fifties and early sixties: black students, often the first in their families to attend college, were the first generation in decades to see opportunities in their own lives and a chance to challenge racism successfully. At the same time, the hold of conservative whites over the southern Democratic party was beginning to slip, as the party's liberal wing began to see the advantages in attracting a black constituency. The civil rights movement won the vote for blacks in the South and made racism a public issue in the United States as it had never been before, but beyond this point progress on racial issues was blocked, perhaps because the structures of racial inequality are so deeply embedded, and those who suffer most from them still have too little power.[16]

Among the other great changes of the postwar era, the existence of the bomb has made old ways of thinking about war and peace obsolete. The Truman administration believed that the atom bomb would give the United States the ability to set the terms for international relations.[17] Subsequent administrations have been reluctant to give up this idea, in spite of extensive evidence to the contrary. Before the advent of nuclear weapons, foreign policy could be conducted on the assumption that increased military power translated more or less directly into increased international influence and security. Nuclear weapons have undermined this logic. Because their use is virtually unthinkable, international relations proceed largely as if they did not exist. The trend toward Third World independence continues without regard to superpower nuclear stockpiles; economic self-sufficiency and nonnuclear weaponry take precedence over military capabilities that refer to what is thus far an imaginary nuclear war.[18] At the same time, because nuclear weapons *could* be used, their existence threatens everyone's security. The war in Vietnam demonstrated that the United States could be defeated in spite of its enormous military strength. As both the United States and the Soviets have gained the capacity to destroy the human race many times over, the irrationality of the arms race has become increasingly apparent. Until recently pacifism was only a very small current in the United States, even in the peace movement. But as conventional military assumptions break down, many people have become open to new ways of thinking about international relations and the use of force, and the audience for pacifism has grown. On the left, especially, disappointment with the results of violent revolutions in the Third World has led to increased interest in nonviolent forms of struggle.[19]

The movements of the thirties flourished because they challenged economic and political structures and demanded a place for labor in the political life of the nation. There were elements of a social or cultural critique in Communist politics: the attack on racism, the campaign to organize blacks, took the Party beyond narrowly defined economic and political realms. So did its insistence on a multiethnic, multiracial definition of American identity.[20] The fact that there was room inside the Party for discussion of male chauvinism created some small opening for a challenge to male dominance, at least in the realm of political activity.[21] But on the whole neither the Communist Party nor the other major organizations of the thirties felt the need to challenge the organization of social life or the ideas that governed it. The concept of revolutionary change that guided the Party had to do with the transfer of economic and political power from one class to another rather than the elimination of hierarchies or a rethinking of what power should mean and how it should be defined and exercised. The concepts of reform that governed the movements that surrounded the Party were limited in the same ways.

Democracy, Revolution, and the Search for Agency

Unlike the activists of the thirties, who gravitated to the issues of political and economic power, the activists of the sixties tended to gravitate to what seemed more fundamental issues of how social life as a whole should be organized, what ideas it should be ruled by. The movements of the sixties could not ignore those questions without losing their constituencies, any more than the movements of the thirties could have ignored questions of working-class organization. The very size of the young generation of the sixties added momentum to cultural revolution. But what precisely this cultural revolution was about, few were able to say. The activists of the sixties were better at articulating what they

were against—the war in Vietnam, inequality, racism, sexism—
than what they were for, what a better society would look like.

In the New Left's early years, a certain vagueness in goals was
not necessarily a bad thing; it allowed people to explore their
intuitions and a new kind of politics to unfold gradually. Paul
Potter, an early president of SDS writing later about the movement's process of self-definition, argued that the radicalism of the
early New Left was based on the idea that politics must bridge
the immediately personal and the broadly social. "What we want
most from life," he wrote, "is love . . . to be whole and free. What
we want is to find peace through overcoming the conflict between
ourselves and others, to find a way to be open with at least one
other person, even though that desire symbolizes our desire to be
open with all of our world." The task of the movement, he argued, was to "learn to think about love in a new way . . . to look
at the society and our action in it in a totally new way. I do not
claim to have that new way of thinking about love. But I do have
beginning images I think I can share—because I think they are
shared."[22]

Another early New Left activist, Dick Flacks, expressed similar
ideas in a paper delivered to an SDS conference in 1965, in which
he tried to define what the movement was about.

If I understand what we are trying to work on when we say we are
building a "movement," I think it has to do with two types of goals.
One, which we might call "existential humanism," is expressed by
the desire to change the way we, as individuals, actually live and deal
with other people. . . . Secondly, we say that we seek a radical transformation of the social order. In short, that we act politically because
our values cannot be realized in any durable sense without a recon-
struction of the political and social system. . . . I think it is inescap-
able that our movement must encompass both sets of orientation. It
is clear that politics apart from an existential ethic becomes increasingly manipulative, power-oriented, sacrificial of human lives and
souls—it is corrupted. The danger involved in a social movement
that is apolitical is . . . that of irresponsibility . . . and consequently
. . . disillusionment.[23]

The movements of the sixties began not with revolution but
with the goal of making democracy real. The civil rights movement made it impossible to ignore black inequality; the northern

student movement challenged a political culture that valued private gain over collective good, justified the Cold War, and discouraged dissent. In the process of exposing the hypocrisy of what passed for democracy, the movements of the sixties began to develop new definitions of it. Early SNCC activists spoke of the "beloved community" in which mutual commitment to transcendent goals of social justice would outweigh narrow personal aims. In the early years of SDS, the term "participatory democracy" meant a movement and ultimately a society in which everyone would have an equal voice. By the mid-sixties many activists had become convinced that these goals were incompatible with mainstream liberalism. The resilience of racism and the reluctance of Democratic liberals to challenge it openly radicalized SNCC activists. The responsibility of liberal presidents Kennedy and Johnson for U.S. involvement in Vietnam did the same for SDS.[24]

Though the New Left turned against liberalism, it did not at first identify itself with any concrete alternative. In a speech at the 1965 March on Washington, Paul Potter, then president of SDS, pointed out that the war was the product of a system run by liberals and called on the movement to name that system, but did not suggest what the name might be.[25] In a speech given at the same spot during the next year's March on Washington, the next president of SDS, Carl Oglesby, described the system as "corporate liberalism."[26] Potter later wrote that he had left the definition open because any description seemed to narrow the complexity of the social reality that the movement confronted. "I refused to call the system capitalism," he wrote, "because capitalism was for me and my generation an inadequate description of the evils of America—a hollow, dead word tied to the thirties and a movement that had used it freely but apparently without comprehending it.... I wanted ambiguity.... I sensed there was something new afoot in the world ... that made rejection of the old terminology part of the new hope for radical change in America."[27]

Both these formulations indicate something of the difference between the political vocabulary the New Left was trying to construct and the Old Left language it was consciously leaving behind. New Leftists were more comfortable with the vagueness of "the system" than with the sharply defined class analysis implicit in the term "capitalism," which implied also a revolutionary goal for socialism. Early New Leftists, in most cases sympathetic to socialism, were unwilling to limit their vision. Their language captured the exploratory quality of the movement and its distaste for accepted ideologies, including those of the left; it also captured something of the social reality of the sixties. "The system" and "the establishment" were much more suggestive of a faceless bureaucracy, run by liberals who ruled by manipulation of consensus, than the terms "capitalism" and "the ruling class," which conjured up greedy industrialists exercising control over a resistant working class.

The open, nonideological vocabulary of SDS allowed for creative exploration of new ideas but also imposed an innocence on the theoretical language of the left, reflecting the movement's reluctance to commit itself to particular goals or to find a particular standpoint from which a revolutionary strategy could be put forward. A conceptual apparatus that might have worked for a small movement involved in gradual development quickly became insufficient with the dramatic expansion of the New Left into an angry antiwar movement, as Vietnam drove tens of thousands of young people to radical protest. The betrayal of the antiwar forces at the 1968 Democratic National Convention and the brutal repression of the antiwar movement outside the convention hall was for many activists the final proof that there was no place in the system for dissent. The breadth of popular opposition to the war and the growth and influence of the radical antiwar movement made revolution seem possible. American society seemed to be coming apart at the seams, but in fact the basis for revolution was lacking: young activists were turning toward revolution, but the larger public was only turning against the war. The student movement represented only one generation, and one generation was not enough for a revolution.

Student activists knew that a revolution would require a base beyond themselves. The search for a revolutionary agency and theory had begun in the mid-sixties. As the war expanded but the path to revolution did not open up, the search became desperate. Innocence of radical history and theory may have been an asset in the early years of the movement, when it allowed the New Left to explore new ideas without bias, but as the movement turned toward revolution, innocence meant lack of sophistication and a vulnerability to the revolutionary posturing of sects such as Progressive Labor that sought an audience in SDS and elsewhere in the movement.

In the late sixties, in the absence of any theoretical alternative, the movement was swept up by models of revolution based on orthodox Marxist theory and Third World experience. But these models were not appropriate for the situation the movement faced in the United States. Marx identified socialist revolution with the working classes of the advanced capitalist societies, not foreseeing the possibility of revolution in societies where capitalism had not entirely taken hold and the working class was still small. Lenin developed the theory of imperialism in part to account for the possibility of socialist revolution in the less developed societies of the periphery and revised Marx's model of the revolutionary process in keeping with the conditions his movement faced in tsarist Russia. There the small size of the working class required an organizational form that would allow it, or at least those representing it, to create an alliance with the peasantry and with other groups over which those identified with the working class could maintain control. Tsarist repression made it necessary to create a highly centralized and secretive organization to lead the revolution. Because Russia lacked a tradition of democracy, this necessity did not jeopardize popular support. Lenin never claimed that the organizational form he created should be copied by revolutionary movements in developed capitalist nations with extensive democratic structures; nor would it necessarily be appropriate for other Third World nations. But the desire of revolutionaries around the world to identify themselves with the Bolshevik revolution led many to copy its ideology and structure. The Soviet leadership, especially under Stalin, encouraged this trend, because it helped the Soviets maintain control over the international communist movement.

The American activists of the late sixties did not inherit the Bolshevik model directly from the Soviet Union, which the great majority of them held in contempt, but indirectly, from the Cuban, Chinese, and to a lesser extent the Vietnamese Communist parties. By the late sixties, Progressive Labor, the Revolutionary Union, and other groups that aspired to become vanguard parties had gained a good deal of influence within SDS and the antiwar movement. Both Progressive Labor and the Revolutionary Union called themselves Marxist-Leninist, by which they meant that they believed that only a tightly disciplined vanguard party, based on the working class, could lead to revolution. In fact, the most influential of the Marxist-Leninist groups (including the Revolutionary Union and Progressive Labor in its early days) were Maoist. They took the Chinese revolution as their model. They tended not to distinguish between Third World nationalism and revolution; they regarded anti-imperialism as the central revolutionary dynamic; they admired the Chinese Cultural Revolution and were accordingly skeptical about "bourgeois democracy," including the electoral process and civil liberties. They also admired the Chinese renunciation of the Soviet Union and regarded the Soviet government as little better than that of the United States. Weatherman (which soon dropped the "man" in its name in deference to feminism, becoming "the Weatherpeople" and ultimately "the Weather Underground") shared the Marxist-Leninists' revolutionary aspirations and their desire to emulate Third World struggles, but it was more anarchist than Maoist. Weatherman had no interest in tightly controlled organization, and it incorporated many aspects of the counterculture, in contrast to the Marxist-Leninist organizations that ordered their members to cut their hair and get married in order to make themselves acceptable to the working class.

Despite their differences, all these groups were convinced that the revolution would involve armed struggle and that anyone who was unwilling to countenance violence could not be serious about revolution or even about ending the war. The rhetoric of the Maoists linked violence with party discipline; that of Weatherman linked violence with antiauthoritarian revolt. None of the sectarian groups actually engaged in much violence, except that thrust on them by the police, but they did play a substantial role in undermining arguments for nonviolence within the antiwar movement and in destroying concern for democratic processes. Little coherent opposition was expressed to the politics of the sectarian groups. Many people found the movement an increasingly difficult place to be; some thought their discomfort showed that they were not revolutionary enough, felt guilty, but stayed in the movement anyway.[28] Women, who were among the prime targets of movement authoritarianism, began to turn to feminism; some formed autonomous women's organizations. Others, including both women and men, left SDS or other organizations with similar approaches to become part of the Trotskyist, but ironically less militant, Mobilization to End the War (Mobe), detached themselves from the organized antiwar organizations to form smaller groups, or drifted away from the movement altogether.

By the end of the decade, SDS, so recently the leading organization within the movement, was dominated by sectarian groups that argued among themselves about exactly who in the United States should be regarded as the agents of revolution. Some said the working class as a whole; some said Third World people; some said young people, especially nonwhite and working-class young people. These groups agreed, however, that the movement must turn to revolution and that the revolution would be violent. At the 1969 SDS convention, the organization fell apart in sectarian conflicts over competing revolutionary scenarios, none of which was in fact remotely likely in the United States at that time. The influence of the black movement, especially the Black Panthers, was a factor in SDS's turn toward a violent rhetoric; many SDS members regarded the Panthers as a model of revolutionary militance. Probably only a fraction of the hundred thousand or so SDS members around the country understood clearly what these debates were about. The movement as a whole, however, was strong enough to survive the collapse of its main organization. Many activists were already more closely tied to local organizations than to SDS; others simply shifted their locus of activity. Through the early seventies the plethora of groups that made up the antiwar movement continued to flourish.[29]

The Politics of Liberation and New Models of Revolution

Sectarian politics were strongest in the part of the movement that was most highly organized and most conventionally political in its orientation. SDS (and other national organizations such as Mobe) were surrounded by a vast array of particular constituencies: student groups, women's groups, black and other nonwhite organizations, increasing numbers of gay and lesbian groups, local projects, food co-ops, living collectives. In the late sixties the New Left became, for the first time, a mass movement, and as such it brought together many different, often contradictory, political and cultural impulses.

On the one hand, authoritarianism and moralism were rampant and in no way confined to the sects. Feminism was the strongest basis for a critique of authoritarianism the movement as a whole produced—but within the women's movement, feminism itself could form the basis of authoritarian forms of leadership in which some women defined feminist morality and held other women up to the standard they had constructed. Throughout the movement, politics and personal morality could easily become coercive. Admiration for Third World revolutions and a growing understanding of the oppressive role of the United States produced widespread guilt feelings, which tended to undermine good judgment. To the degree that political activity was an attempt to prove one's dedication (or test that of others), clearminded evaluation of the movement's aims and strategies became difficult. Emulation of Third World models created havoc by encouraging a militaristic style and undermining the values to which the early New Left had dedicated itself, damaging the movement's relations with allies and potential allies outside the student and youth milieu.

The Third World politics of the movement persisted in spite of those negative effects not so much because of the influence of sectarian groups but because the antiwar movement was part of a larger intellectual youth culture that was inspired by, and easily identified its own inarticulate revolutionary impulses with, the Third World example. The impulse to idealize the parts of the world where liberation struggles were taking place was strong enough to keep the antiwar movement from paying serious attention to the fact that Third Worldism and the attendant glorification of violence were isolating it from the working class (and other mainstream) constituencies it hoped to reach. Pacifist organizations such as the Committee for Non-Violent Action kept the tradition of nonviolent protest alive through the sixties, but finally the influence pacifists had on the movement as a whole had more to do with their dedication and militance than with their philosophy of nonviolence.[30]

The movement of the late sixties was also shaped by a liberatory politics that was based on the further development of many of the ideas of the early New Left. The women's movement took the idea of participatory democracy seriously enough to apply it to women as well as men, and as a result was able to put forward a critique of hierarchical social relations with ramifications for all areas of American society. Radical feminists, gays, and lesbians began to challenge the monopoly of marriage and the nuclear family in personal life. In small groups throughout the movement, people began to explore new ways of relating to one another. Sections of the movement began to incorporate feminist ideas into their political practice. Though in many ways sexism in the movement was at its worst in the late sixties—revolutionary ideology was used by many men as one more excuse to tell women what to do—at the same time relations between men and women became for the first time a legitimate terrain of discussion and struggle. Communities were built in which traditional roles were renounced with some success and in which, for the time, ties other than that of the heterosexual couple gained legitimacy and actual importance. There was also some loosening of the barriers created by racism. In spite of considerable conflict, whites and persons of color were sometimes able to work together on relatively equal terms.[31]

The liberatory potential of the movement was not enough to sustain it. As Vietnam began to wind down, in the early 1970s, too many people were convinced that the movement had failed because it could not turn immediately to a Third Worldist revolution, and too many people were burnt out by pursuit of a hopeless goal for too many years. If the American left had had a different history, if the antiwar movement had understood itself as part of a long-term tradition, if it had realized that revolution was not going to take place soon and had been capable of thinking about what a longer-term revolution would entail in a sophisticated and creative way, perhaps a viable politics could have been constructed. A decline of radical activity in the early seventies was not inevitable, even with the end of the war and the national shift to the right; a stronger movement might have been able to accommodate itself to these changed conditions.

But weaknesses that had not seemed important in the sixties, when the movement was bolstered by growing public opposition to the war and widespread sympathy at least for liberal reform at home, had become serious problems. Because the movements of the sixties did not consider themselves part of an ongoing tradition or think of revolution as a long-term goal, they became disoriented. More sophisticated and creative thinking about what a revolution would entail in the late twentieth-century United States probably would not have solved all of the movement's problems but might have prevented the movement's virtual collapse when it became clear that revolution was not an immediate prospect.

The two most comprehensive and thoughtful histories of SDS, Todd Gitlin's *The Sixties: Years of Hope, Days of Rage* and James Miller's *"Democracy Is in the Streets": From Port Huron to the Siege of Chicago*, both see the promise of the early New Left burning out in the late sixties; both suggest that it was the turn to revolution that destroyed the movement.[32] Miller argues that the vagueness of the concept of participatory democracy left SDS open to infiltration and its domination by Marxist sects. Gitlin sees the turn toward revolution as a distortion of the liberal democratic politics of the early New Left and an impediment to effective opposition to the war. It is true that SDS, and much of the rest of the movement, destroyed itself in an attempt to make a revolution in the United States, but an analysis that condemns the revolutionary politics of the late sixties misses what was legitimate about the impulse that shaped those politics.

One may criticize a movement's strategies and disagree with its aims, but any politics passionately espoused by masses of people deserves to be examined respectfully. Tens of thousands of committed activists in the late sixties and early seventies, and the hundreds of thousands who constituted the movement's periphery in those years, were not only against the war; they wanted revolution. Precisely what was meant by revolution was never clearly defined, and in fact different people meant quite different things by it; but for many, probably most, it included cultural revolution. The revolutionary politics of the sixties were given their particular form by anger about the war and romanticism about the Third World, but they were also more than that. The impulse toward revolution was rooted in the turmoil and unresolved tensions that were being felt in virtually every area of American life, most sharply by the young, but also by older persons, especially women and people of color. These groups of course had different complaints against American society; but for each, revolution meant some sort of fundamental change. The vagueness of the conception did nothing to diminish the passion with which the goal was held. It is quite possible for large numbers of people to be willing to fight and die for a social transformation whose character is only in the process of being defined, as the example of the Chinese students' movement for democracy, in 1989, makes clear.

What revolution meant for the late twentieth-century United States was never a significant issue among activists. Only in the early seventies, as the war in Vietnam receded, was there public debate about this question. The movement was preoccupied with the war and, to a lesser degree, with the challenges that women and people of color were raising over white male dominance. Even though the movement was increasingly regarding itself as revolutionary, the question of what revolution would look like seemed too abstract to divert attention from the more urgent issues. As a result, the assumptions of those who put revolution forward as the movement's goal went almost entirely unchallenged.

Within the broad penumbra of the organized antiwar movement many other concepts of revolution began to circulate, and even if no coherent alternative theory of revolution was being put forward, practices were being developed that implicitly challenged Leninist and Third Worldist models. By the late sixties, in virtually every arena of the movement, tensions had arisen between those oriented toward traditional political forms and intellectual discourse and those who occupied the politicized edge of the counterculture. From a variety of standpoints, the attempt was to construct a politics of experience, to give voice to a sense of alienation, and to form communities, or at least personal relationships, that would prefigure a more liberatory society. This impulse was not new. Many early New Leftists had understood radicalism as the attempt to integrate the utopian, visionary impulse with political effectiveness. When Paul Potter called on the movement "to learn to think about love in a new way . . . to look at the society and our action in it in a totally new way," he was pointing to the need for a visionary basis for radical politics. When Richard Flacks said that the movement was trying to unite " 'existential humanism' . . . expressed by the desire to change the way we, as individuals, actually live and deal with other people . . . [with the attempt to achieve] a radical transformation of the social order," he was expressing the hope that these impulses could be contained within one movement in spite of the innate tension between them.[33]

By the late sixties, the politics of experience and utopian vision and the politics of immediate efficacy had largely parted ways and in one arena after another confronted each other as adversaries. In the women's movement, the confrontation was between radical feminists, who rejected all ideological preconceptions and ties to the left and sought a politics based on their own experience, and the Marxist feminists (many of whom later called themselves socialist feminists) who wanted to develop a theory of women's oppression within the context of Marxist categories and retain a connection with the left and the antiwar movement in spite of their criticisms.[34] Radical feminism was much more hospitable to lesbianism than was Marxist feminism. While radical feminists plunged into a critique of the family that led many to a renunciation of heterosexuality in practice as well as theory, Marxist feminists tended to hold back.

Radical feminism contained a separatist conception of the revolutionary process; it remained unclear whether the sexes would be separate in a revolutionary society or whether men and women would live together entirely without the hierarchical relations that radical feminists insisted had their origin in the domination of women. Marxist feminists hoped to integrate the struggle against sexism into the left and make female equality a condition of socialist revolution. Marxist and socialist feminism had the advantage of creating a space between the male-dominated left and separatism for women who remained committed to both socialism and feminism. It was radical feminism, however, that had the sharpest impact on the movement as a whole and that supported the attempt to put different values into practice.

In the antiwar movement, and the "mixed" movement gener-

ally, there were parallel tensions, in this case between the political
realm inhabited by Marxist-Leninists, and by some movement intellectuals who were beginning to call themselves democratic socialists, and a more eclectic realm of cultural rebellion inhabited
by hippies and anarchists. The hippies and anarchists never articulated alternative conceptions of revolution very clearly, partly
because most of them were in flight from intellectual life generally and were as repelled by traditional forms of debate as by the
traditional Marxist-Leninist concepts of revolution. But many of
the groups that intersected with the antiwar movement and the
counterculture developed a practice that suggested a different way
of thinking about revolution. In New York, for instance, the
Motherfuckers, a group of artists and other hippies living on the
Lower East Side, came together around the use of avant-garde
art in protest against the war, and turned to living guerrilla theater as a way of mocking the materialism of mainstream American life and pointing to its inherent violence. The Motherfuckers,
who liked to describe themselves as "a gang with an analysis,"
organized hippies against police raids, marched up Sixth Avenue
with garbage collected from the sidewalks of the Lower East Side
and dumped it in front of Lincoln Center to indicate their opinion of a socially unconcerned high art, and disrupted SDS meetings in an attempt to bring the concerns of hippies and street
people to what they saw as the arid political discussions of the
student movement.[35] Other groups organized around a similar
radical/countercultural politics were forming communes and in
many cases moving to the countryside. Some people took on new
names to suggest the renunciation of mainstream society and the
beginning of a new life; many took names of plants or animals to
indicate a sense of connection with nature.

The alternative culture of the political hippies and anarchists
was laced with contradictions. The countercultural left, like the
more conventional antiwar movement, was fascinated by violence.
Groups such as the Motherfuckers made a point of playing with
violence, using violent imagery as a mirror in which mainstream
America might see itself. A rhetoric of personal and sexual liberation often conflicted with a more complicated reality in which
the rejection of convention allowed machismo to flourish and the
attempt to reestablish a bond with nature reinforced the expec-

tation that women would occupy traditional roles as mothers and nurturers. The counterculture's distaste for formal organization made countercultural communities vulnerable to domination by charismatic leaders, in spite of their ethos of egalitarianism.

Nevertheless, the countercultural wing of the movement sustained the visionary impulse of the early New Left (and the almost forgotten legacy of radical pacifism). It was in the "less political" part of the movement that a concept of revolution began to emerge that was different from the Third Worldist model that was helping the antiwar movement destroy itself. The counterculture's use of guerrilla theater and other forms of creative expression, its lack of interest in the conventional political arena, its emphasis on the creation of alternative communities, all suggested that revolution had more to do with thinking and living differently, and convincing others to make similar changes, than with seizing power. By the early seventies, the focus of the left counterculture had shifted to the countryside. Many of the people who had made up the countercultural wing of the antiwar movement were moving to rural areas in northern New England, Northern California, and elsewhere to construct communities where they hoped to live their values and perhaps begin to build a movement expressive of them.[36]

Nonviolent revolution made sense to many who were trying to build democratic and egalitarian communities in the early seventies. It was in the rural communities of the countercultural left and similarly minded refugees from the antiwar movement that the nonviolent direct action movement against nuclear energy began to emerge in the mid-seventies. The cluster of concepts on which that movement based itself—small-scale community, consensus-process grass roots democracy, the rejection of all hierarchies, nonviolent revolution—had intellectual roots in pacifism, anarchism, and the memory of the early civil rights movement but were grounded in the immediate experience of the left/countercultural politics of the late sixties and its migration to the countryside in the early seventies.

Whatever theory of revolution the antiwar movement followed, it was very unlikely to have led immediately to revolution. The war ended without undermining the legitimacy of the existing system in the minds of most Americans. The desire for revolution did not reach far beyond the activist core of the movement. The size of that core created illusions that would have been shattered in any event once the war ended. Even with a better analysis of American society, the antiwar movement was unlikely to have maintained its strength while turning its attention to other issues. With the end of the war, the aging of the student generation, and economic decline, there was no possibility of maintaining anything like the level of protest activity of the sixties and early seventies.

Nevertheless, the near collapse of the movement could have been avoided. The inappropriateness of its theories of revolution gave that movement a fantastic quality that led to self-doubt, mutual recriminations, and despair. The early New Left understood the importance of the ideal of democracy in the United States, the need to find new forms of democracy to challenge ruling bureaucratic definitions, and the central role of the redefinition of culture in bringing about a new society. By the late sixties the New Left's critique of mainstream culture had been deepened by feminism, and feminists, anarchists, and others were beginning to create alternative models of community, democracy, and revolution. If these tendencies had been developed further, the movement as a whole might have remained intact, although smaller, a focal point for continuing efforts toward social change. And many former activists would not have felt that it would take them years to recover from their experience of movement activity.

Anarchists and hippies were not the only people troubled by some of the political conceptions that took hold of the movement when it rejected liberalism. Many early New Left activists withdrew to the sidelines as a new generation of leaders turned away from democratic aspirations and toward a celebration of violent revolution. In the early seventies some left intellectuals began to challenge openly the movement's reliance on foreign models of revolution and its neglect of the arena of culture. *Studies on the Left,* the most important theoretical journal associated with the movement, split in 1969 over the question of whether the journal should follow the movement or criticize it and introduce a consciously socialist perspective. A new theoretical journal, *Socialist Revolution* (later renamed *Socialist Review*), emerged from this split. James Weinstein and Anne Farrar, both members of the critical tendency within *Studies,* moved to San Francisco to organize a collective where the movement was relatively free of the sectarian tendencies that had taken over the leadership of SDS and much of the antiwar movement on the East Coast and in the Midwest.

Socialist Revolution became the center of an attempt to develop a new analysis of American society and to put forward a more appropriate model of revolution. The journal was influenced by Weinstein's vision of a democratic socialist politics, modeled to a large extent on the history of the Socialist Party in the first decades of the twentieth century and by a feminist vision, put forward by Anne Farrar and others, that placed the transformation of culture and social relations on an equal level with that of political and economic structures.

The journal, and the larger left intellectual tendency it came to represent, was also greatly influenced by the Italian Communist Antonio Gramsci's analysis of domination and revolution in advanced capitalist societies. Gramsci argued that after the basic process of industrialization has been completed, and the economy begins to produce for mass consumption, forms of social control are transformed and revolutionary politics must be reshaped as well. The state expands its role, both as regulator and as provider for the security of a labor force whose allegiance must be obtained to ensure the system's smooth functioning. Control is exercised more through the construction of consent than the use of force. The educational system, the media, and the realm of culture and ideology generally thus take on central importance for the left. The working class becomes diverse in an economy that requires many highly trained workers. New forms of social control create new arenas of protest, some outside the working class, some not defined by class. The process of coalition becomes crucial to revolutionary politics.[37]

The founding of *Socialist Revolution* was part of a broader process taking place in the left in the early seventies—the emergence of a democratic socialist tendency influenced by the legacy of Gramsci, the example of Eurocommunism, and American cultural radicalism, especially feminism. In a position paper written during the formation of *Socialist Revolution,* James Weinstein argued that an independent, democratic socialist left in the United States required three things: a theoretical journal, a newspaper, and an organization. *Socialist Revolution* became that theoretical journal. Weinstein later founded *In These Times,* which became the newspaper of the American democratic socialist left. At about the same time as *Socialist Revolution,* the New American Movement was organized by people with a similar perspective (and to some degree influenced by the journal). By combining independent democratic socialism and socialist feminism, the organization hoped to attract movement activists critical of Marxist-Leninist strategies and to transform the antiwar movement into a mass movement for socialism.[38]

The New American Movement (NAM) did not succeed in the latter aim. The antiwar movement faded away, leaving a small number of committed activists. NAM helped to keep the radical impulse alive and to develop a more sophisticated and sober approach to left politics than that which had dominated the antiwar movement. The Gramscian/feminist perspective provided a new basis for a nonsectarian radical politics. NAM brought men and women into the same organization on the terrain of socialist feminism and helped to reestablish the link between socialism and democracy. But over the course of the seventies NAM became increasingly cautious and unwilling to look for new constituencies. As the hopes for a mass socialist movement faded, NAM shifted to the right. Membership declined. In the late seventies NAM merged with the Democratic Socialist Organizing Committee (DSOC)—a group of leading social democratic intellectuals, labor leaders, and politicians—to form the Democratic Socialists of America (DSA). DSOC had regarded itself as the left wing of the Democratic party and the AFL-CIO; it valued its status as left adviser in both organizations and cultivated the respectability that allowed it to play this role. In merging with DSOC, NAM committed itself to a focus on electoral politics and to the pursuit of respectability.

Neither the Democratic party nor the organized labor movement was a promising arena for the development of a new radical politics. By tying itself to these institutions DSA had more or less abandoned the cultural radicalism and the militant style of the movements of the sixties. DSA's politics, however, attracted many former antiwar activists who had concluded that the movement needed to tone down its radicalism to be effective. DSA members and supporters overlapped with the readership of *Socialist Review,* which included former activists who had entered the professions and academics whose views had been affected by the movements of the sixties. Many of those who made up the radical wings of the new movements of the mid to late seventies—the environmental movement, the antinuclear movement, the lesbian and gay movements, and the women's movement—were aware of *Socialist Review*. But they did not consider it their journal, and the Marxist discourse to which it referred did not play a significant part in their thinking. In the categories that had been established in the late sixties, the New American Movement and *Socialist Review* spoke the language of the "politicos"; the new movements spoke the language of the left counterculture.

Reviving the Cultural Revolution

Though many of the new movements of the late 1970s and 1980s criticize existing American culture and are trying to construct more liberatory relationships, the nonviolent direct action movement addresses this task most explicitly and has played the largest role in articulating the concepts that have shaped the thinking of large numbers of activists. In comparison with the more conventional wings of the peace, environmental, and women's movements, the nonviolent direct action movement has been small. Though nonviolent direct action is likely to be a component of movements yet to emerge, it is unlikely that it will dominate them as the New Left and specifically SDS dominated the movements of the sixties, or as the Old Left and specifically the Communist Party dominated the movements of the thirties. The nonviolent direct action movement has been hard to delineate. Its organizations have not been formally linked in any way; the movement has been internally diverse and has overlapped many other movements and communities. It has also been quite elastic. Most of its organizations have had no formal membership; the movement has oscillated between day-to-day reliance on a relatively small core of linked communities of activists and periodic large-scale mobilizations. Though the nonviolent direct action movement eludes attempts to measure or define it, it has had great influence on movements around it, largely by giving political expression to a widely shared sensibility.

The direct action movement speaks to large numbers of people because of the issues addressed and the way it has addressed them. The idea of a revolution that operates in some sphere larger than the state makes sense to many people. Earlier in the twentieth century, it was possible to imagine that state control was the key to a better society, but no longer. Poverty, violence, crime, and widespread disaffection call for changes in public policy, but they also require much deeper social and ideological changes. The failure of the socialist world to solve these problems makes it clear that even control of state and economy is not sufficient. As nations are increasingly subsumed within a global economy and political order, states lose their ability to control the forces that affect their societies. The sense grows that no one is in control, that the traditional forms of power no longer serve their purpose, that genuine power must come from some different source.

The widespread attraction to nonviolence reflects a sense that in the late twentieth century violence is a problem, not a solution to problems. Nuclear weapons have made it impossible to support the idea of another world war. Many areas of the Third World are mired in protracted wars with no end in sight: under these conditions, even though democratic and radical movements are often compelled to defend themselves by the use of force, the concept of "war of national liberation" loses a good deal of its appeal, and the ability of a party to establish peace becomes as attractive as the promise of progressive reforms. For those viewing the world scene from the United States, the argument for nonviolence as the principled basis for international relations becomes increasingly compelling. Government support for or collusion with violent repression in the Third World has led to massive anti-American sentiments and is hard for the American public to condone. Although military spending eats up a large portion of its economy, the United States faces no danger of attack except that created and sustained by the Cold War.

The direct action movement's commitment to creating non-hierarchical structures and relationships is attractive to many people because it expresses the desire for a deepening of democracy and reflects the protest against subordination that has been pressed by women and people of color. Such movements have gained enormous momentum in the postwar years and have been reinforced by the emergence of women's movements around the world and by the growing power and autonomy of Third World nations and movements, as the superpowers decline.

The early New Left understood that postwar society required a new kind of politics, but it was reluctant to say exactly what that politics would be. In part it feared closing the process of exploration too quickly; in part it feared the radical implications of its stance. The early New Left was especially strong on the elite college campuses; it drew heavily from successful upper-middle-class students. Though these students were very sensitive to the hypocrisies and tensions of American life, many of them were made somewhat uneasy by the idea of revolution—either on the traditional political/economic model or one that would encompass social relations and culture broadly. When the antiwar movement turned toward revolution, many early New Leftists simply pulled back; few argued against this approach. The nonviolent direct action movement may have a better chance of developing a viable radical politics for late twentieth-century America because it is not afraid to explore the revolutionary implications of its critique of American society. It also has a deeper understanding of the relationship between democracy, egalitarianism, and revolution, partly because it has learned from the mistakes of the movements of the sixties and partly because of its education in the principles of feminism. The direct action movement's affiliation with environmentalism has also strengthened its vision of a liberatory society.

The nonviolent direct action movement has had problems of its own: in its pursuit of a prefigurative politics it has tended to neglect the arena of political economy, and it has failed to confront the question of political power. In 1966 Richard Flacks called for the integration of what he called "existential politics" and "social change" and argued that movements become distorted when they emphasize one over the other. The direct action movement's cultivation of an experiential, morally based politics has submerged concerns for political efficacy. In spite of these problems, the movement has the advantage of speaking a language that makes sense to increasing numbers of people in the United States, especially the young, women, and religious people, all of whom are likely to be important components of emerging movements for social change.

Chapter Two

The Clamshell Alliance

Consensus and Utopian Democracy

The nonviolent direct action movement of the late 1970s and the 1980s began in 1976 with the formation of the Clamshell Alliance to oppose the construction of a nuclear energy plant near the town of Seabrook, on the New Hampshire coast, through massive civil disobedience. The Clamshell arose from a coalition of local environmentalists who turned to civil disobedience after legal efforts to block the construction of the plant failed and activists who moved to New England in the late sixties and early seventies, disappointed by the antiwar movement and hoping to build a movement in the countryside more in line with the values of the countercultural left. Antinuclear civil disobedience drew massive support from young activists throughout New England and beyond. The Clamshell combined small-group structure and consensus process with nonviolent civil disobedience on a large scale. The Clamshell's mass occupation of the proposed plant site in 1977 led to 1,401 arrests, a euphoric experience of community at the site and in the armories that served as jails, and the creation of alliances around the country modeled on the Clamshell.[1]

Though the Clamshell was unable to stop the construction of the plant at Seabrook through direct action, the nuclear power industry was nevertheless stalled by the early seventies, partly by intraindustry problems: growing evidence that nuclear power was costly, inefficient, and dangerous, as dramatically demonstrated by the accident at Three Mile Island in 1981, and partly by growing popular opposition. The Clamshell, along with other, more conventional antinuclear and environmental organizations, played an important role in generating that opposition.

The greatest contribution of the Clamshell, however, lay not in containing the growth of the nuclear power industry, but in the creation of a mass movement based on nonviolent direct action and infused with a vision of a better world, which it attempted to prefigure in its own practice. Other than the early civil rights movement, on which it was modeled to some degree, the Clamshell represented the first effort in American history to base a mass movement on nonviolent direct action. It continued the New Left impulse toward a politics of living out one's values and rejected the antiwar movement's machismo and authoritarianism. For many of its members the Clamshell was a realization of the hope that had seemed to fade in the late sixties for a movement based on shared commitments and mutual trust. Many younger people who had not been directly involved in the antiwar movement came out of their experience in the Clamshell determined to be part of radical politics for the rest of their lives.

Participation in the Clamshell was, for many people, a transformative experience; but the way the Clamshell ended was shattering. The euphoria did not last. Plans for a second occupation that promised to be much larger than the first were highly publicized, and it seemed likely that this time the gate would be locked. A small group of Clams argued that occupiers should be prepared to cut through the fences, regardless of the police response. Clamshell founders and local seacoast activists argued for strict adherence to nonviolence on principled and practical grounds. With both groups determined to stand fast, there could be no resolution through consensus process. State intervention led the informal leadership of Clamshell founders and others to circumvent consensus process, violating the Clamshell's basic principles. The organization fell apart, leaving deep hostilities and raising the question of whether the radical egalitarianism of consensus process and the ecstatic experience of direct action were viable bases for a political movement.

Years later Anna Gyorgy, a founder of the Clamshell, told me that she would never again become part of an organization that was open to anyone who wanted to join and gave every member power to block the decisions of the majority.[2] Cathy Wolff, Clam media representative and seacoast activist, blamed the deterioration of the Clamshell on the turn toward pursuit of community for its own sake. "We started out wanting to stop Seabrook," she said.

The sense of community was a side benefit. We were all working in unison, we were all motivated. The primary motivation was stopping the nukes, the secondary one, how good it felt. That secondary motivation became primary for a lot of people. Happiness has to be a side benefit. For a lot of people, the process became more important than the product, the means became an end. People said, "I just want to lay my body on the line." They got involved as an opportunity for community, for self-expression, for a sense of purpose—and especially as an opportunity to stay in jail for two weeks.[3]

Cindy Leerer, another seacoast activist, added, "It was magic. Magic doesn't last."[4]

The environmental activists on the New Hampshire seacoast, at least, turned to civil disobedience only after extensive efforts to stop the plant by more conventional means. Since the early seventies there had been talk that the Public Service Corporation (abbreviated PSCo, and pronounced "Pisco") might establish a nuclear power plant in Seabrook, on a piece of land jutting out into the ocean. Preventing this had been a principal concern of the environmental organizations in the seacoast towns. A nuclear power plant, recycling water into the ocean, would have polluted the seacoast and destroyed the ecology of the area. The possibility of a nuclear accident placed residents of the seacoast area in particular jeopardy.

The Seacoast Anti-Pollution League had taken the lead in opposing PSCo's plans for a nuclear plant. Later, the Granite State Alliance brought together environmental and antinuclear activists from around the state. In 1975, Guy Chichester, a staff worker for the Seacoast Anti-Pollution League (and soon to be a founder of the Clamshell Alliance), initiated a referendum on the question in Seabrook, which ran against the plant, 767 to 432. Referenda were then held in about a dozen nearby towns. Voters were asked whether or not they supported the people of Seabrook in their vote against the PSCo plant. All but a few towns that tabled the issue endorsed the Seabrook vote.

Local votes against the plant were not enough to stop its construction, and when the license for the plant was granted by the New Hampshire Nuclear Regulatory Commission in June 1976, many local activists felt it was time to move from electoral and legal activity to direct action. Antinuclear activists were inspired by the example of Wyhl, Germany, where in 1975 a site proposed by the government for a nuclear plant was occupied by 28,000 people. That occupation was begun by several hundred from the local farming community and joined by thousands of antinuclear activists from Germany, France, and Switzerland.[5] It was maintained for a year, halting and finally canceling construction of the plant. The occupation at Wyhl, and others like it elsewhere in Europe, reinforced the belief of radicals in the antinuclear movement that it was time to turn from electoral to direct action.

A Signal to the Movement

By 1976, when the Clamshell was formed, there was already considerable interest in rural New England circles of countercultural leftists in civil disobedience as the focal point of a new kind of politics. In February 1974, Sam Lovejoy, a member of the Montague Farm, outside the town of Montague in northwestern Massachusetts, took a crowbar and knocked down a tower erected by Northeast Utilities as part of a projected nuclear power plant. Lovejoy then hitchhiked to the Montague police station and handed the police a written statement explaining and taking responsibility for the action. Lovejoy was charged with "malicious destruction of personal property" and went on trial in September. He presented expert witnesses who testified to the dangers posed by nuclear power and to the legitimacy of civil disobedience as a form of protest. After a nine-day trial before a packed courthouse, Lovejoy was acquitted by the judge on grounds that the charge was erroneous: it should have been "destruction of real [rather than personal] property," which would have been a misdemeanor, not a felony. Later interviews with the jurors made it clear that even if Lovejoy had not been acquitted on a technicality, they would have found him innocent on the ground that they did not regard his action as malicious.[6]

Sam Lovejoy's action became something of a legend in New

England, especially among activists and the counterculture. Montague Farm had been established after a split in the Boston-based Liberation News Service (LNS) in the early 1970s. One group moved to Montague and had established an organic farm, supporting themselves mostly by writing until the farm was producing to capacity. The fact that the Montague group had taken the LNS press, which sat in the barn unused, provoked some skepticism among other rural New England activists, but Lovejoy's action and the local political work of other Montague Farm people nevertheless placed them in the leadership of the emerging New England antinuclear movement.

Lovejoy's action had, in fact, been intended to encourage that movement and to give it some direction. Lovejoy argued that through the issue of nuclear power, the antiwar movement would be able to establish itself in local communities and find a strength that the student base and the national focus of the antiwar movement had not allowed.

To dump the tower was to send a signal to the politicians, and also to the movement. Not just the upper-middle-class antinuclear power movement but also to the New Left, which I was a member of, that the war was ending, there were other issues. The single biggest failure of the New Left was that it never had a home base. It had a student base. But movements don't last unless they have home base, a population base, not just an age-segment base. To the antinuclear power movement I was saying, there are other tactics. If you lose every legal fight, there are other tactics. Civil disobedience is one way to invigorate, empower younger people.[7]

Other strains of nonviolent civil disobedience contributed to the formation of an antinuclear movement in rural New England. Ware, New Hampshire, was the home of the Greenleaf Harvesters' Guild, a farming collective organized on pacifist principles by Arthur Harvey, a Gandhi scholar. Harvey and others from the Guild participated in the activities of the People's Energy Project, one of the environmentalist groups on the seacoast. In January 1976, Ron Rieck, one of the Guild's apple pickers, erected a sleeping platform on top of a pole on the site designated for the nuclear plant. To bear witness against the projected plant, Rieck climbed up to the platform and stayed there two days and nights, with supporters bringing food and comfort, until he was arrested. His supporters included not only local activists but also a few people from the Cambridge office of the American Friends Service Committee, which had, since the mid-sixties, been more willing than any other to involve itself in active protest. The AFSC members who went to New Hampshire to encourage Ron Rieck hoped that his action might be one more step toward a nonviolent antinuclear movement. Two staff members from the Cambridge AFSC, Elizabeth Boardman and Suki Rice, were invited back to the seacoast by local activists to give training in nonviolent direct action.

The Creation of the Clamshell Alliance

In June 1976, when PSCo was granted a license to begin construction of the plant, the networks already existed for the formation of an antinuclear movement that would focus on the use of nonviolent direct action. A small meeting was held at Guy Chichester's house in the seacoast town of Rye. Soon after, a somewhat larger meeting of about fifty people was held to ratify and expand the decisions made at the first meeting. Seacoast activists made up most participants in those early meetings, joined by Sam Lovejoy from the Montague Farm. Two other Montague people, Anna Gyorgy and Harvey Wasserman, were to become members of the Clamshell steering committee, but neither was present at the initial meetings. Anna was coordinating antinuclear efforts in Western Massachusetts, and Harvey Wasserman was in Europe; he became involved in the Clamshell on his return, nearly a year later. Two staff members from the Cambridge office of the AFSC, Elizabeth Boardman and Suki Rice, drove up to New Hampshire to participate in forming the organization. Boardman and Rice had the support of Cambridge AFSC but were not representing it: the AFSC cannot join a coalition or officially lend its support to another organization without a decision of the board of directors, which had been neither requested nor given. Nevertheless, Boardman and Rice continued to be among the most active of the inner circle. All of the founding members of the Clamshell were in their twenties or early thirties, with the exception of Elizabeth Boardman, a long-time Quaker and peace activist a generation older than most of her fellow Clams.

The name Clamshell Alliance (often shortened to "the Clam")
referred to the clams living in sand and mud flats along the seacoast, which would have been destroyed by nuclear wastewater.
The Clamshell's adherence to nonviolent direct action, semiau-
tonomous local groups, and decision making by consensus emerged
more or less spontaneously at its first meetings. The organization
had been formed out of a shared sense that the limits of electoral
and legal action had been reached; and nonviolence made sense
to everyone, for various reasons. "I was not a pacifist, but I was a
committed nonviolentist when it came to nuclear power," Sam
Lovejoy remembered. "Elizabeth [Boardman] is a committed
nonviolentist; they believe in it as a religion. The principle of
nonviolence was laid out at our first meeting, ratified at the second. As for consensus, it went from 'it's operating this way' to
'there's got to be a word for it,' so Elizabeth said, 'it's consensus.'
She laid out how it was used in the AFSC and earlier movements.
It was legitimized at our second, large meeting."[8]

Although nonviolence and consensus decision making were articulated by the Quakers, they were also identified with the early
civil rights movement, in which some founding members of the
Clamshell had participated, and which many, including the
Quakers, regarded as a model for political action. Guy Chichester
recalled that "nonviolence came [into the Clamshell] because of
the trainings [conducted by the Quakers]. We knew that the AFSC
people knew about nonviolence. Also, I had grown up through
the civil rights marches in the South, and I saw nonviolence as a
way for people to come together."[9]

The First Occupation

The focus of the Clamshell's activity was a series of occupations
of the site of the proposed Seabrook plant, leading up to the
massive occupation of the spring of 1977. These occupations
combined dramatic political action with an intense experience of
community; they attracted public attention to the issue of nuclear
power, and they drew to the Clamshell a constituency in search
of a morally charged experiential politics. At the first meetings of
the Clamshell, it was decided that the first occupation should be
small and made up only of New Hampshire residents. The sec-

ond should be larger and should include people from other states as well, and the third should be a mass occupation. One local activist, Rennie Cushing, proposed a "power of ten" rule: the first occupation should be limited to 18 people, the second to 180, and the third, it was hoped, would draw 1,800 willing to be arrested. The reality turned out to be surprisingly close to this projection. On August 1, 1976, 18 people walked down the abandoned railway tracks leading into the site and were arrested. On August 22, in pouring rain, 180 people, some of them from Boston and Western Massachusetts, were arrested. Suki Rice provided nonviolence training before each action.

After the August 22 occupation, planning began for the mass occupation, originally scheduled for October but put off to the following spring because of the possibility of bad weather, and because it had become clear that the occupation would draw a large number of people and more time was needed for preparation. In the meantime, an Alternative Energy Fair was held to introduce local residents to the idea of safe energy as opposed to nuclear energy. Through the winter, intensive nonviolence trainings were held. On April 30 and May 1, 1977, some 2,400 people, mostly from New England, gathered at Seabrook. Only members of affinity groups were allowed to participate; this rule ensured that the action would be restricted to people who had been introduced to the ideas of nonviolence and were part of a collective structure. Elizabeth Boardman remembered that one man, "roaring drunk," tried to join at the last minute but was turned away by marshals trained for the event on the ground that he was not attached to an affinity group. When he tried to push the marshals away they "hugged him out of the way."[10]

The protesters walked onto the site, which, because it was Saturday, was empty of workers. The occupation was set up on a village model, with several affinity groups in each space marked out as a camping area, and with "roads" laid out between the encampments. Each "village" of affinity groups chose a representative to attend a "spokescouncil," which would attempt to arrive at consensus on any issues that arose and would convey those decisions to the police when they arrived. Saturday afternoon was spent digging latrines and setting up camp. The next morning the occupiers awoke to find the National Guard on the other side of the fence that surrounded the site. Around noon a helicopter arrived bringing New Hampshire governor Meldrim Thompson. The occupiers were told that anyone not off the site within twenty minutes would be arrested. About a thousand left, while 1,401 remained to be arrested. The protesters were taken by bus to be arraigned at the Portsmouth armory. Some were kept there, but the majority were again placed in buses and distributed among six other armories throughout New Hampshire, where they stayed until they were released two weeks later.

A Community of Protest

The occupation and the armory experience built a strong sense of community among the protesters, an important source of which was the affinity group. The Clamshell Alliance was made up of local groups that might be of any size; it had been agreed that civil disobedience actions should be based on affinity groups made up of roughly eight to fifteen people who already knew one another and could work well together and rely on one another. Those who participated in the first small action did so as individuals; the second, larger action was based on affinity groups. The concept of an affinity group had been introduced to the New Left in the mid-sixties by the philosopher Murray Bookchin, who found it in his studies of Spanish anarchism. Though Bookchin was to become involved with the Clamshell Alliance, along with others at his Institute for Social Ecology in Burlington, Vermont, it was in fact the Quakers who introduced the idea of affinity groups to the Clamshell. Guy Chichester remembered, "Before I met Elizabeth and Suki I never in my life had heard of any such thing as an affinity group, and I was a fairly well read person. They showed us the special protections afforded by an affinity group in times of stress, when there might be violence by the police. The affinity group evolved into something that included that part, and also the part that Bookchin described [in his account of Spanish anarchism], the spirit of community."[11]

The bonds among members of affinity groups helped many people through the frightening aspects of arrest. Some groups waited for hours to be arrested and then were kept in the buses for sixteen or twenty hours before being arraigned. In some cases the police confiscated the food the protesters had brought with them. After arraignment, the protesters endured long bus rides to the armories where they were to stay. People from the Movement for a New Society (MNS), a Philadelphia-based group with Quaker origins that had for many years brought nonviolent training and a Quaker process to various protest groups, participated in the occupation and played an important role in bringing a sense of community to the armories.

Meg Simonds, a member of Boston Clam, was separated from her affinity group and without sleep for thirty-six hours before she was deposited at the Manchester armory, where the rest of her affinity group had been brought earlier. "There were seven hundred people," she remembered. "It looked like a mass of bodies. I didn't see one person that I knew. I began to lose it. A man came over and welcomed me to the Manchester armory; he was from MNS. He took me around; 'We'll find your affinity group,' he said. I don't know if I would have made it without that. I was on the verge of hysteria. Once I found my affinity group I was okay."[12]

The experience in the armories quickly created a sense of community among protesters. In the Manchester armory, the MNS people called a meeting of facilitators from the various affinity groups to discuss whether to accept bail or demand release on "own recognizance" (OR). Each affinity group was asked to decide this question separately. When the affinity groups came together for a mass meeting, spokespersons (spokes) from the various affinity groups were asked to stand up to indicate their groups' decisions. No one stood up when asked which groups wanted to go out on bail. When asked which groups would demand OR, all the spokes stood up. "Once we got that done, we were united as a group," Meg Simonds said. "You need a unifying decision that you can make quickly and easily at the beginning."

This demonstration of the capacity of the consensus process to affirm solidarity strengthened the protesters' determination to insist on their right to use it. "The authorities were always coming in and saying we had to make some decision now," Meg Simonds recalled. "We would say, that's not enough time. We're going to use our process. They had to allow us to do what we wanted. The officers said, 'We want to talk to your leader.' We said no, we have a committee of two men and two women, which will rotate daily; that's who will speak with you. The first time we said it the officers walked out. But several hours later they came back and said okay."

For several days the protesters had no beds, but slept on the concrete floors. Finally someone remembered that the state of New Hampshire had cots stored away for civil defense, and these were brought in. In spite of relatively difficult physical conditions, a spirit of euphoric community developed quickly. Workshops were organized. Elizabeth Boardman, who was also being held in the Manchester armory, recalled that "one group led singing, another gave lessons in journal writing. We were as busy and organized as you please, running around and taking our lessons." Boardman was on the liaison committee when the authorities raised the issue of "immorality" in the armory. If it did not stop, the officers said, men and women would be separated. "It was evidently supposed to be my role as an older woman to be shocked about this," Boardman said. "I said to the lieutenant, 'If you break up our arrangement of affinity groups, if you separate us from our affinity groups, we are not going to be responsible for what hell breaks loose.' "[13] The protesters eventually found a solution in the cardboard boxes in which the cots had been delivered. Two structures of cardboard boxes were erected, each with a little curtained door. One was for privacy for women, the other was for couples. There were no more complaints about immorality.

The protesters were released after two weeks, pending their trials. A few trials were held during the winter but most were put off; finally, in most cases, the charges were dismissed. The occupation and the experience in the armories put the Clamshell on the front page of newspapers, especially in New England. Dick Bell, at the time managing editor of the Boston *Real Paper,* and beginning to get involved in the Clam, points out that the reporting of those events did not highlight the issue of nuclear power. "There was likely to be one paragraph about nuclear power in thousands of inches of coverage. Nevertheless, it was a tremendous spectacle, the people moving onto the site, digging the latrines, being taken to the armories, the legal process. It could not have been a better media event."[14]

Soft and Hard Clams

The occupation and the armory experience showed that the Clamshell represented a new kind of politics, one that many people, especially young people, found attractive. Over the summer and fall of 1977 the Clamshell was flooded with new members. The occupation had been extremely successful, but of course it had not stopped PSCo's plans to construct a nuclear plant at Seabrook. The Clamshell decided to hold another mass occupation in June 1978, with the hope that this one would be two or three times as large as the last. By December, conflicts about what form the occupation should take were breaking out in Boston Clam, which was an important group because of the large number of occupiers from Boston in the April occupation and because of the numbers of people joining the Clam in Boston. A committee had been set up by Boston Clam, called the Occupation/Restoration Task Force, to plan the upcoming occupation (and the subsequent "restoration" of the site); the committee drew a number of Clams who called themselves anarchists.

The term "anarchist" was a slippery one in the Clamshell, because many—probably most—Clams regarded themselves as anarchists. The rejection of hierarchy, the espousal of the consensus process, the affinity group structure, spokes and spokescouncils, were all regarded as coming directly or indirectly out of an anarchist tradition. But the Boston anarchists brought a new element into the Clamshell. Associated with groups such as the Black Rose, which ran an anarchist lecture series at MIT, and Hard Rain, a Boston affinity group, they put themselves forward as representing militancy against what they regarded as the prevailing timidity. Some argued later that the Boston anarchists never believed in nonviolence. Whether or not this was true, they were willing to stretch the limits of nonviolence considerably further than the Quakers and other founding members of the Clamshell.

The terms "soft Clams" and "hard Clams" began to be used to distinguish the two approaches. As the Hard Rain affinity group moved to the center of debate, its name came to be identified with the hard Clam position, even though not all hard Clams were members of Hard Rain. The debate focused on the question of what the Clamshell should do if, as seemed likely, the gate to the Seabrook site were locked when the next occupation was attempted. In April, the demonstrators had been permitted onto the site on Saturday as long as they were prepared to leave on Sunday, to allow the workers to enter. The demonstrators' refusal to leave had been the signal for the arrests. After the success of the first action, PSCo was unlikely to leave the gate open on the date of a planned Clamshell occupation. And it seemed very likely that the New Hampshire police, under the direction of Governor Thompson, a vociferous supporter of nuclear power, would back up PSCo.

The Hard Rain people argued that the demonstrators should take wire cutters and be prepared to cut through the fence. Others objected that to do so was contrary to their principles, because it was more or less guaranteed to provoke police violence for which the Clamshell could be regarded as responsible. The Hard Rain people argued that the American working class would never take an organization seriously that was not willing to confront the police. The opposition feared that the prospect of violence would severely limit the numbers of people who would be willing to take part in the occupation.[15]

Guidelines for the June 24 action required nonviolence training and adherence to a code of nonviolence by all participants:

1. Everyone must receive preparation in nonviolent direct action before taking part in the action—either in support or as an occupier.
2. No weapons of any kind.
3. No damage or destruction of PSCo or Seabrook property.
4. No running at any time.
5. No strategic or tactical movement after dark.
6. No breaking through police lines.
7. No dogs.
8. No drugs or alcohol.
9. In case of confrontation, we will sit down.
10. We will not block workers' personal access to the site.[16]

In a further elaboration of nonviolence, occupiers were asked to adopt an "attitude towards officials and others who may oppose us . . . of sympathetic understanding of the burdens and responsibilities that they carry" and to "speak to the best in all people, rather than seeking to exploit their weakness to what we may believe is our advantage. . . . No matter what the circumstances or provocation, we should not respond with violence to acts directed against us."[17]

The most controversial item in the guidelines was the proscription against destruction of property. It was argued in favor of cutting fences that an assault on property rather than on people was acceptable and that anyway the fences would be repaired as soon as the demonstrators were on the other side. Some Clams suggested other ways of getting in, such as digging under the fences or using large ladders to climb over them. But there were practical problems with each of these proposals. Ultimately the debate about fence cutting was a debate about the relationship between militance and nonviolence, about whether the Clam should adopt the confrontational style that had been the measure of commitment for many in the antiwar movement or attempt to construct a different kind of politics.

Conflicts about Leadership and Decision Making

The debate about fence cutting raised the questions how decisions should be made in an organization that described itself as leaderless and what the content of those decisions should be. Through the winter and spring of 1978 the organization grew rapidly. Week-to-week direction was provided by a coordinating committee centered on the Portsmouth office staff and other seacoast and Western Massachusetts activists, most of whom had been part of the Clamshell since its earliest days. As the debate about fence cutting proceeded, the Hard Rain people argued that it was the old guard, especially the "Montague Farm gang" (or, less affectionately, the "Montague Farm mafia") that was holding back militancy. This argument hit home in many quarters because there were others, many with no sympathy for fence cutting, who for other reasons had doubts about the role of Montague Farm in the Clamshell. By that time Sam Lovejoy of the Montague group was spending most of his time traveling around the country, speaking about nuclear power and encouraging resistance to it, in the effort to start a national movement. Lovejoy's efforts, although instrumental in organizing a number of other antinuclear alliances, did little to endear him to critics in the Clamshell who regarded him as "star-tripping." Harvey Wasserman and Anna Gyorgy, also of Montague Farm, were traveling frequently for the antinuclear movement at that time.

The Montague people's assumption of what amounted to leadership roles in a movement that purported to have no leadership caused resentment. The fact that neither Lovejoy nor Wasserman nor Gyorgy had taken part in any of the Clamshell's occupations provided further rationale for animosity toward them. The Montague Farm people, along with many of the founders of the Clamshell, regarded civil disobedience as only one of a number of tactics that should be used to oppose nuclear power. But most of those who joined the Clamshell after the 1977 occupation were inspired by civil disobedience and regarded it as central to what the organization was about.

Tensions over leadership were heightened by the media's seeming to choose leaders. Sam Lovejoy drew the attention of the press after he knocked over the tower. Lovejoy, Gyorgy, and Wasserman all had forceful, charismatic personalities that attracted media attention. After the Montague gang, the media focused on a few activists on the seacoast, Guy Chichester and Rennie Cushing in particular, whose self-confidence and flair for public speaking made them good subjects. It was easy for rank-and-file Clams in other parts of New England to feel that their organization was being dominated by leaders they had never chosen.

If not for the leadership question, and if it had not been seen as a challenge to the "old guard," the Hard Rain call for cutting fences probably would have made less headway. The conflict was fed by confusion over the Clamshell's decision-making process. The founding group had agreed that the Clamshell should be run by consensus, with Quaker process as a working model. In the Clamshell's first year, when it was still relatively small and there was a great deal of good will and agreement on basic aims, consensus had worked wonderfully. It had also worked well in the armories, even when large numbers of people tried to make decisions together. Relatively brief but intense experiences of community building, such as the occupation and the time spent in the armories, can generate either sharp conflict or a euphoric spirit of cooperation. In the armories, consensus process worked well because everyone wanted it to work and because there was plenty of time to work out every question.

There were, however, structural problems in the decision-making process, which went unnoticed as long as it worked well, no factions arose in the organization, and power struggles were not prominent. If someone could not agree on a particular point, it was possible to "stand aside" and allow a decision to be made without giving assent but also without impeding the will of the group. When, in the fall of 1978, the Clamshell began to expand rapidly and nonviolence training began to take place on a large scale, the concept of the "block" was introduced: a person with strong principled objections could stand in the way of a group decision. The block was a departure from the Quaker practice of putting aside a seemingly unresolvable conflict for a time and allowing the disputants to rethink it. During the fall of 1977 and the spring of 1978, the MNS was heavily involved in nonviolence training. The block was included as an element of consensus process in MNS sessions, and no one seems to have given much thought to the problems that could arise if every individual had the power to halt the whole organization.

In the context of the debate over fence cutting, blocking consensus assumed an important role within the Clamshell. Hard Rain and the people who came together around them had no stake in arriving at consensus. They saw their differences with the old guard as fundamental and based on principle. As Harvey Halpern, not a member of Hard Rain but one of the leading proponents of fence cutting, told me, the question was whether to sit down and be arrested or to "physically stop the nuke, to act in concert with others to stop the nuke ourselves."[18] The question was whether to "appeal to the authorities" through a symbolic action or to pull down the fences, get onto the site, and build villages, as the Germans had done at Wyhl. Halpern told me that this could have been done if fifty or seventy thousand people had come to Seabrook to occupy the site. Others recall that in the debates that took place at the time, the Hard Rain people had also argued that part of the question was how to draw working-class people into the antinuclear movement. The working class, they claimed, had no patience with merely symbolic protest or with middle-class protesters who were afraid to confront police violence.[19]

The fence-cutting proposal was an attempt to revive the confrontational style of the antiwar movement in an organization that had been formed in the hope of finding a different approach to protest. Faced with sharp disagreements, the Hard Rain people did not hesitate to block any consensus that would exclude fence cutting from the occupation. There were perhaps ten or fifteen people actively arguing for the Hard Rain approach. Within Boston Clam a roughly equal number of people argued strongly against it, primarily on the ground that a threat of violence would deter many people who might otherwise join the occupation. These two groups contained the most vocal people in Boston Clam; between them were those who were reluctant to come down firmly on either side.

The middle group, whose allegiance was sought by both sides, consisted of people who did not especially like the idea of fence cutting but sympathized with Hard Rain's hostility to the Clamshell's unofficial leadership on the seacoast and in Western Massachusetts, and tended to see the Hard Rain group as a minority trying to make themselves heard. In Boston, the anti-fence-cutting group began to regard Hard Rain as troublemakers, turned to heavy-handed tactics against them, and became increasingly impatient with the middle group and its continued sympathy for Hard Rain. Out of frustration, the anti-fence-cutting group proposed that the Clamshell's process should be revised. When consensus could not be reached, the vote should be resorted to, with an 80 percent majority required for a decision to stand.

The middle group opposed this modification on the ground that it would disempower the 20 percent whose votes were not necessary to arrive at a decision. In proposing that consensus process be modified, the anti-fence-cutting group managed to cast itself as the opponents of what the Clamshell stood for, namely, a political process in which everyone's voice would be heard. Dick Bell, a leading opponent of fence cutting, argues that resistance was based on a general identification with that remaining 20 percent as a disenfranchised minority (and by implication with the fence cutters, who would undoubtedly have found themselves in that percentage). There was a widespread feeling, Bell said, that to overrule a minority would not be nice. Feelings would be hurt. "What we had was the politics of niceness. For a significant group, being nice was more important than being right. To argue for a position was not nice. It was difficult, under these conditions, to have a simple principled argument. People who argued strongly would be condemned for not being nice, not for whether their argument was right or not."[20]

The Rath Proposal: State Intervention

The debate over fence cutting raised three crucial issues for the Clamshell: where the line between violence and nonviolence should be drawn, what to do when consensus could not be reached on a major issue, and whether there was any legitimate role for leadership. Any one of these questions had the potential to divide the organization; the three combined led to an explosion that destroyed the organization. If the organization as a whole had seriously addressed these issues as soon as they arose there might have been some chance of resolving them. But conflicts were allowed to simmer within Boston Clam for a very long time before the rest of the organization paid any attention.

The anti-fence-cutting group in Boston appealed to the unofficial leadership on the seacoast and at Montague Farm to come to Boston and help resolve the debate. But the coordinating committee and the people in the Portsmouth office were busy trying to pull together a rapidly growing regional movement. Furthermore, in an organization that officially had no leadership, in which the coordinating committee was regarded as simply expressing the accumulated will of the various local groups, no one had the authority to intervene. Many people at the center of the Clamshell had been doing little but Clamshell work for a year and a half or more and were tired of being told that they were dominating the organization. They had no desire to travel to Boston and subject themselves to a barrage of such criticisms. Furthermore, many of the Clamshell activists in northern New England believed that the rural roots of the movement mattered most, that what went on in Boston should not be given undue weight. The view circulated among the rural people (most of whom had recently fled the cities themselves) that the behavior of the Hard Rain people could be put down to urban stress: city life drives people crazy.

As the estimated number of those who would join the occupation grew and the debate about fence cutting continued unabated, the activists on the seacoast grew uneasy. The seacoast communities had voted their opposition to nuclear power, and those towns contained a reservoir of good feeling for the Clamshell because of its prominence in the effort to keep the plant from being constructed. But the Clamshell had never had a strong local base of support for civil disobedience. Many of the seacoast activists had themselves either grown up in the area or lived there for many years. But the majority even of the local activists were young people who had led relatively mobile lives and were not integrated into the older, more stable seacoast communities. Some older residents gave active support to the Clamshell: a number had made their houses available to organizers and had allowed protesters to camp on their land before the occupation of 1977. But there were few such people. The Clamshell could count on the support of the rural countercultural left, but the more tenuous support of the indigenous communities could easily be destroyed by the threat of a violent action.

In the late spring of 1978, signs of trouble appeared. Supporters of the Clamshell along the seacoast who had volunteered their land as staging grounds for the occupation were warned by the state that their property might be reassessed for increased taxes. A few reported fires on their property. At this point New Hampshire attorney general Tom Rath publicly proposed that the Clamshell hold a demonstration on the site over an agreed-upon weekend, with the stipulation that the demonstrators would leave at the end of that time. The Governor's council endorsed this proposal. The Clamshell coordinating committee was in touch with Rath and other state officials, and began to discuss how to respond to Rath's proposal.

Pressures for a rapid decision were created by the fact that Rath announced his proposal through the media rather than going to the Clamshell first, and the fact that the proposal came in May, close to the planned occupation of the site. Members of the coordinating committee canvassed Clamshell supporters on the seacoast and reported that few remained willing to let occupiers use their land. Critics of the coordinating committee later claimed that some of these canvassers were not merely polling Clamshell supporters but trying also to convince them that it would be unwise to allow their land to be used for an occupation. It is possible that some members of the coordinating committee, having concluded that the occupation should not take place, wanted to make their position as strong as possible. But it is hard to believe that the seacoast communities were very enthusiastic about an occupation that was likely to lead to violence.

The core members of the coordinating committee felt that it would be a bad idea to go ahead with the occupation; they were afraid that the Hard Rain people would do something to cost the Clamshell its local support. The problem was not so much that the coordinating committee decided to abandon the action that had been the focus of Clamshell organizing for a year (though that in itself would have been very difficult for the organization to have absorbed) but that their lack of confidence in the possibility of resolving the issue led them to violate Clamshell procedures. An expanded coordinating committee meeting was held with spokes from Clamshell groups throughout the region. Consensus was reached to accept the attorney general's proposal. As soon as the meeting was over, before the decision could be relayed back to the local groups and discussed there, the media were informed that the occupation had been canceled.

In both form and spirit, Clamshell procedure had been violated. Some spokes were genuinely persuaded to support the Rath proposal, but others had agreed only under pressure. The decision was reached, according to one seacoast activist, by "an arm-twisting type of consensus." Many spokes went against the instructions of local groups in giving their support. The failure to relay the decision back to the local groups presumed that the coordinating committee had the authority to make final decisions, contrary to the idea that power should be decentralized and that the purpose of the coordinating committee was to facilitate decision making by the organization as a whole, not to make decisions itself. The fact that the decision had been announced in the press made it irreversible. For local groups to reject the decision of the coordinating committee would have been meaningless, because there was no time to revive the occupation.

Many members of the coordinating committee and other activists on the seacoast and in Western Massachusetts believed that Clamshell groups in the seacoast communities had a special right to veto Clam actions. The local people, the argument went, had special concerns about a nuclear plant because of the damage it would do to their area and because they would be most vulnerable. Furthermore, a badly planned action would have more impact on the local activists than anyone else. According to this line of thinking, the coordinating committee was within its rights to stop the occupation, since local Clamshell groups and supporters were against it.

The founders of the Clamshell understood that people living near the Seabrook site had a privileged place in Clamshell decision making, but this understanding had never been formally endorsed by the Clamshell as a whole. Many newer Clams in other areas of New England were unaware of it and assumed, during the months of preparation for the occupation, that the action belonged as much to them as to the seacoast people. Murray Bookchin, who played an important role in organizing the Clamshell in Vermont, pointed out that an accident would have endangered everyone in the region and beyond. In that sense, the local communities had no special claim to a veto over actions.[21] In fact the idea of the special veto came partly from a commitment to local autonomy and partly from the understanding that to retain its legitimacy and political clout, the Clamshell must maintain support in the communities close to the site.

The decision not to hold an occupation effectively destroyed the Clamshell. Members of the coordinating committee, along with seacoast activists, went to local groups throughout the region to try to explain the decision. Angry meetings were followed by demoralization. Throughout New England, people began to leave the Clamshell. In Vermont, Murray Bookchin recalls, a meeting was addressed by two activists from the seacoast who had been involved in the decision to call off the occupation. Making a personal appeal for trust, they called for unity and tried to revive commitment to the aims of the movement, but their arguments fell on deaf ears. People drifted out of the meeting and then out of the movement entirely.

Division and Collapse of the Clamshell

The shift from occupation to a legal demonstration was the signal for the Hard Rain people, and others who had become disillusioned with the existing informal leadership of the Clamshell, to form their own organization, Clams for Direct Action at Seabrook (CDAS), committed to continuing militant occupations of the Seabrook site. But the constituency for such actions was in fact considerably more limited than when the original Clamshell mobilized, with its clear commitment to nonviolence and its attempt to find a nonconfrontational style of protest. The Hard Rain people had said that they were committed to physically preventing the construction of the plant while the old guard was only interested in symbolic politics. But the first occupation they mobilized was much too small to have any effect on the plant, and the second was smaller than the first.

CDAS was unable to sustain a return to the militant style of the late sixties: the people who came to occupy the plant site could not bring themselves to engage in such confrontational politics. The new series of actions slipped into the style of politics the Clamshell had originally embraced, without being able to articulate the process or acknowledge that it was happening. In fact the appeal of CDAS had more to do with the opportunity to occupy the site, and disaffection with the regular Clamshell for its violation of democratic process, than with enthusiasm for late-sixties-style militancy. The founders of CDAS, and much of its constituency, identified themselves as anarchist much more vehemently than had the founders of the Clamshell, for most of whom nonviolence had been the central term. But anarchism and nonviolence were nevertheless linked in many people's minds as components of a new kind of democratic politics. The CDAS actions were shaped by the same new spirit of radicalism as the earlier Clamshell.

In accordance with the Rath proposal, a legal demonstration was held at the site in place of an occupation. Twenty thousand people came. It was the largest demonstration the Clamshell had ever held and on that ground alone could be considered a success. Meanwhile, local groups were dwindling. Clamshell held an action in Washington, D.C., in which several hundred people camped out in front of the Nuclear Regulatory Commission for several days, demanding that the plant at Seabrook not be constructed. The sit-in culminated in the announcement of a temporary halt in construction, which overjoyed the demonstrators and led to what one described as "the most incredible street party."[22] But the Clamshell as a whole was crumbling, and no single demonstration could revive it.

At the legal demonstration at Seabrook in June, the Hard Rain/ Black Rose people passed out a leaflet calling for occupation and signed "Clams for Democracy." A month later, activists were unhappy enough about the direction being taken by the Clamshell to meet and set up what amounted to a rival organization. Out of this meeting came CDAS and a call for an occupation in October. The publicity did not make the distinction between CDAS and the Clamshell clear. The Clamshell office in Portsmouth, fearing that there would be violence at the CDAS occupation, sent a letter to peace groups around the country denying any connection with that action. This denial caused further hard feelings between the Clamshell leadership and CDAS.

In October, the first CDAS occupation of Seabrook took place. About two thousand people came, many from outside New England. Some wore helmets and other military-style protective gear. Many brought fence-cutting tools. The demonstrators stood outside the fence; the police stood on the site, inside the fence. A number of demonstrators began cutting into the fence. As sections of the fence fell to the ground, removing the barrier between them, the police were standing directly in front of the demonstrators. Aikos Barton, a demonstrator from Boston, recalls that the results were not what the organizers of the action had expected.

Now the police were standing in front of us. So everyone stepped back. That summarizes the whole year-long debate. If there had been thirty thousand people there, or more German-style alienation [of the sort that characterized the German antinuclear movement of the time], maybe there would have been a confrontation. But people never walked through the fence. We decided to circle the site, walking around the fence. That's not a Hard Rain thing to do. The police inside didn't really know what was going on. But they didn't want to arrest people, they wanted to disperse us. When we finished circling the site, we went back to camp.[23]

CDAS attempted a second occupation of the site in the spring, and some five hundred people came. Having failed to mobilize effective direct action at Seabrook, CDAS disbanded. The Clamshell office continued to exist and to mount local efforts against nuclear power, at Seabrook and elsewhere. Many Clamshell activists on the seacoast returned to electorally oriented activities, similar to those in which they had been involved before the formation of the Clamshell. Clams played a major role in mobilizing public opinion to defeat a state ballot initiative, "Construction Work in Progress," which would have allowed PSCo to charge consumers for the cost of construction while a nuclear energy plant was being built. The initiative's failure was a prime factor in the deferral of the Seabrook plant to the indefinite future. A number of the Clams who took part in that campaign had been involved in electoral struggles against nuclear energy before the Clamshell emerged. Their return to electoral activity reflected some degree of disillusionment with civil disobedience.

Nonviolent Direct Action: Democracy and a Better World

The Clamshell was the first important political expression of an anarchist/countercultural tendency that emerged from the movements of the sixties and flowered in the seventies. It drew on a philosophy and tradition that had been pushed aside by much of the antiwar movement: the nonviolent direct action of Gandhi and of Christian pacifism, the Quaker devotion to consensus and community, and the example of civil rights in creating a mass movement based on these principles. The Quakers in the founding Clamshell group, especially Elizabeth Boardman, played a key role in articulating nonviolence and consensus and in pointing to their historical roots.

The fundamental reason nonviolence and consensus were adopted by the Clamshell was that the culture of which it was a part was already imbued with those values. The Clamshell's commitment to feminism deepened the democratic component of nonviolence, and opened up more space for female leadership than had been present in the movements that had preceded it. That commitment was particularly important for a movement that relied on the support of local constituencies: in the seacoast communities, women were at the center of the opposition to the plant and played a larger role than men in holding the movement together. The Clamshell's commitment to environmentalism was an important addition to the tradition of nonviolence. Feminism and environmentalism were both elements in the better world the Clamshell envisioned. The broad appeal of the Clamshell had a great deal to do with its ability to bring together values that were held by many people, and to associate them with the specific and seemingly winnable issue of nuclear power.

The concept of democracy was at the heart of the Clamshell's vision, and its rapid growth and public appeal were based to a large extent on the fact that it spoke directly to people's ability to make the decisions that would shape their environment. The postwar era has seen the emergence of a national security state that has shielded U.S. foreign policy from democratic intervention to a greater degree than ever before. The atom bomb has been the rationale for this shift, and questions involving nuclear power have in particular been made the province of the national security community. To the founders of the Clamshell, nuclear weapons seemed too large and too abstract to be a promising basis for building a mass movement. Nuclear power, on the other hand, was concrete and local. Unlike nuclear weapons, which threaten everyone more or less equally, nuclear power plants pose special dangers for those living near them. Furthermore, victories seemed more easily attainable in the arena of nuclear power. It is easier to halt the construction of a particular plant than to take on the arms race.

Protest against nuclear power tapped emotions engendered by the larger nuclear issue and the public's lack of control over it. The Clamshell attempted to be an embryonic grass roots democracy, accepting everyone who pledged nonviolence and open to the press, the state, or anyone else who asked about its plans. The question of democracy was highlighted by the contrast between an organization of this sort and a nuclear energy corporation with a great deal of power over the lives of people living in the vicinity of the plant and little if any accountability to them. Unlike the more electorally oriented antinuclear organizations, the Clamshell was thoroughly aware of the larger implications of its work. The committee planning the June 1978 occupation of the site tried to express the relation between these two goals:

The reason why we face the problem of nuclear power is because a small group of people are in control of, amongst other aspects of people's lives, their energy policy. To try all on our own to force the ruling class to stop nukes through the actions of our presently small and unrepresentative group of members and supporters would be elitist and would probably prove counter-productive to our effort to stop nukes and furthermore to our effort to create a better world. The best and most effective way to fight the problem of nukes in such a way that the world does get better is to help the vast majority of the country to take control over the energy aspect of their lives.[24]

In addition to giving expression to anger about the infringement of democratic rights, the Clamshell did a great deal to give its members a sense of having some control over their own lives—in the language of the movement, to empower them. It gave them a way of making themselves heard on an issue ordinarily restricted to those claiming scientific expertise. It gave them the hope that if they could be heard on this issue, they could be heard on other issues as well. As the movement grew, it gave them hope that their views might make a difference.

The movement was also prefigurative of a community in which one could construct a life based on one's highest values. The occupations of the site seemed to be opportunities to put ideas about a better society into practice. The handbook for the June 1978 action urged each affinity group to develop an alternative energy project to bring to the site. "Returning the land to its former condition will be difficult and in some cases impossible, but we can make a start. We can plant trees and grain and vegetable crops and fish the river to demonstrate that the land has other uses. Instead of just taking things away from the earth and marshland, we can build a model of a sane, energy independent society on a restored and venerated land." The handbook suggested that occupiers might want to bring solar cookers and ovens, small windmills, or compost toilets. A supplement to the handbook further suggested that each occupier might want to bring a packet of sunflower or other hardy seeds to spread around the site, that kites could be used to demonstrate wind power, and that "theater, music, dance, painting, all have a place in the restoration. These, in conjunction with signs and banners, can help clusters to begin to establish a genuine sense of community."[25]

The Clamshell attracted a sympathetic audience that, although mainly white and of middle-class origin, included people of all ages. But the largest numbers of those who became Clamshell activists were in their twenties or early thirties; the distinctive character of the Clamshell came from the particular outlook of this group, who were in a broad sense the younger brothers and sisters of the antiwar protesters. They had been infected by the idealism of the sixties, but they had also seen the weaknesses of the antiwar movement, its tendency to resort to internal hierarchy and violent rhetoric, its sexism. Many of them had come to the Clamshell from the women's movement or the environmental/ecology movement, or had been deeply influenced by them.

Many of the young people drawn to the Clamshell expected that their life's work would be to create a better world. But in the late seventies the nation was moving toward the right, and the professional and academic jobs that often attract people with such aspirations were not as available as they had been. The Clamshell provided community in a society from which many of these people felt alienated and an arena in which people could, however indirectly, begin to address what they would do with their lives. Many Clams, especially those who became central activists, gained skills that enabled them to go on to jobs in alternative energy or to do other kinds of organizing or political work. Even those who went on to more conventional work in many cases carried with them a strong belief in social change and a determination to mold their jobs so as to allow them to contribute to it.

Experience of a movement dedicated to egalitarian democracy had at least a temporary effect on the personal lives of those involved. The movement's commitment to feminism undermined patterns of male dominance and mitigated assumptions that the nuclear family was superior to other forms of personal life. If any social form was privileged in the movement, it was the collective. The influence of the Montague Farm people was enhanced by the fact that they represented a rural commune in which family merged with community and manual labor was interspersed with political work. Anna Gyorgy expressed an ideal widely held in the Clamshell community when she admiringly described Sam Lovejoy, a fellow member of the Montague Farm, as one who "believe[d] that the struggle against nukes begins at home."[26]

The Limits of Consensus: Efficacy Versus Community

In view of the many strengths of the Clamshell, why did it break apart so dramatically and so rapidly? One answer is that in certain respects it recapitulated the history of the antiwar movement on which it was hoping to improve. The Clamshell's spontaneity, its lack of firm organization, made it unable to absorb rapid growth easily or to ride out sharp internal divisions. Like the New Left, the Clamshell was most harmonious in its early phase, when its members were more aware of what drew them together than of their differences and the organization was suffused with the generosity of people working in harmony, who value each other's contributions and want to protect the movement they have constructed.

The almost ecstatic sense of community the Clamshell enjoyed in its first year or so led Clams to believe that internal harmony was the automatic result of consensus process and a philosophy of nonviolence. But in fact consensus probably worked best among people who were more or less like-minded, as the original group was, or in the special circumstances of incarceration in which power struggles were not at issue and there was both the time and the desire to work out differences. The Hard Rain people brought the sectarian style of the late sixties into the Clamshell. The Clamshell decision-making process could not absorb a group who were more interested in shifting the organization toward their point of view, and in gaining power themselves, than in arriving at consensus.

The Clamshell's process made it vulnerable to disruption. Many of the people who joined the Clamshell after the spring 1977 occupation regarded the Clamshell as being fundamentally about organizing another occupation. They viewed the coordinating committee's decision to call off the projected occupation as, at the very least, a huge mistake—and at most, a sign of an overly cautious and conciliatory approach to politics. Nonviolence, many would point out, did not mean vacillation or compromise. Aikos Barton, for instance, believed that the old guard made a serious error in agreeing to the Rath proposal and substituting a legal demonstration for the planned occupation. "They failed to see that we needed a dramatic action," he said. But he argued that it was Hard Rain, and the contentious spirit they brought to the Clamshell, that was most destructive. "People came in to be a community of resistance, to see if nonviolence would work. They left once the Clamshell stopped being a community. After October 1979, we were no longer seen as sincere antinuclear people. When we lost that friendly nonviolent spirit, in the CDAS action, we lost a lot of our capital. Hard Rain was crucial in destroying that spirit of good will."[27]

The Clamshell might have withstood the conflict over fence cutting (and the issue of the limits of nonviolence more generally) if it had not already been somewhat fragile. In the wake of the successful occupation of May 1978, a number of issues emerged in the Clamshell that were not addressed in any systematic way, partly because so much energy was going into the occupation planned for June of 1978, and partly because the issues were difficult, possibly unresolvable. One was the existence of an informal, unelected leading group in an organization that claimed to be leaderless. Another was the place of local autonomy within a regional organization—whether groups near the plant site should have a veto over actions of the organization as a whole and, if not, how their relationship with the local community could be protected. Many of the newer people were unhappy with the informal leadership because they had played no role in choosing it, because those leaders claimed special rights for the seacoast people (especially suspect because the two groups were seen as allied), and perhaps most substantively because both the informal leadership and the seacoast activists seemed reluctant to go beyond the issue of safe energy, content to leave the larger implications of their critique implicit.

The tensions over the questions of leadership and local autonomy reflected a deeper division over the Clamshell's political orientation—the balance between a focus on nuclear energy and a broader attack on the system of power relations in which nuclear energy is embedded. Hard Rain gained the sympathy of many of the newer activists not only because it challenged a firmly entrenched (though unacknowledged) leadership but also because it seemed willing to go beyond the critique of nuclear power to a larger critique of power relations in the United States.

Many of the seacoast activists joined the Clamshell because conventional challenges to nuclear power were not working and it seemed that it was time to try direct action. For those from other parts of New England, especially those inspired to join the Clamshell by the 1977 occupation, the Seabrook plant was an example of what was wrong with American society and the appeal of the Clamshell lay in its radical environmental and social vision. Among the newer Clams were some who were dissatisfied with both the narrowness of the concerns of the old Clams and Hard Rain's confrontational style and failure to understand the concept of nonviolent revolution. According to Crystal Gray, a member of an anarcha-feminist group from the West Coast that attended the CDAS action in 1979 (and that used the spelling "anarcha-feminist" intentionally to underline its rejection of the masculine universal), many anarcha-feminists were attracted to CDAS initially because of its anarchism but were disappointed to find how little the group had been influenced by the feminist critique of the macho style.[28] The appeal of the Clamshell to local environmentalists and to activists from the radical counterculture lay in its novel approach to political action—its use of civil disobedience and the consensus process. But both elements of the Clamshell's politics raised problems that were never resolved. The founders of the Clamshell intended to create an organization that would engage in a variety of nonelectoral forms of action against nuclear power. But occupations were much more dramatic and compelling than the other activities the Clamshell engaged in. Civil disobedience on the site quickly came to define what the Clamshell was about. The focus on civil disobedience created a confrontational atmosphere in which commitment was measured by one's determination to occupy the site regardless of the potential for the destruction of property or of police violence.

The Clamshell's emphasis on civil disobedience made it difficult to answer the Hard Rain challenge and committed the organization to the notion that nuclear power could be defeated by occupation. Some Clams in fact believed that an ongoing, massive occupation could force PSCo to abandon its plans. That most Clams probably did not believe it was ultimately beside the point. The intoxicating, almost addictive nature of civil disobedience made it difficult for the organization to engage deeply in any other form of political activity. Thus it would have been virtually impossible for the organization to survive the cancellation of a major occupation, regardless of the reasons for it or the process by which the decision was made.

Many people came out of their experience in the Clamshell believing that the consensus process was partly responsible for its demise, that consensus might work in small groups but needed modification to be effective in large organizations. The Clamshell's rigid commitment to its process, its unwillingness to consider such alternatives as the 80 percent majority when consensus could not be reached, froze the tensions within the organization.

The Clamshell wanted both political efficacy and community. In its early history these aims reinforced one another easily; after the first large occupation, continuing to build community seemed to require putting aside practical political considerations. Hard Rain's maximalist position was based on the argument that occupation was not symbolic politics but a real threat to nuclear energy, that if the Clamshell took a sufficiently militant approach, enough people would stay on the site long enough to make construction of the plant impossible, just as thousands of Germans had prevented the building of a nuclear plant at Wyhl. In fact, a repeat of the Wyhl experience in the United States was highly unlikely. The American antinuclear movement was not nearly as large as its German counterpart.

Nevertheless, Hard Rain's argument that no obstacles should be allowed to prevent occupation of the site resonated in the Clamshell because it legitimized the Clam's focus on civil disobedience, and it was in the experience of civil disobedience that community was most vividly realized. Dick Bell, a Boston Clam and a leading opponent of the Hard Rain group, argued that the Clamshell's emphasis on civil disobedience laid it open to these problems. There is an important difference, he argued, between civil disobedience (CD) as a tactic to be used when political analysis suggests that it is appropriate and CD as a life-style.

If you say, this is a CD organization, people come in because they want to do CD; the organization is very limited in what it can do. You have this internal double bind that's sitting there waiting for you when you have a successful action. People come in based on what you already did, not what you might want to do next. New people are hooked on your past. Now you have three clumps of people, people who went through the last action and liked it, want to do it again, new people who think it was nifty and want to do it, and a small group of people who want to discuss what to do next. That's when debate gets sticky, even if you don't have a group of anarchists around.[29]

Cathy Wolff, part of the Clam's informal leadership and much more sympathetic to the organization's anarchist/countercultural ambiance than Bell, nevertheless believed that that ambiance caused serious problems, some of which could not be attributed to the influence of Hard Rain. In the context of the Clamshell's claim that it had no leaders and that decisions were made by consensus, it was irresponsible for the leadership to step into the breach and make decisions before consensus was reached. It was in the same vein, she said, "as people saying we would stop Seabrook by sitting there. There was magic in the Clam, but the magic was not that we would stop Seabrook by sitting there. People believing that made the magic stronger, but then the magic doubled back on us."[30]

The promise of community had much to do with the Clamshell's magic. Like the focus on CD, it caused problems, in particular a reluctance to confront potentially divisive issues or firmly to reject a minority position. Even in Boston, where Hard Rain was based, most Clams did not think that cutting fences or other actions that might provoke police violence were a good idea. Nevertheless, Bell argued, the majority of Boston Clams were unwilling to take a stand on the issue, because Hard Rain was perceived as the underdog, a beleaguered minority, and because they feared that sharp debate would disrupt the Clamshell.

One of the messages that the Clam put out, and the armory experience fed into, was, here is a way for you to find the community you have always longed for. If you are isolated, lonely, living in an apartment in Boston, come to this meeting and it'll be better; here are people who care about you. Then you come to the meeting and discover conflict. The debate was threatening on two levels. It threatened the concept of community that a significant minority had come to the Clam to find. Also, to the extent that people felt unable to participate [in the debate] themselves, it was threatening. Clamshell clearly was perceived as a dialectical response to the failures of the New Left. This is one of the reasons consensus decision making was such a sacred cow. If you put out the message that this is a community, sharp debate is jarring, alarming, people say this isn't what they want.[31]

One of the strengths of the Clamshell was that it linked the specific, immediate issue of nuclear energy with a vision of a society in which policy would be democratically decided, people would treat the environment and one another with respect, and technology would be appropriately scaled to its tasks. But the Clamshell never developed a strategy for achieving such a society. Instead it remained content with the assumption that the values it espoused would be adopted by more and more people and would somehow lead to the transformation of society. The fact that the Clamshell's constituency was almost entirely white and middle-class, and that it was dominated by the counterculture, made it unlikely that its values would spread to the rest of the population easily or straightforwardly. Many Clams were aware of the problem but unable to solve it.[32]

At the heart of the Clamshell's difficulties was the tension between moral witness and political efficacy. Moral witness and civil disobedience have always had a place in American protest: the American Revolution, for instance, rested in large part on the tactics of civil disobedience. In the late twentieth century, the centralization of power in the state and the corporate elite, and the often sharp contrast between human needs and the official policies, give the politics of moral witness a special resonance. As Noël Sturgeon argues in her discussion of the political theory of nonviolent direct action, there is something about placing one's body in the way of "progress" that expresses a truth about our relation to the state and to corporate power. In the late twentieth century, as we confront the large issues of the fates of the environment and of the human race, moral witness is an important ground for political action. But by itself, moral witness is a fragile basis for a lasting movement. It does not recognize the question of political efficacy or the fact that movements need victories to survive.

The Clamshell wanted efficacy, but it relied largely on the politics of morality. Some Clams recognized the contradiction. Activist Marty Jezer wrote, at the height of Clamshell activity,

Historically, moral witness has proven itself an effective way of starting a movement, but inadequate in sustaining or building a movement already in existence. During the 1950s, for instance, when there was no radical movement, individual actions (like sailing small ships into nuclear testing zones) had a profound effect in making people aware of the nuclear issue and inspiring them into action. But once people are mobilized to act in a political way, individual witness loses its effect.[33]

Jezer's point of reference was individual moral witness. Collective moral witness, especially when it involves thousands of people, is more likely to get results. It can produce a movement with staying power, especially if it is combined with other approaches and forms of action. But the Clamshell was unable to solve the problem to which Jezer pointed. The Clamshell had a brilliant beginning but a short history and an end that left much bitterness. Antinuclear alliances around the country inspired in part by the Clamshell, and following its philosophy and organization, dealt more successfully with similar issues. The largest and most prominent of the Clamshell's immediate successors was the Abalone Alliance, which emerged from the struggle against the Diablo nuclear plant near San Luis Obispo, California.

Chapter Three

The Abalone Alliance

Anarcha-Feminism and the Politics of Prefigurative Revolution

The Abalone Alliance was modeled on the Clamshell and had a similar history: like the Clamshell, the Abalone involved a regional effort to shut down a particular nuclear plant, in this case PG & E's Diablo Canyon plant, near San Luis Obispo on the central California coast. As in the Clamshell, there were conflicts between activists at the local site and elsewhere over decision making, which raised the questions of whether consensus process could be made to work and, implicitly, of what should be regarded as the central aim of Abalone: shutting down the Diablo plant, challenging nuclear power on a regional or perhaps a national scale, or creating a movement that would work toward an environmentally balanced, decentralized, egalitarian society while at the same time living out those values.

The Abalone lasted longer than the Clamshell, and its experience was more benign. Abalone activists developed the same commitment to radical politics that the Clamshell had produced in its members, but without the bitterness that the Clamshell's internal conflicts created. Like the Clamshell, the Abalone held a series of progressively larger occupations; the largest and most dramatic, in 1981, led to 1,900 arrests. The Clamshell equivalent, the occupation of 1977, led to factionalism and an explosion that destroyed the organization. There were conflicts in the Abalone, but they were less wrenching. After the Diablo occupation the Abalone declined rapidly, but by then it had trained a generation of activists and created networks to serve as bases for other movements.

The differences between the two organizations have to do with what the Abalone was able to learn from the experience of the Clamshell. The Abalone made the consensus process more flexible by introducing some modifications, making it easier for the organization to live with ongoing internal differences. The fact that the Abalone's 1981 occupation of Diablo indirectly led to the shutting down of the plant for an extended period was also significant. The Clamshell ended in mutual recriminations over the failure of the movement to attain its goal; Abalone activists were able to leave for other struggles feeling that they had won at least a partial victory.

The Abalone's most important contribution to the direct action movement was the internal culture it created—a commitment to nonviolence combined with a utopian vision of a radically democratic society in which everyone's views would have equal weight and all relationships would be strictly egalitarian. The Clamshell Alliance had envisioned such a culture but had not been able to develop or extend it widely enough to provide a framework for dealing with serious internal differences. Though most Clams had identified with both nonviolence and anarchism, on some level the two were in conflict: anarchism, which for many Clams was synonymous with revolution, required a militancy that seemed incompatible with nonviolence. In the debate over fence cutting, the two principles seemed to come into opposition, partly because there was no agreement about what revolution meant, what kind of society the movement looked toward creating, or even whether such a revolutionary vision should be a prominent aspect of the movement's politics.

The founders of the Clamshell shared a vision of a radically egalitarian society but finally were less interested in that vision than in organizing around issues of local control. The Boston anarchists were more interested in a concept of revolution influenced by the sectarianism and confrontational style of the late sixties. The fact that the leaders of the Boston anarchists were mostly men also molded the group's political style. Most Clams fell between the two poles, more concerned than the old guard with revolution, more likely than the Boston anarchists to think in terms of a nonviolent revolution. Not only were these differences very deep, but there was no generally accepted set of principles against which the claims of each side could be measured. The question of who in the Clamshell represented nonviolence is as difficult as the question of who represented anarchism: virtually everyone subscribed to both. But like anarchism, nonviolence had different meanings for different groups. There was no agreement in the Clamshell about whether nonviolence meant refraining from damaging property or refraining from behavior that might provoke police violence. On a deeper level, there was no agreement about whether nonviolence meant conducting politics in a spirit of goodwill even toward opponents or included the confrontational style of the antiwar movement.

Clamshell's inability to resolve these differences raised the questions of what the movement meant by democracy and whether a mass movement could operate on consensus, without leadership. The Clamshell founders believed that a radically democratic organization of this sort could function effectively. The collapse of the Clamshell convinced many of its founders and early members that consensus could not work beyond small groups of people who knew each other well; it convinced many of those who joined later that the existence of even an informal leadership was dangerous to democratic process. In either case, the Clamshell's experience made it clear that the movement did not yet have a process or a conception of democracy that both empowered each member and allowed for effective functioning.

The concept of democracy could not decide the conflict between revolution and nonviolence. There is a commonsense presumption, to which the Quakers and other "soft Clams" were deeply committed, that democratic process must be nonviolent. But antielitism came into conflict with the organization's need for some sort of leadership and restraint in its political practice. In the end, the old guard was not willing either to restrict Clamshell membership to those who agreed with them or to ride out the democratic process within an open organization. Thus the fence cutters came to represent antielitism, egalitarianism, and community; they seemed the more credible representatives of revolutionary anarchism and the radical democratic impulse that drew many people into the Clamshell. The old guard's decision to put aside the principles of decentralized democracy to save nonviolence sealed the fence cutters' claim that it was they who represented the Clamshell's vision.

The Abalone Alliance did not solve these problems, but it did manage to function much more harmoniously than the Clamshell Alliance. The Abalone lasted only a few years longer than the Clamshell, but it ended because it achieved part of its aim—the closing of the Diablo nuclear plant and weakening of the nuclear industry as a whole—not because of internal differences. The Abalone sustained itself better than the Clamshell partly by adopting some changes in the consensus process, but chiefly because it created a much more explicitly defined movement culture linking nonviolence and revolutionary aspirations through commitment to feminism and prefigurative politics. It was the anarchist contingent in the Abalone Alliance, the activists who called themselves anarcha-feminists, who were most responsible for developing this culture.

The anarcha-feminists joined Abalone while the mass blockade of Diablo, toward which the organization had been moving since its inception, was being planned. They assumed much of the responsibility for organizing and carrying out this action, linking local activists determined to close down the plant through civil disobedience and activists elsewhere, who were beginning to resist the subordination of the Abalone as a whole to local needs and were in some cases skeptical about the usefulness of direct action. The anarcha-feminists insisted that an anarchist or revolutionary egalitarian politics must be feminist, meaning that it must transcend the division between public and private by putting its political principles into practice in daily life, and that those principles must include nonviolence, respect for all human beings and the natural environment, and a rejection of the machismo that had undermined the antiwar movement and had infected the Clamshell Alliance. The argument that feminism required revolutionary nonviolence gave nonviolence a legitimacy that was hard to challenge and that undermined the association between revolution and a willingness to engage in violence.

Through their role in the blockade the anarcha-feminists were able to do a great deal to define the political culture that the Abalone would bequeath to subsequent incarnations of the direct action movement. That political culture helped to create more space for internal differences in the Abalone, and in later organizations, than there had been in the Clamshell. It strengthened the role of the counterculture within the direct action movement, and it opened the movement to the spirituality that later became one of its most salient aspects. The influence of anarcha-feminism did not settle the questions that had divided the Clamshell: in the Abalone and in later organizations there continued to be disagreements about what nonviolence meant, how decisions should be made in the movement and how much power each participant should have, and whether the movement's radically democratic process and its rejection of leadership hindered its ability to function effectively. But anarcha-feminism reinforced the commitment to a utopian democratic vision and a political practice based on the values it contained.

Diablo Canyon and the Formation of the Abalone Alliance

Protest against PG & E's Diablo Canyon Nuclear Power Plant began in the early 1970s when the Mothers for Peace in San Luis Obispo, who had organized years earlier to protest the war in Vietnam, learned that there was a fault line immediately offshore from the plant and decided to prevent the plant's licensing. In 1974 the Mothers for Peace became legal intervenors against the plant by petitioning the Atomic Energy Commission (AEC), which then had authority over the plant. Despite the AEC's denial of their petition, the Mothers continued to press their case against the plant, both through legal action and by educating the community to the dangers of nuclear power.

The protest against Diablo might have remained a local effort if it had not been for the Continental Peace Walk, planned by the Santa Cruz Resource Center for Nonviolence, which passed through San Luis Obispo in 1976. Four participants in the walk, including one member of the Resource Center, committed civil disobedience at the Diablo plant. The Continental Walk put the Mothers for Peace in contact with a network of peace centers and organizations around the state, including the American Friends Service Committee in San Francisco, the Santa Cruz Resource

Center for Nonviolence, and the Modesto Peace Center. Raye Fleming, a member of Mothers for Peace, had become impatient with legal action as the vehicle for protest. She and other local antinuclear activists took up the idea of civil disobedience, and invited Liz Walker and David Hartsough, AFSC staff workers, to conduct a nonviolence training in San Luis Obispo. This training led to the formation of People Generating Energy, which looked toward the use of civil disobedience as a means of protest against the plant.

The interest of some of the Mothers and other local antinuclear activists in civil disobedience meshed with the peace activists' interest in a mass antinuclear movement based on nonviolent civil disobedience. David Hartsough was connected with the Movement for a New Society (MNS) in Philadelphia, which was at that time working with the Clamshell in the hope that the antinuclear movement would prove to be the basis for a mass movement for nonviolent revolution. Hartsough and the other peace activists who came together around Diablo shared the view that nonviolent civil disobedience had been confined for too long to small, highly dedicated groups. He and others in MNS on the East Coast had participated in the civil rights movement, which, at least in its early years, was a model of a mass movement based on nonviolent civil disobedience. The West Coast peace activists were drawn to Diablo Canyon by environmental concerns and opposition to nuclear power, and also by the belief that a movement to oppose Diablo could connect nuclear energy and nuclear weapons and ultimately become the basis for mass opposition to militarism and the social structure that supports it. Though the Mothers for Peace were primarily interested in stopping the Diablo plant, all these ideas were quite congenial to them. The beliefs the peace activists brought with them—opposition to the corporations and to capitalism, antimilitarism, nonviolence, and consensus—were all in the air, and the Mothers welcomed the ability of the AFSC, the Resource Center for Nonviolence, and others to show how they could form the basis for a movement.

The first Abalone conference was held in 1976. The name "Abalone Alliance" referred to the thousands of abalone killed when Diablo's cooling system was first tested. David Hartsough and Liz Walker from the AFSC and Scott Kennedy from the Re-

source Center played a leading role in setting out the basic principles of the organization, which committed the Abalone to nonviolence and to the guidelines for nonviolent action adhered to
by the Clamshell. In following the model presented by the Clamshell, the Abalone inherited an approach to politics that went back
to the early civil rights movement and the tradition of radical
pacifism. The Abalone also adopted the Clamshell structure: the
affiliation of local groups; the organization of affinity groups for
civil disobedience actions; feminist process, or consensus; and the
discouragement of any institutionalized leadership through the
rotation of representatives, or spokes, who would convey the decisions of the local group to a spokescouncil. Like the founders
of the Clamshell, those who formed the Abalone were inspired
by the recent antinuclear protest at Wyhl, Germany. They also
drew upon the example of the affinity groups employed by the
Spanish anarchists and, more broadly, the anarchist legacy of small
communities and decentralized power.

In addition to playing an important role in shaping the ideology and structure of the Abalone, the peace activists, especially
the AFSC members, brought important resources. Liz and David
had argued to an AFSC board meeting that the struggle against
Diablo could extend the nonviolent movement and should be
supported; the AFSC assigned the two activists to work full-time
to develop that movement. David, as a member of MNS, had connections with the Clamshell Alliance; he and Liz followed the
progress of the Clamshell closely and hoped that something similar might develop on the West Coast.[1] Their interest in building
such an organization came from both their opposition to nuclear
energy and their belief that a movement against nuclear energy
would form the basis for protest against nuclear arms as well.

The Abalone remained relatively small for some time. Ten or
twelve local groups were formed, mostly in Northern California;
regional conferences drew fifty people or so. A strong sense of
community developed, although there were differences within the
Abalone, especially between those closer to the counterculture,
who tended to emphasize civil disobedience (CD), and others who
supported CD but were more comfortable engaging in legal forms
of political pressure, at least until these were exhausted. Especially in the early years, these differences never became sharp

enough to threaten a split. Abalone members were committed to building a movement with room for people oriented toward a variety of modes of protest, and a good deal of effort was put into working out differences. When differences emerged at the periodic regional conferences, those taking the strongest positions were asked to form a committee and work out a common approach. Such groups often stayed up all night to arrive at a mutual understanding that could be presented the next morning. The Abalone could tolerate differences in part because it was so close-knit: the strong bonds of common purpose, the monthly conferences at which people shared meals, partied together, and spent nights side by side in sleeping bags on the floor, created ties that transcended differences of political approach.

In its first years, the Abalone organized two quite successful actions. On August 7, 1977, 1,500 people attended a rally at Diablo; forty-seven people were arrested for occupying the plant site. By prior agreement, most of those arrested were local residents; outlying Abalone groups were each allowed to have two representatives arrested. Over the next year there was debate over how prominent a place in Abalone's work CD should occupy. While some groups focused on public education, outreach to labor and other groups, and electoral strategies, others continued to organize for the next year's occupation. On August 6 and 7, 1978, 5,000 people attended a rally outside the gate to the Diablo plant, and 487 were arrested. Of these, twenty were chosen for a representative trial. In the end, they were found guilty of failure to disperse and given sentences, applicable to everyone arrested, of fifteen days in jail and a \$300 fine.[2]

Shutting Diablo Down

The 1977 and 1978 blockades were designed as symbolic gestures, to publicize the dangers posed by the Diablo plant, not actually to shut it down. Like the Clamshell, which held two small, symbolic protests before attempting a massive blockade of Seabrook, the Abalone intended to follow its early blockades with a much more massive one, which, it was hoped, would shut the plant down as the occupation in Wyhl had prevented the construction of a nuclear plant there. The question was whether to hold such a massive occupation before or after the plant was granted an operating license. The CD-oriented contingent argued for a fixed date, for an occupation sometime in the near future, regardless of the status of the license. Others favored a floating date, with the Abalone ready to occupy as soon as the license was granted. A blockade held sooner, they argued, would be seen as less legitimate, and would attract fewer people. The floating date won, partly because it was generally agreed that the Abalone should try every legal means of protest before resorting to a massive blockade, and partly because it was expected that the license would be granted soon. If they had known that licensing would be delayed until September of 1981, the proponents of a fixed date might not have given in so easily.

The discussion was interrupted by the accident at Three Mile Island in early April 1979. Suddenly nuclear power became a national concern. Before the accident, Abalone had been working toward an antinuclear rally to be held in San Francisco. That rally, held as planned on April 7, only days after the accident, attracted some 25,000 people. In the aftermath of Three Mile Island local protests against nuclear power proliferated. *The China Syndrome,* a film depicting an accident at a nuclear plant, was playing in San Luis Obispo; local Abalone people led a march from the movie theater to the local PG & E office, carrying a casket that they delivered to PG & E officials. On May 25, ninety-three PG & E offices around the state were picketed. On June 30, 40,000 people came to San Luis Obispo for the largest antinuclear power rally ever held in the United States. In the fall, sixty teach-ins were held in thirty-five cities throughout the state. The Abalone grew rapidly. Soon the organization had sixty local groups.

Because the license had not yet been granted (the Three Mile Island accident had, in fact, resulted in a temporary halt in the granting of any new licenses), the Abalone had no single immediate focus. Over the next year and a half, local groups turned increasingly to work on local issues, including actions at other plants, such as Rancho Seco, near Sacramento, opposition to plans for plants elsewhere, and nonnuclear issues such as the draft. As the Abalone grew, a variety of special projects were established: *It's About Times,* a newspaper published every month and a half, which came to serve the whole California antinuclear and peace community; the Labor Task Force, which developed contacts with labor unions and organized a conference that encouraged union members to rethink their positions on nuclear power; the Diablo Conversion Project, which drafted plans for the conversion of Diablo to other purposes; and the Media Service, which developed the skills required to bring antinuclear material to the media.

One of the attractions of the Abalone was that it was getting to be very good at what it did. People with expertise about nuclear power or organizing media experience were drawn to the organization; the inexperienced learned fast. Soon the Abalone was functioning skillfully in a number of areas. The proliferation of projects made it possible for people with different political orientations to coexist peacefully and to use their talents in the same organization. The fact that the Abalone took many directions at once allowed it to function as an ostensibly leaderless organization; there could be many leaders, in many areas, without a need to identify any particular leadership group. A statewide Abalone office was established in San Francisco to coordinate these efforts; the San Francisco office and the Diablo Project Office in San Luis Obispo remained Abalone's two centers.

As the Abalone became larger and more professional, however, it lost some of the sense of family that marked its early days. In the absence of an immediate common focus of activity, the various groupings within the organization operated more or less autonomously; different political tendencies were increasingly pulling apart. Though there was still a strong latticework of personal connections in the organization, the actual basis for unity—the agreement that local groups would do everything possible to oppose the plant within the bounds of legality, and unite to organize a massive blockade only as a last resort—was becoming fragile. Statewide conferences were becoming increasingly contentious; consensus process was breaking down. The Alliance for Survival, a Los Angeles organization structured much more conventionally than the rest of the organization, which emphasized large concerts at which prominent rock stars performed, found itself in conflict with the nonhierarchical, CD-oriented groups from Northern California.

These problems reached a peak at a statewide conference held in Santa Barbara in the summer of 1981, where it became clear that consensus was impossible. The organization was in danger of becoming paralyzed. Members from around the state joined a committee to work on a proposal for a new decision-making structure, which finally modified the consensus process. Individuals would no longer be able to block consensus at a statewide meeting; only a member group would have that power, and only if the group had reached consensus internally to block a proposal. The modification also distinguished between an enthusiastic consensus, in which a proposal was backed by every local group, and a lukewarm consensus, in which it was backed by only two-thirds of the local groups but not blocked by any. The committee's proposal achieved 100 percent consensus and was adopted, making it easier for proposals to go through without the active support of everyone in the organization and less likely that the power to block a proposal would be used casually or irresponsibly.

Early in the summer of 1981 it became clear that the licensing of the Diablo plant was imminent. The pace of nonviolence trainings accelerated; by the end of the summer, as many as five thousand people around the state had gone through the training sessions required of anyone who wanted to participate in the blockade. The training introduced the philosophy of nonviolence; methods of handling confrontations so that they would not escalate; the process of decision making by consensus, which would be used during the blockade; what to expect if arrested; and the process by which collective decisions would be made in jail. Many Abalone members around the state attended special workshops to become nonviolence trainers. People new to the Abalone learned about nonviolent civil disobedience and consensus chiefly from the nonviolence training and frequently formed affinity groups with people in their sessions. Even those who did not go on to commit CD or remain active members of Abalone often carried these ideas with them into other arenas.

Abalone members around the state were asked to make themselves ready to go occupy the plant site as soon as the license was granted, which happened on September 10. PG & E, publicly taking the position that Abalone was no threat, nevertheless prepared for a worst-case scenario of 60,000 demonstrators. A large security force was put in place in observation posts scattered through the mountains near Diablo. Governor Brown ordered out the California National Guard, which set up temporary headquarters on the plant site. Demonstrators began to arrive; tents were set up on a piece of land made available to Abalone by a sympathetic local rancher.

On September 15, with about 2,100 protesters present, the blockade began.[3] Some blockaded the main gate of the plant, stepping over a blue line that marked the boundary of PG & E's property. These people were promptly arrested and taken to jail. Others blockaded back roads into the plant grounds; some hiked into the backcountry in an attempt to reach the plant itself. In some cases, it took days before those in the backcountry were discovered and arrested. Some protesters arrived by sea: a fleet of ships headed by Greenpeace's *Stone Witch* deposited rafts full of protesters in the sea near the plant; those people were arrested shortly after landing on shore.

Meanwhile, the camp served as home base to protesters who had not yet joined the blockade and those leaving jail who wanted to do support work for the blockade, to rest before blockading and being arrested a second time, or simply to participate in the communal life of the camp. Food and supplies were brought to the camp every day by local supporters; a temporary kitchen was set up in one large tent, where meals were cooked every day for the entire camp. The Diablo Project Office (DPO) staff and others involved in planning the action had decided early on to limit the camp to blockaders, fearing that it would become a haven for those who simply wanted free food and lodging. Some people were uncomfortable with this decision because it seemed to deny legitimacy to forms of protest other than civil disobedience. In spite of the DPO's and Abalone's single-minded focus on the blockade and their failure to organize a simultaneous legal protest, six days into the action, on Sunday, September 21, 5,000 local residents marched outside the gates of Diablo carrying placards proclaiming their opposition to the plant and their support of the blockade.

Two weeks into the blockade, more than 1,900 arrests had been made, but the daily number of arrests was declining and protesters were beginning to leave the camp. It was becoming clear that the blockade was not going to stop the plant. By that time people were entering the camp who had had little to do with Abalone and were more interested in living at the camp than in stopping the plant. There had never been any discussions of how to end the blockade, short of victory; some on the office staff were afraid that they had created a monster over which they might lose control. The DPO came up with the idea of announcing "stage two," a plan according to which protesters would return home, recuperate, and then jointly consider what should be done next. Fortunately, most people remaining in the camp realized that it was necessary for the blockade to end. Stage two was accepted, and on September 27 the last residents of the camp began to leave.

As the camp emptied, a PG & E plant superintendent announced that he had discovered, the day before, a serious mistake in the plant blueprint: certain pipes in Unit One, crucial to the plant's safety system, were duplicates of corresponding pipes in Unit Two, rather than mirror images of those pipes as they should have been. The plant could not be safely operated without extensive and costly repairs. Though the blockade itself had not stopped the plant, many blockaders felt that their protest led the superintendent to check the blueprint and created an atmosphere in which he felt impelled to make his findings public. Operation of the plant was now put off into the indefinite future.

The Abalone Alliance faded away after the blockade. In the men's jail at Diablo, a list was passed around for those interested in forming a CD-based organization to oppose the weapons-producing Lawrence Livermore National Laboratory; that list was the seed of the Livermore Action Group (LAG), the center of the next concerted effort of the nonviolent direct action movement— opposition to the arms race. Many Abalone affinity groups participated in LAG actions and gradually shifted affiliations to that organization. Some Abalone groups turned to local organizing around a variety of issues. Many groups disappeared. Many former Abalone members, especially the informal leadership, for whom Abalone had been a consuming activity over a number of years, took a respite from political activity to devote some attention to other parts of their lives. Over the next several years many of those who had held the DPO together moved away from San

Luis Obispo, as many had said they would do if the plant were not stopped. In Santa Cruz and in the San Francisco Bay Area, many of the central Abalone activists formed families, went back to school, and started careers, often finding their way into jobs that involved environmental concerns, organizing, or community politics. In spite of continued pressure against the plant, most of it local, Diablo was ultimately licensed and went on-line in late 1984. But by that time many former Abalone activists had found other arenas of political involvement. Everyone, except perhaps those who remained in San Luis Obispo and faced the eventual opening of the plant, viewed the struggle against Diablo as a success: the credibility of the nuclear industry had been seriously damaged, a powerful movement had been built, and participants had moved on to other things with a sense of accomplishment. If Abalone members had seen themselves as engaged in building a lasting organization, there might have been more disappointment; but many, especially the anarchists, believed that once an organization had served its purpose it should fade away, allowing affinity groups to refocus on local concerns or move on to new broad issues.

One reason the Abalone ended with a sense of accomplishment rather than of failure, in spite of the fact that PG & E had not been forced to abandon the plant, was that Abalone was not entirely about Diablo or even nuclear power. For most Abalone members, Diablo was a concrete instance of a series of larger problems: the exploitation and destruction of the environment, the abuses of nature and society resulting from the concentration of power in the hands of profit-oriented corporations, the role of the state in fostering those abuses. Diablo was regarded as a window onto the nexus of nuclear power, militarism, and nuclear war. Many of the founders of the Abalone had those issues in mind. Many who joined later either shared their general perspective or came to it through their involvement in the organization. In view of the breadth of the issues, and the fact that not everyone saw them in the same way, it is not surprising that there were substantial differences within the organization. What is surprising is that Abalone proved flexible enough to incorporate those differences into an environment in which people with different reasons for opposing nuclear power could work together productively. And what is particularly surprising is that the anarchists, in spite of their lack of interest in building an enduring organization, provided the glue for the different tendencies within the organization while it lasted.

Old and New Abalones: Incorporating Differences

Abalone members, discussing the differences within their own organization, tended to distinguish between "old Abalones" and "new Abalones," the founders and first members and those who entered in the wake of the Three Mile Island accident. The old Abalones included the people in San Luis Obispo, the early peace activists, and those who joined out of environmental concerns, an attraction to nonviolence, and, often, a desire to find some way of welding CD with more conventional forms of protest. The new Abalones tended on the whole to be somewhat younger than the old Abalones, more closely identified with the counterculture, and more focused on CD, often to the exclusion of other forms of political activity.

In fact, the differences between old and new Abalones were by no means clear-cut. The DPO people had from the beginning been strongly supportive of CD as long as actions were carefully planned and organized. There was considerable tension between the DPO and the Mothers for Peace over this issue. The Mothers were, for several years, officially part of Abalone; though they never engaged in CD as a group (a few did as individuals), they did a good deal of support work for Abalone blockades, especially providing food and housing for blockaders from out of town. Eventually, the Mothers publicly withdrew from Abalone, explaining that since CD had become the focus of Abalone's work, and they were not willing to endorse CD as an organization, they could not remain. The Mothers' public withdrawal angered some women in the DPO; Raye Fleming believed that because of their respectability, their endorsement of CD would have strengthened the Abalone greatly and made a real difference in the effectiveness of the 1981 blockade.[4] Many of the Mothers, meanwhile, were angry that so little appreciation was expressed for their years of work against the plant. Sandy Silver, a Mother who was always supportive of the blockades, argues that the Mothers provided a space in which women who would not under any circumstances have done CD were able to do other kinds of work to stop the plant.[5] The Mothers and the DPO women were all part of the same relatively small liberal and professional social grouping; their differences were in their relationship to the conservative community in which they lived. The DPO women were willing to step beyond what were regarded as the bounds of respectable behavior by the San Luis Obispo middle and upper classes. The fact that the DPO operated in a considerably less hospitable climate than the rest of the Abalone gave them a fierce dedication to CD and at the same time a great concern that it should be carried out carefully and effectively.

Meanwhile, some other old Abalones were increasingly skeptical of CD, or at least of the idea, implicit in the plans for the blockade, that CD itself could shut the plant down. Scott Kennedy and others from the Resource Center for Nonviolence believed that it would be difficult to repeat the Wyhl victory against nuclear power because the effort at Wyhl had been to prevent the construction of a plant; at Diablo, the plant already existed, and PG & E had an enormous investment in it. Furthermore, it was not clear that the antinuclear movement in the United States could produce as many blockaders, or blockaders as persistent, as the German movement. The Resource Center people and some other old Abalones believed that blockading Diablo should be part of a larger strategy that would include other forms of political pressure and would have as its aim not just dismantling Diablo (which might not happen) but also building a strong antinuclear movement.[6] This point of view was reasonable. The prediction about Diablo turned out to be correct, but did not take into account the magnetism of CD, the tendency for the prospect of a massive CD action to drive other forms of political activity to the margin, the tendency for the enthusiasm about CD to produce the assumption that the blockade could stop the plant. Some old Abalones fully shared that enthusiasm; others held back questions about how much the blockade could accomplish, for fear of putting a wet blanket on the action.

The question of what would happen if the blockade did not succeed in shutting the plant down was not addressed before the action. Some new Abalones argued later that there was no point in asking: the point was to make the best possible attempt, to see if it could be done. In any event, the bigger the blockade, the bigger the dent it would put in the nuclear industry as a whole.[7] The basic difference between the skepticism of old Abalones and the enthusiasm of the new Abalones was not about estimates of the possible impact of a blockade on Diablo. As CD became the central focus of Abalone's activity, it attracted groups who regarded Diablo as an arena in which a particular political vision could be played out, groups for whom CD was more an emblem of that vision than a vehicle for political efficacy. The politics of the new and old Abalones overlapped in many respects. But the old Abalones were more concerned with practical results than the new Abalones, for whom the vision, and the construction of a community around that vision, took precedence.

Prefigurative Politics:
The Emergence of Anarcha-Feminism

Many of the new Abalones called themselves anarchists without any reservations; some, deeply influenced by the women's movement, coined the term "anarcha-feminist." The most cohesive such grouping originated in Palo Alto as a group of Stanford students. Working together for the university's divestment from South Africa and living together in a series of student cooperatives, they had become committed to consensus process, feminism, the anarchist vision of an ecologically balanced, decentralized society, and to propaganda by the deed, including civil disobedience.[8] Many became knowledgeable about anarchist history and philosophy; an extensive anarchist library was maintained in one household, and everyone in the larger circle was encouraged to use it. After Three Mile Island, members of this group turned their attention to nuclear power and Diablo, and as Roses Against Nuclear Energy (RANE), connoting the anarchist black rose, they became part of the Abalone.

The Stanford anarchists began to come together in 1976; by the spring of 1979, many of them had graduated or would soon do so. Especially in the context of the emerging antinuclear movement, more or less full-time political work looked much more appealing than graduate school. Furthermore, the restricted academic market of the late seventies made graduate school less attractive than it might otherwise have been. Living in a collective household, one could support oneself through a series of jobs in gas stations or cafes and devote a good deal of time and attention to the movement.

Some of the Stanford group stayed in Palo Alto; some moved to San Francisco, where the Urban Stonehenge household became a center of political activity; and some established a network of households in Santa Cruz. Especially in Santa Cruz, where the counterculture was strong and many people in their twenties and thirties were sympathetic to anarchism, newcomers were easily drawn into the community. A shared Paganism provided the basis for community celebrations and rituals. Jackrabbit, who was a member of Love and Rage, the Santa Cruz affinity group that emerged out of RANE, describes it as "a nebulous but real community, a series of households connected through May Day picnics, through shopping for community foods, through politics; the politics was sort of like the motor. The sense of community, of people holding certain ideas and being willing to act on them, grew really fast."[9]

Many anarchists marked the change that becoming part of the movement meant for them by taking new names: Jackrabbit, Crystal, Crazy Jane (or Juana Loca), Shoshoni, Mariposa. These *noms de guerre* provided anonymity at an arrest. Assumed names always had a special significance. "Jackrabbit," for instance, from a character in Marge Piercy's novel *Woman on the Edge of Time,* suggested an animal that lived by its wits, moved fast, and survived any threat. Names were used singly as a rule; in Abalone meetings, people often identified themselves by their first or adopted names, with the name of the affinity group as a kind of family name. The practice of taking new names showed the Abalone anarchists' roots in the counterculture and demonstrated the importance of self-transformation in Abalone anarchist political culture.

For the anarchists, creating a community that would both prefigure the better society and give its members a sense of power in the present was a major goal of political activity. Anarcha-feminists from Santa Cruz cite an experience they had when a group

of them went to Boston to help organize for the 1979 CDAS action at Seabrook. Walking down the street one night after having
dinner together, Jackrabbit recounts,

We saw a man, holding a woman under his arm, slam her against a
streetlight. His hand was on her neck. Jason sees it; he says, "We
can't allow this to happen." We all ran back and confronted the guy.
The guy was flipped; he said it was none of our business, she was
his wife. Other guys were hanging around; they said, "Leave him
alone." We confronted them, especially the women [in our group].
It was like, we can own the part of the city that we're in. It was sort
of like having power.[10]

For the anarcha-feminists, the 1981 blockade was an opportunity to try out political action and community on a much larger
scale. Members of Love and Rage staffed the Guides' Collective,
the group that drew up plans for backcountry actions and helped
other affinity groups through the experience. The anarcha-feminists did not want to simply stand at the front gate and be arrested; it was, as Jackrabbit said, "the idea of going over the land,
of looking for ways to get into the plant, that captured our imagination. We looked at it as a mini-war; we were into a nonviolent
guerrilla mentality. We were ecowarriors going into the woods
with an electronic communications network." Along with several
other affinity groups, Love and Rage hiked into the backcountry
at night; they narrowly missed being seen several times during
the night and were discovered and arrested in the morning close
to the plant. "It was an incredibly successful direct action," Jackrabbit said, "both really fun and also you feel it's like playing it
out, it's like a role play for what you'd really like to do, stopping
business as usual."[11]

Many who joined the Diablo blockade were able to develop a
bond with the land itself. Several affinity groups, including the
anarcha-feminist (Antinuclear Civil Disobedience Community
(ACDC) decided to blockade a back gate, on state parkland.
Blockaders at the front gate were being arrested as soon as they
stepped over the line; the backcountry blockaders camped out
for four days. They held the gate open for blockaders heading
into the backcountry; meanwhile, they lived on food they brought

with them and pizzas brought out by local residents. Noël Sturgeon, one of the blockaders, recalls excitement and a sense of adventure fed by radio reports of the blockade's progress and by the participants' own view of the sea blockade, of boats dodging the Coast Guard to let off protesters. While the blockaders waited, they debated whether to go back to the front gate and be arrested immediately or continue to blockade: as Noël points out, a discussion of the purposes of civil disobedience. "Eventually," she recalls, "the police came and arrested us. It was a really moving experience; people were crying. Because we had been there so long, we had made the place our own. I've never had so much feeling of connection with the land."[12]

Noël Sturgeon argues that the sense of place, the opportunity to create a different kind of community and a different relationship to the land, was fundamental to what Diablo (and the antinuclear movement as a whole) was about. The camp, she points out, became an alternative society, with town meetings and a community kitchen. "It took enormous organizing and fundraising to create that city, but when you got there it seemed so easy, a self-supporting, mutualistic community where all the decisions were made by consensus, with people sharing things. I felt, this is a way I could live."[13]

The camp seemed to many people, not only those steeped in anarchist philosophy, to be a model of a future society. Jackie Cabasso, who had come with a group from Walnut Creek, and had only recently become involved in the Abalone, remembers the camp as "literally a utopian society. This was a town with no discernible leaders; everyone was equal, everyone was walking around hugging each other, there was incredible bonding." In spite of the utter chaos, it was a functioning society. The counterpoint to the camp, Jackie said, was the police surveillance. Police were watching the camp from low-flying helicopters; they seemed especially interested in the shower area. The blockaders responded collectively, and in the spirit of nonviolence, by flying kites, which made it impossible for the helicopters to come down so low.[14] The same community spirit prevailed in jail. Lawyers came in and out bringing news; each piece of information required another meeting. "It was like an overstimulated New England town," Jackrabbit recalls. "Part of what Diablo was about was just that: self-government. We were using a model that we really had faith in. It was our ideology in action."[15]

Daily evidence of outside support strengthened the blockader's sense of being part of a larger community of purpose. Jackie Cabasso remembers that one night in the wash truck, she turned a faucet, saw blood all over her hand, and realized that she had been badly cut. She went to the medical tent, where the doctor bandaged her hand but did not have the supplies to give her a tetanus shot. A group of people took her to the hospital; Jackie had no money with her and was afraid that she would not be treated. A nurse came into the hospital waiting room when they arrived. They explained the problem, and she said, "You're protesters, aren't you?" She went into an office and reappeared with a paper bag, which she handed to them. "Don't tell anyone I gave this to you," she said. It turned out to be supplies for tetanus shots. "That was an example of how powerful it felt," Jackie said. "The outside world was responding as if something important was happening. When I went back home, it was hard to get back into daily life. For days, people told me I was just glowing."[16] Noël Sturgeon describes the atmosphere at the camp as one of "mutual admiration. A lot of people fell in love," she remembers.[17]

For many people, nonviolence and the self-respect it generated were fundamental to the sense of community created by civil disobedience. Charlotte Davis, a San Francisco Abalone member, was arrested at the front gate along with seventeen others; it was her first arrest. The protesters were surrounded by what looked like four hundred police as they boarded the bus to go to jail. Charlotte, who was at the end of the line, found herself separated from the others and facing the head policeman. She looked at him and said, "You look very tired." "Tired!" he blurted out angrily, "I haven't slept in thirty-six hours." "I'm sorry," Charlotte said. "Our intention isn't to have you guys working overtime. I'm sorry we're doing this to you, but we have to do this."

His whole face changed, his whole nasty mask fell off, and he said, "I know." Something had happened in that moment. He was a human being and I was a human being and we were smiling at each other. That made me feel we were doing something right. I was handcuffed, I was alone with this man, I was absolutely terrified. But I felt very much not alone. That spoke to me of the strength of what we were doing. I felt that there were thousands of people who would come to my defense if he did anything to me. I carry that moment with me. It's the nonviolent part of it that makes me feel part of a community.[18]

At Diablo, the atmosphere of nonviolence was contagious; people who in other circumstances might have caused trouble were absorbed into the prevailing spirit of the protest. Jackie Cabasso was a monitor at one of the backcountry gates. She remembers that "a real wide-eyed guy turned up. He had tattoos; it turned out that he was an ex-convict. We were worried. But as the day wore on, just being around the other people he calmed down and became real mellow and loving. He wasn't a problem. I saw a lot of other people go through that transformation."[19]

Though nonviolence was infectious, it was a credit to the planning of the action that there were no violent incidents, in spite of the numbers of people involved and the intensity of feelings on both sides. The fact that every blockader had been required to go through a nonviolence training session undoubtedly helped; those who had not had training before coming to the camp attended sessions held at the camp. Some people resisted; some anarchists felt that it was authoritarian to require it, and many people with experience in the antiwar movement scoffed at the idea. For the most part the blockade was planned by a collective of six or seven people that included two DPO staff members, Raye Fleming and Joyce Howarton, and others drawn primarily from San Luis Obispo Abalone (for a time, a member of Love and Rage who had moved to San Luis Obispo was part of this group). The planning collective insisted that nonviolence training was crucial. Anarchist groups such as Love and Rage that had been deeply involved in organizing the action agreed and conducted many of the sessions themselves. Thus everyone who participated in the blockade acted on a common set of rules. The blockaders' confidence in their own unity reduced the likelihood of panic. Furthermore, monitors, who had received special training, were stationed everywhere, prepared to step in if anything began to get out of hand.

The required trainings and the high level of organization of the blockade earned the planning collective and the DPO (two distinct but overlapping entities, incorrectly viewed as one throughout Abalone) a reputation for high-handedness. It seemed to Abalone members from elsewhere in the state that when it came to Diablo, the consensus process did not stop the DPO leadership from getting whatever they wanted. In view of the stakes, it is understandable that the planning collective connected to the DPO did not want to leave much to chance. Furthermore, their disproportionate power in decisions having to do with the blockade had some legitimacy; they were the ones doing most of the work, and they knew local conditions best. There was nevertheless some justice in the argument that the DPO leadership was unwilling to tolerate the egalitarianism to which the Abalone was officially dedicated. Joyce Howarton, for years a member both of the DPO staff and the larger planning collective, admitted that she generally knew how to get the decision that she wanted out of a meeting, consensus process or no consensus process. At the time of the blockade, she said, the DPO people felt that they had the right to insist on nonviolence trainings, to set the standard of behavior for the blockaders. "We had made a commitment; we wanted other people to show they had a commitment too. We required a lot. Some of it may have been a little much. In some ways we built a bureaucracy, our own nonviolent civil disobedience bureaucracy."[20]

The DPO people were "straighter" than many of the blockaders, skeptical about aspects of the counterculture that seemed to put the blockade at risk. For many of the blockaders the camp kitchen was the center of the Diablo community and a symbol of communal sharing. To Joyce Howarton of the DPO it was a health hazard. A group of people had taken it upon themselves to set up a kitchen; the DPO was having problems with the state Department of Health and would have liked to shut it down but could not. "We heard reports," she said, "that there was a man with open herpes lesions on his lips doing the cooking. I went down to the camp and made the man with herpes leave the kitchen. Some people thought I was being unfair. People came to live in the camp without supplies, without bedding. One of the beauties of the movement is that you will take care of people, but it's also one of the problems."[21]

Some people in the Abalone, especially some of the old Abalones, were seriously disillusioned by the experience of the blockade. Some had distanced themselves from the Abalone before the blockade took place; the Resource Center for Nonviolence, for instance, was much less involved in the blockade than in previous phases of the Abalone's activity, partly because they felt that the Abalone was now on its feet and no longer needed special help, and partly because they doubted that civil disobedience alone could stop the plant. Other old Abalones who participated in the blockade came to the same conclusion. Mark Evanoff, a leading Bay Area member, had been arrested in the 1978 blockade of Diablo and continued to be a strong supporter of CD. "My switch," he said, "came during the 1981 blockade, when I was media representative. I realized I was hyping. It was silly to say that this was the action that would shut Diablo down if I didn't believe it. I was also saying that the affinity groups controlled the action, when they didn't. It was a select group in San Luis Obispo that controlled it. For a lot of people it was a very upbeat action, it was the crescendo of the movement, but I was bitter after the action."[22] Susan Lawrence, another leading Bay Area activist, said that though she believed in nonviolence and was drawn to civil disobedience because she believed that people would feel safe participating in it, by the time of the 1981 blockade she had come to the conclusion that it excluded too many people to serve as the basis of a movement; only those with a certain amount of privilege could risk arrest. "The eighty-one action was a media event," she said, "it was not Abalone any more. By that time I saw that CD was not a way of building a mass movement. The race and class stuff had gotten to me."[23]

The old Abalones who doubted that the blockade could close the plant down and feared that the focus on CD had changed Abalone were proved right. Some of them began to see CD as a kind of entry-level political experience, drawing people into the movement but soon revealing its own limitations. Certainly by 1981 the old Abalones wanted results that CD alone could not produce. Though most worked hard for the blockade and participated in it, often in crucial roles, their ambivalence about it prevented them from collectively exercising the kind of leadership they had earlier.

The blockade was ultimately held together by an uneasy coalition between the DPO people and the new Abalones, especially those who explicitly identified themselves as anarchists. The DPO led in organizing and preparing the blockade and guided it through the two weeks of the action; the anarchists provided much of the spirit that went into the action. The anarchists had tended to regard the DPO people as rule-bound bureaucrats; the DPO had been suspicious of the anarchist tendency to use the consensus process to challenge existing leadership groups (meaning, often, the DPO itself). But both groups, for slightly different reasons, had large stakes in the blockade, so they worked well together around that event.

Not only did the anarchists do a good deal to hold the blockade together, they also played an important role in showing participants what Abalone was about. The anarchists were able to articulate what was central to Abalone as a whole: the experience of total engagement, of politics merged with personal life, that came with dedication to visionary politics and with the attempt to build a prefigurative community. The quality of human relationships and the attempt to realize shared goals in the practice of the movement itself gave old and new Abalones alike the energy to keep going, rather than fear of nuclear power plants or the desire to replace them with something safer. Even though Californians in general, and certainly residents of San Luis Obispo in particular, had good reason to be worried about an accident at the Diablo plant, such fears would not in themselves have produced a movement with Abalone's momentum. The threat that Diablo posed to the environment was the occasion, rather than the impetus, for a movement that was fundamentally about social, communal, and personal transformation.

The consensus process worked best in small groups of people who knew and trusted one another. It worked during a blockade or in jail because of the heightened sense of solidarity and the strong desire for harmony and cooperation among the protesters. In more routine large meetings, consensus could break down quite painfully. Even in smaller settings some were willing to use the block manipulatively or egotistically. But the central experience of the Abalone was that of working with small groups and developing the blend of solidarity, intimacy, and mutual respect that occurs only in the heat of common struggle.

Joyce Howarton, for instance, says that despite her strong feelings about the Diablo plant, what held her was the personal involvement. In the core DPO group, she remembers, each built on the contributions of the others. In discussions each would go one step beyond the last. That the core group was made up entirely of women may be one reason for that sense of connection. A few men joined for short periods, but none really became a part of the group. One man, after sitting in on several meetings, gave his impressions to Joyce: "He pointed out that no one in the collective ever finished a sentence; everyone knew where everyone else was going. It was just working together and having the same goals. We're all different individuals, there was no problem disagreeing or criticizing each other, yet when we came together we were able to work together in a way that I miss. I don't have that in my life any more. We brought out the best in everyone." The intensity of this experience produced not just a tight working group but close personal relationships as well. "There was incredible tension," Joyce recalls. "We would meet until ten, then go out dancing or drinking. We had to do it. We became best personal friends. When we started out we hardly knew each other. By the end, we were all each other's best friends—and worst enemies."[24]

Utopian Democracy and Leadership

Abalone's experience raises two questions. First, what gave the Abalone the strength that carried it to and through that blockade? In particular, what explains the broad appeal of the anarchist/utopian vision that was expressed through the struggle against Diablo? Second, why did it decline so abruptly after its most successful action?

Abalone did continue to exist after the 1981 blockade. Both the DPO and the San Francisco office functioned on an ever reduced scale and local actions against Diablo were held sporadically. But the statewide movement dissipated, in part because no one knew what to do next. The blockade had drawn what was probably a very large proportion of the Californians who were willing to commit civil disobedience for an environmental issue, and though the blockade had succeeded in drawing attention to the dangers of nuclear power, the plant had not been closed down. That fact was softened by the discovery of a serious flaw in the design of the plant on the day the blockade ended. The coincidence between the blockade and the discovery of the plant's internal weakness allowed the blockaders to go home with a sense of satisfaction. Even when it was made clear that the flaw would be repaired and Diablo would eventually go on-line, those who had been part of the blockade continued to feel, with justification, that their efforts had not been wasted. The publicity the action generated put a large dent in the reputation of the nuclear power industry and contributed to its economic decline. In addition, the Abalone had built a strong movement and trained a generation of activists, many of whom went on to do other kinds of political work.

Some Abalone members, especially the anarchists, saw nothing wrong with the decline of their organization but argued that that was the way political organizations should work: small, autonomous groups should come together for a particular purpose and then return to work in their own local communities—or move on to another large issue—once that purpose had been served. This classical anarchist view of political organization reflected a distrust of large organizations whose structures were held intact between surges of movement activity. The anarchists not only feared that the movement might create its own bureaucracy but also believed that such a bureaucracy was unnecessary, that an underlying political culture existed that could emerge and assert itself at moments of struggle, then retreat to its local bases, without losing its constituencies, until the need for unity arose again. The anarchist view, however, did not entirely describe how the Abalone had come together, nor was it a reliable judge of the impact of the organization's dissolution. It was true that Abalone had drawn on several preexisting political cultures, especially the women's movement, the counterculture, and some remnants of the antiwar movement. It was also true that the formal autonomy of Abalone's local affiliates and affinity groups made it easier than it would otherwise have been to disengage and move on to other arenas. In the men's jail, at Diablo, a list was passed around of those interested in opposing the nuclear-weapons-producing Livermore Laboratory. The Livermore Action Group (LAG), which was to be at the center of the next wave of the nonviolent civil disobedience movement, began with that list. Many Abalone affinity groups participated in LAG actions and gradually attached themselves to that organization. But most people had joined the Abalone not as members of preexisting groups but as individuals, forming affinity groups in the process. Many affinity groups were not strong enough to survive the demise of the organization that had created them.

The Abalone dwindled not only because the blockade was an end itself and no one knew what to do afterward, but also because the leadership was tired and ready for a rest. Because there were officially no leaders, there were of course no mechanisms for putting a new stratum of leadership in its place. More important, there was no structure within which to consider what should be done next. The belief that the organization was, or at least should be, leaderless added to the burdens of the central activists who were in fact exercising leadership; it created a situation in which the normal grumbling of the rank and file about those with more power or influence had an ideological legitimacy, whereas the self-defense of the leaders did not. Furthermore, in the absence of formal constraints on the behavior of leaders (who had no more accountability to the organization as a whole than any other members), there were frequent opportunities for abuses of power.

If the role of the leaders had been understood, and if there had been some mechanism for a transition in leadership, the newer Abalones could have supplied the next generation. When there is no such mechanism for transition, new leadership groups tend to be identified through a process of challenging the old leadership, rather than trained and welcomed by it. This pattern started to be played out between the new and the old Abalones and was only aggravated by the scornful attitude of the new Abalones toward leadership generally. These strains had been eased temporarily by the unity of the blockade and by the fact that the new Abalones took a prominent role in organizing it.

Failure to acknowledge the place of leadership caused problems but was not the reason for the Abalone's decline. If the Diablo plant had not been shut down for repair and the Abalone had carried out a series of massive blockades, the anarcha-feminists might well have continued to play a leading role as organizers and thus might have become the next informal leadership. The Abalone came to an end because it had no strategy for pursuing the struggle either against nuclear power or for the broader social transformation regarded by most Abalones as their fundamental goal. If the old Abalones had remained enthusiastic about the organization, they might have found answers to the question of what to do next. Many of them had seen the Abalone as the first step in the creation of a nonviolent movement with widening concerns. But after the 1981 blockade most of them had become too disenchanted with civil disobedience and the consensus process to do anything but drift away from the organization they had created. The new Abalones did not see a problem: the Abalone's purpose had been the blockade; if there were to be no more blockades, then there was no further reason for the Abalone to exist.

The demise of the Abalone was not on the whole as damaging as it might have been. The collapse of the Clamshell had left many embittered people and permanent rifts in movement circles. In the early eighties many activists were turning their attention toward the arms race, and the fact that LAG had grown out of and was modeled on the Clamshell made it a magnet for Abalone participants who remained enthusiastic about its approach to politics. Nevertheless, a movement that sheds its organizational structure when it moves away from an issue loses something in the process. When an organization that has been a focus of many of its members' lives dissolves, those lives change, often in ways that leave less room for political activity. Some people remain in touch, but many fall away. The next time around, the institutions, the networks, the patterns of life that form the basis of political commitment will have to be rebuilt. Lessons that might have been learned, if people had stayed long enough to evaluate their experiences, are lost. Many of the old Abalones who, by the end of the blockade, had become aware of some of the limitations of civil disobedience, saw LAG as repeating the mistakes of the Abalone and doomed to come to a similar end.

It is not especially surprising that the Abalone's utopian anarchism created an organization that could not last. Anarchism has never been known for its ability to create stable and long-lived organizations. What is surprising is the broad appeal of utopian anarchist politics. Even in the Abalone's period of greatest growth and public visibility its appeal had as much to do with utopian vision as with opposition to nuclear energy. The large numbers of activists who were drawn in by that appeal were quite ready to move on to the next issue, taking with them the politics and organizational structure that had evolved in the Abalone. Many of the people who supported the Abalone without participating in its actions were probably responding to the same vision. During the 1980s the ideas of nonviolence, consensus decision making, and affinity group structure spread very widely in California, especially among activists, but also among people who are far from the left and the counterculture; to the degree that they have a connection to political activity, it is likely to be through their churches, or through "socially concerned" professional organizations. In the summer of 1985, for instance, I spoke at a summer workshop on peace education for Orange County elementary school teachers. I was astounded to find that they had adopted consensus decision-making structure and were speaking the language of nonviolence and the politics of example, with which I was familiar from the direct action movement. Those women were influenced more directly by the peace movement than the antinuclear movement; they may not have been aware of the history of the Abalone. Nevertheless, in California the Abalone was the first to try out these ideas on a mass scale.

In "Direct Action as Living Theater," Marcy Darnovsky, a former Abalone activist, points out that the Abalone was caught in the contradictions of symbolic politics.[25] The direct action movement, Darnovsky suggests, has a special appeal to activists and left intellectuals who see the need for a movement that can challenge not only the prevailing power relations but the ideology that sustains them. But, Darnovsky argues, Abalone's ability to create such a politics was undermined by the fact that it was torn between two concepts of direct action, each of them incomplete and therefore inadequate as the basis for challenging ideological hegemony. Some people took the idea of direct action literally: a massive blockade would close down Diablo; and if this scenario could be repeated at enough nuclear plants around the country, the nuclear industry would come to a halt. Anyone who believed this scenario could not but be enormously disappointed when it did not work. Others did not believe that even Diablo, much less the whole nuclear industry, could be stopped this way. They understood direct action as a way of drawing public attention to an issue, by arousing the interest of the media. The view of direct action as symbolic protest thus led to a politics based on manipulation of the media. To play the game of media politics meant abandoning the principled stance that was the movement's greatest strength. Probably most people in the Abalone never thought very clearly about what they meant by direct action. They knew that the blockade itself was not likely to cause PG & E to close down the plant, but they were unwilling to adopt the cynical view that the blockade was simply a way of catching media attention. In the end, Darnovsky argues, the Abalone was overtaken by a collective myopia: the blockade was planned as if it would close down the plant, even though few people seriously thought that this would happen.

Symbolic politics can mean various things, not all of which pose the dilemma the Abalone faced. Many movements placed considerable emphasis on symbolism as a way of dramatizing an issue and persuading the public. The Abalone did not merely employ symbolism and theater in the pursuit of an immediate objective: the 1981 blockade of Diablo, for many, probably most, participants, *was* symbolism and theater—an opportunity to act out a vision of a better world. Symbolism and theater merged with prefigurative politics; both were based on dedication to a set of values that revolved around nonviolence, egalitarianism, and democracy. There is always a prefigurative element in radical politics, or at least a pull toward prefigurative politics, because without an effort to live one's values radical claims collapse into hypocrisy. There is also a pull to accommodate to the existing system so as to be able to operate effectively in it. Each movement finds its own balance between these opposing forces.

Though anarchism has roots deep in the history of American protest, most mass movements in the United States, at least in the twentieth century, have subordinated the prefigurative aspect of their politics to a particular objective. This was certainly true of the Communist Party and the movement to build the CIO in the

1930s. Symbolic and prefigurative politics were a part of the student and youth movements of the sixties but ultimately were subordinated to the goal of ending the war in Vietnam. The early civil rights movement made extensive use of symbolism, but it did so differently from the Abalone (and the Clamshell). The image of blacks being beaten and arrested for walking down a public road in daylight, or for sitting down at a counter and ordering a cup of coffee, conveys a different message from the image of antinuclear protesters being arrested for blockading a nuclear plant. In the first case the action is legal; the response illustrates the fact that fundamental, accepted rights are being violated. In the second case the action is illegal; the protest is designed to show that the rules need to be changed, that citizens must gain the power to stop grave threats to the environment. The "beloved community" was a very important aspect of the civil rights movement. It helped give civil rights workers the strength to go on under extraordinarily difficult circumstances, and it left many with a permanently altered sense of what human relations could be. But community never became the object of the movement.

What was new about the Clamshell and the Abalone was that for each organization, at its moment of greatest mass participation, the opportunity to act out a vision and to build community was at least as important as the immediate objective of stopping nuclear power. Many activists, including early Clamshell and Abalone members, found this fact disturbing, because they knew that vision alone could not sustain a movement and that the pursuit of community for its own sake could lead to bitter disappointment. The prominence of symbolic and prefigurative politics in the Clamshell and the Abalone made them virtually incomprehensible to many students of social movements, especially those trained in the Resource Mobilization school, which dominated the academic study of social movements through the seventies. Resource Mobilization argued, against an earlier conservative view of protest movements as mass irrationality, that protest movements were a legitimate part of the political process because they pursued well-defined and reasonable objectives in a rational manner. This model had difficulty with the cultural aspects of the movements of the sixties; and the Clamshell and the Abalone simply did not fit it. The opportunity to engage in living theater was not the sort of objective that the Resource Mobilization analysts had in mind when they defended protest movements as legitimate and rational.

The failure to resolve contradictory ideas about what direct action meant, the uneasy balance between the imperatives of symbolic and prefigurative politics on the one hand and practical objectives on the other, gave the Clamshell an underlying fragility. The Abalone did not suffer as much from these problems because it did have a concrete objective—closing down the Diablo plant—and because the nuclear industry was already in so much trouble that mass action could have a real, if indirect, impact not only on that plant but on the standing of nuclear power with the American public. As the direct action movement turned to the larger, vaguer, and less immediately tractable issue of the arms race, the movement's own contradictions would become a more serious problem.

Chapter Four

The Livermore
Action Group

Direct Action and the Arms Race

The Livermore Action Group (LAG), which from 1981 through 1984 mobilized a mass effort to shut down the nuclear-weapons-producing Lawrence Livermore National Laboratory, affiliated with the University of California, was inspired by the Abalone Alliance and inherited its philosophy and organizational structure. Some former Abalone members, disenchanted with the consensus process and with a politics that relied on massive civil disobedience, thought it was a mistake to accept that inheritance. The founders of LAG were for the most part not longtime Abalone members but people who had participated in the Diablo blockade or witnessed it from the outside, had been impressed by the Abalone's ability to combine mass action with nonviolence, and believed that this style of politics should now be brought to the movement against the arms race.

LAG had strengths that both the Clamshell and the Abalone lacked. It attracted a more diverse constituency than either of its predecessors. As in the earlier organizations, the majority of LAG's activists were in their twenties and thirties—the great majority of them white and middle-class—and the left counterculture was an important presence. But there were considerably larger numbers of older people in LAG, and the range of subcultures was much broader than in either of its predecessors. LAG brought together former Abalone affinity groups, especially anarcha-feminist ones, a more spiritually oriented section of the counterculture that identified with Paganism and witchcraft; activists who leaned more strongly toward Marxism than any groups in the Clamshell or the Abalone; Quakers; Catholic and Protestant pacifists; feminists; environmentalists; lesbian activists; rural countercultural groups; veterans of the antiwar movement of the sixties; peace activists who had been involved in left politics since the thirties; and middle-class, middle-aged people who had never been involved in political activity before, many of whom came to LAG through San Francisco Bay Area churches. For several years, these disparate elements showed a remarkable ability to work together in spite of often deep differences.

Perhaps because LAG reached into a larger number of existing communities than had either the Clamshell or the Abalone, LAG affinity groups were more likely to have a degree of autonomy. Many engaged in actions beyond those called by LAG as a whole; some were able to survive LAG's collapse, at least for a time. The fact that some LAG affinity groups had come into existence in the context of the Abalone encouraged greater independence: large organizations might come and go but the affinity group would remain. Another factor was the strength of anarchism in LAG, which encouraged the autonomy of affinity groups and clusters of affinity groups. That autonomy made it possible for quite different styles to coexist in the same movement. The Christians, for example, regularly held actions at the "labs" (as the laboratory was called within the movement) that were steeped in religious ritual, but they felt no necessity to introduce the same ritual into actions held by the organization as a whole. Because LAG affinity groups participated simultaneously in, for example, the ecology, feminist, and lesbian and gay movements, LAG developed broader connections than it would otherwise have had. But the most dramatic of LAG's actions were those called by the organization as a whole, especially the mass blockades of the Livermore labs that took place in 1982 and 1983.

The Clamshell and Abalone Alliances had been torn by conflicts between local activists working within conservative communities to shut down specific plants and activists more interested in building a regional or national movement and more willing to emphasize broad visionary goals. LAG avoided that problem by taking up an issue with no equivalent local constituency and by making its commitment to nonviolent revolution explicit and central to its politics. Drawing on the Abalone's anarcha-feminism, LAG activists created a political culture based on nonviolence, feminism, and spirituality, a mixture that enabled a broad range of groups to come together around a politics of moral witness. LAG also modified the organizational structure it had inherited from the Abalone to make it stronger and more flexible. The introduction of clusters, which drew together like-minded affinity groups, gave legitimacy to the variety of perspectives in the organization and provided forums for expressing and developing a variety of approaches. The creation of "working groups" that, unlike affinity groups, addressed themselves to specific organizational tasks legitimated functions that in another movement would have come under the heading of leadership.

Some problems that had been apparent in the Clamshell and the Abalone became more serious in LAG. The fact that nuclear plants seemed particularly threatening to the people who lived near them had given the antinuclear movement access to local constituencies; the pressure to reach accommodation with those communities gave the movement a grounding in political reality. Because the arms race is equally threatening to everyone, and the peace movement has no specific constituency (except those who have taken it upon themselves to act on this threat), LAG had no equivalent political ground. Many Abalone activists, especially those who lived in and around San Luis Obispo, had been interested mainly in shutting down the Diablo Canyon plant. LAG activists wanted to shut down the Livermore Laboratory, but they chose that object more to attack the arms race than to drive the labs out of the vicinity. The labs were not likely to be closed down, without drastic changes in national security policy. LAG's target was larger and ultimately less tangible than the Clamshell's and the Abalone's, and it was also less vulnerable.

The conflicting conceptions of direct action that the Clamshell and the Abalone had managed not to address were avoided equally in LAG, where they caused equally serious problems. Was LAG's purpose literally to shut down the labs, not just during a blockade but permanently? If so, the organization was setting itself up for failure. Was the purpose to raise the cost of the arms race by shutting the labs down for as long as the blockade could be sustained? If so, it hardly seemed worth the effort, because many workers simply arrived early to avoid the blockade, and in any event much of the work could go on with a reduced work force. Did LAG hope to reach the workers in the labs and change their thinking? If so, the actions were failures; the workers needed their jobs and were a very unlikely audience for the message of the peace movement. There is little evidence that their thinking was much influenced by LAG. Was the purpose of LAG actions to attract the media and thus bring public attention to the arms race? Many LAG activists assumed that publicity was the main purpose of mass civil disobedience. There was little discussion of the issue, however, because it suggested that massive civil disobedience was not really "direct action," at least not in the anarchist sense: it would not, directly, stop the machine.

To acknowledge that what the movement called direct action was really symbolic action and that winning over the media was a crucial part of the process would have raised very difficult questions about moral witness and the creation of alternative community as political acts. The commitment to prefigurative politics was even stronger in LAG than it had been in the Clamshell and the Abalone, whose constituents had mostly been secular, though they had some appreciation for spiritual values. LAG was dominated by two forms of spirituality, Christianity and Pagan anarchism. LAG's commitment to prefigurative politics, inherited from the anarcha-feminists in the Abalone, was reinforced from both sides—by the Pagan-anarchists, whose concept of political action was living theater, and by the Christians, who thought of politics in terms of moral witness. Both the Pagan anarchists and the Christians believed that creating a community in which authentic human relations could take place was central to radical politics. Though the two groups had different ideas of what such a community would be like, their net effect was to place prefigurative politics and moral witness at the core of LAG's identity. To discuss direct action in instrumental terms, or for that matter to address the related issue of strategy, was therefore all but impossible.

In the end LAG's problem was the same as the Abalone's: it had no strategy beyond mass direct action, in this case, two massive blockades of the Livermore Laboratory. Drawing what was probably the largest number of people in the San Francisco Bay Area and vicinity willing to go to jail over the issue of nuclear arms, those blockades were highlights of radical peace activity in the Bay Area in the early 1980s. They invigorated the entire peace movement, greatly strengthened the direct action movement, and helped to politicize the extensive local alternative subculture. But the second blockade was somewhat smaller than the first, and a third, held a year later, was considerably smaller. It was clear that LAG could not organize a blockade that would actually shut the labs down, and to repeat the same action year after year, with dwindling numbers of participants, might even damage the peace movement by suggesting that opposition to the labs was waning. LAG had no idea what to do next. Like the Clamshell and the Abalone, LAG gradually declined, many of its activists taking the political culture and the skills that they had acquired in LAG to the anti-intervention movement, the next focus of nonviolent direct action.[1]

Building the Movement

The Livermore Action Group was born in jail, at the Abalone's 1981 occupation of Diablo Canyon.[2] Long-time peace activists Ken Nightingale and Eldred Schneider, along with a handful of others in an affinity group called the Sea Cucumbers, joined the blockade at Diablo and subsequently went to jail. In jail they collected the signatures of those interested in establishing an organization that would apply nonviolent direct action to the Livermore Laboratory in particular and the arms race in general. Ken, Eldred, and the others began working on the project as soon as they returned to Berkeley from Diablo. One such organization already existed, the University of California Nuclear Weapons Lab Conversion Project, which had done considerable research and worked hard to expose the labs' role in producing nuclear weapons. In spite of educational work and several protests, the Conversion Project shrank to a dozen or so people by the fall of 1981. They nevertheless decided to organize a blockade of the Livermore labs for the following June and welcomed the opportunity to increase their numbers. After a small blockade in February (about 1,000 people demonstrated and 170 were arrested), the two groups became the Livermore Action Group, established an office, and began to work toward a much larger blockade in June.

LAG adopted the organizational form of the Abalone Alliance: affinity groups and a spokescouncil made up of spokes from each of the groups. In addition, LAG set up working groups to take charge of particular tasks, such as organizing actions and relations with the media. Office staff and working groups overlapped to a considerable degree: collectively these people were regarded as LAG's core, the informal leadership.

Before June, several groups within LAG held their own smaller actions. On Ash Wednesday a group of Christian pacifists, mostly from the Graduate Theological Union, in Berkeley, organized a blockade. Thirty-one people, including Catholic nuns, Dominican priests, and a Lutheran minister, were arrested. Spirit, a radical Christian affinity group, took shape in this action and remained an important presence in LAG. A year later three members of Spirit, Darla Rucker, Terry Messman, and Pat Runo, were confirmed in the Catholic church in a ceremony held before the Livermore gates. Immediately after the ceremony Darla, Terry, and Pat, along with nine others from Spirit, chained themselves to the model of a missile in the shape of a cross and blocked the gates. Fifty-nine others knelt in the road holding black crosses. All seventy-one were arrested. This action made a strong impression, not only on the priest who had conducted the service (who later committed civil disobedience and went to jail himself), but also on many other Catholics, who began to join LAG actions in increasing numbers.

In May of 1982 a group of LAG women organized a Mother's Day action. Only women were to blockade; men were to participate in a legal demonstration of support. This action was more confrontational than any that had gone before. The women who had planned the event, especially the Feminist Cluster, gained a reputation for a militancy that pushed the nonviolence code to its limits. In previous actions, people stood in front of the gate and waited to be arrested. The eighty-one Mother's Day blockaders found the police blocking the gates when they arrived. They decided on the spot to sit down in the middle of the road, inaugurating what became standard LAG practice. Evidently such a response had not been anticipated. The police were members of the Livermore Laboratory Security Force, who had the authority to make arrests at the gate on Laboratory property but not to arrest people sitting in the county roadway. Two hours elapsed before the appropriate police force arrived. During that time the women were able to prevent anyone from entering the labs. Drivers left their cars to argue with the women, and a few even tried to disrupt the blockade by edging their cars toward women sitting in the road. Four women chained themselves to the front gate and poured blood on the ground. The police were quite rough when they arrived. They dragged some women to the side of the road without arresting them, hoping to be done with them. Those women rejoined the blockade and were arrested.

When the June action finally came about it was a huge success, even by San Francisco Bay Area standards. It drew over thirteen hundred blockaders and a demonstration of support of over five thousand people. LAG required that everyone in the blockade be a member of an affinity group and go through nonviolence training conducted by one of the LAG "preparers." The blockade covered the four roads leading to the labs. One road was designated the site for a women's blockade, another the place where props would be allowed (balloons, banners, floats); a third was for people willing to take special risks, such as climbing the fence if the opportunity presented itself; and the fourth was for people who wanted a simple blockade with no special risks and no props (which some people feared might accelerate violence in any clash with the police). Clusters of affinity groups arrived in waves beginning at five in the morning. The arrests, which lasted into the afternoon, went smoothly. Those arrested were given the option of "citing out"—being released after signing citation papers—or going to jail. Those who went to jail were arraigned on the second and third days, after negotiating a charge of jaywalking.

This action established LAG as the radical wing of the peace movement in the Bay Area. Many affinity groups formed for the action continued to function afterward. LAG now had an extensive constituency and a reputation for imagination, creativity, and organizing skill. Between June 1982 and the next major blockade of the labs in June 1983, a number of smaller actions were held, of which the most important were three at the Vandenberg Air

Force Base in Lompoc, California, where a test launch of the MX missile was planned. Security regulations precluded the launch's taking place if unauthorized people were within a certain radius of the pad. Thus the opportunity existed actually to delay a missile test. The launch date was announced for January 1983, but after plans for a January action had been set in motion, the launch was delayed.

A number of the affinity groups most involved in the planning of the Vandenberg action wanted to cancel the January protest and hold one instead at the time of the launch, whenever that might be. People in the office and the working groups, already committed to a major action at Livermore in June, wanted to hold the Vandenberg action and be done with it. In the end, three actions took place. In January, in addition to a large legal demonstration, some people blockaded the front gate of the installation and others hiked into the backcountry in order to enter the test site. Two hundred were arrested. The missile test was rescheduled for March; although it was called off, a second action, sponsored by the Vandenberg Action Coalition, was nevertheless carried out by the affinity groups involved. Pagan anarchist affinity groups were especially prominent in this action, which was virtually run out of Urban Stonehenge, a Pagan anarchist household in San Francisco. The fact that the LAG office contributed only material resources and that staff and working groups did not plan the action, except, in a few cases, as individuals, sharpened the tensions between the affinity groups and the informal leadership.

In the March action, 777 people who hiked into the backcountry and entered the test site were arrested. There were some frightening incidents. A man walking down a backcountry road toward the site encountered a rancher on horseback who recognized him as a protester, lassoed him, and dragged him for some distance. When the test launch was finally held in June, a third and smaller action was held; forty people went onto the test site and were arrested. The June action went on for a week and succeeded in delaying the launch for several days. The missile was finally launched in violation of security rules while blockaders watched from positions close to the pad.

By the time of the June 1983 blockade, it seemed that LAG

led a charmed life. Operating more on political intuition than detailed political analysis, LAG was able, time after time, to draw impressive numbers of people for its actions, to maintain an unsullied reputation for nonviolent and principled behavior in the face of large-scale confrontations with the police, and to gain substantial and often favorable media attention. People in other sections of the Bay Area peace movement, such as the Nuclear Freeze, often criticized LAG for abstaining from electoral politics; many of the more respectable peace groups were put off by the scruffy appearance of LAG members and the eccentricity of their style. Nevertheless, LAG won the respect of a great many people, not only for the success of its actions but for its ability to hold together a very diverse coalition.[3]

Ideology and Affinity

LAG differed from the more conventional wings of the peace movement not only in its emphasis on direct action but also because it was able to bring "respectable" constituencies, including people with very little prior experience of protest movements, together with experienced radicals and members of the Bay Area counterculture and to create a movement with a strong sense of cohesion. LAG's identity was based primarily on the bond among people willing to take nonviolent direct action against militarism. That bond, forged in the act of civil disobedience and in jail, transcended differences of philosophy and life-style. It created a sense of comradeship among people who outside the direct action movement might have had very little in common. An understanding of the political culture created out of this common commitment and experience requires a look at the particular constituencies of which LAG was composed.

Several of the major groupings in LAG defined themselves in religious terms. First there were the Christians: although Quaker tradition remained an important influence, when LAG activists used the term "Christians" they usually meant Catholics and Protestants other than Quakers. Differences between Catholics and Protestants were not very important within LAG, but those between radical and mainstream Christians were. Spirit was an affinity group of radical Christians, both Catholic and Protestant.

It found inspiration from Jonah House, the community centering on the Berrigans, and from the related Pacific Life Community in the Northwest.

Like other radical Christians, Spirit upheld an ideal of resistance that included moral witness and a willingness to make sacrifices and take risks, including physical danger and long jail sentences. At the time of the blockade of the Livermore Laboratory on Good Friday 1982, when Spirit was formed, Terry Messman decided that sitting in the road was "not enough of a witness." He climbed over the fence, unobserved by the police, and walked to the building where, he knew, high-security research was conducted. He climbed up an outside stairwell and at the top found the door to an unoccupied nuclear research and design office open. Terry went in and began gathering papers off the desk and throwing them out the window. A security guard came in and pointed a pistol at Terry, who lay down on the floor and began to recite the Lord's Prayer. The guard dragged him down the hall and into the parking lot and put him in a police van. Terry was given a thirty-day sentence.[4]

Spirit has taken collective actions involving considerable risk. In August of 1982, along with others, Spirit blockaded a Trident nuclear submarine that was entering the Port of Seattle. First the members of Spirit spent five days in prayer with members of the Pacific Life Community in Seattle; then for two weeks they waited in boats for the submarine. Its approach was preceded by the Coast Guard, who directed water cannons at the protesters, boarded their ships, and arrested them at gunpoint. Charges were eventually dropped because the Coast Guard had assaulted the protesters without first giving them warning. Members of Spirit believe that they are called upon to risk more than others, Terry Messman told me, and that it is the role of Christians in the movement to be at its cutting edge. Spirit recognizes that many people in the organization would rather avoid long jail sentences. The radical Christians were often critical of such people, who, as Terry described them, "want[ed] to negotiate light little sentences and waltz out of jail."[5]

Spirit, like Jonah House and the Pacific Life Community, was not only a group of political actors but also a religious community and a support network. The group met regularly for worship.

Most members lived in the same neighborhood, and when someone went to jail, others would take over such responsibilities as child care and rent. Spirit regarded the building of a tightly knit community, going beyond the nuclear family, not only as a way of enabling people to take political action, but also as a step toward the kind of society they believed in. Pamela Osgood, a radical Christian who was a member of Spiderwomyn, an all-women affinity group, told me that it was through the expansion of this kind of community and the extension of its values that she foresaw the movement gaining power. Its values, she said, included questioning the sanctity of private property and the primacy and self-sufficiency of the nuclear family.[6]

There were other, less radical Christian groups in LAG as well. Mustard Seed, an affinity group of Catholics and Protestants closer to the mainstreams of their congregations than members of Spirit usually were, played an important role in bringing older, more conventional churchgoers into the direct action movement. Blockades of the labs attracted support also from such Christian groups as the Ecumenical Peace Institute, Unitarians, and the American Friends Service Committee. The members of Spirit, however, were most likely to work with LAG on a day-to-day basis. They were more willing to accept the poverty-level salaries that the LAG office provided (when it had any money at all) than the older, more conventional Christians. The radical Christians shared with other core LAG activists a deeply critical view of American middle-class culture and a willingness to do without its comforts.

The Christians were not the only groups in LAG to define themselves at least partially in religious terms. There were many Jews in LAG, and some of them came together for particular actions. Small groups of Jews connected with LAG held civil disobedience actions in front of the Israeli consulate in San Francisco, protesting the Israeli invasion of Lebanon. In 1984, during Passover, Jews held an action in front of the Livermore gates in which a revised seder was read before the protesters committed civil disobedience. For the most part, however, Jews did not represent a separate grouping within LAG. We were scattered among the organization's various constituencies. What was striking was that here, in contrast to many other left and peace organizations,

Jews seem to have had relatively little impact on the organization's cultural and intellectual tone. LAG's predominant spirituality ran counter to the secularism that most progressive Jews have been accustomed to, especially in organizations of the left, and many were uncomfortable with the aversion to debate that they found among other LAG members. Many of the Jews whom I interviewed, including those who were very much a part of LAG, spoke of feeling a degree of cultural alienation from the organization. They sensed the existence of implicit rules against expressing sharp political differences and against being too intellectually quick. One Jewish woman told me that when she said what she thought in an uninhibited way, she was often accused of being too aggressive.[7] Several Jews said that they found LAG emotionally flat and that they found the emphasis on "niceness" inhibiting.

The Pagans, another religious influence within LAG, came together in a cluster called the Web to participate in important actions. Within the Web, the affinity group of witches (men as well as women) called Matrix played a particularly prominent role. One or two people from this group were always involved in LAG, but for the most part Matrix, and the broader group of Pagans, were somewhat detached from LAG between actions. The witches had an influence in LAG out of proportion to their numbers. They stood at the intersection of several movements, as part of a network of covens stretching across northern America and Europe that adheres to a tradition either inherited or reconstructed from pre-Christian religions. During the 1970s, many American feminists were drawn to religion or spirituality who could not bring themselves to be part of any conventional churches, with their hierarchical organizations and their devotion to an all-powerful, transcendent, male god. Some of these women formed covens and affiliated themselves with "the Craft."

Matrix was one such group. Its members created and performed rituals that derived from their study of Native American as well as European pre-Christian traditions. These rituals centered on the concept of a Goddess understood not as a transcendent being but as an immanent presence in nature and in human beings. Members of Matrix see witchcraft as a way of being in tune with the powers of nature, human consciousness, and collectivity. The values of the witches (and of the broader group of Pagans) fit easily with those of the nonviolent direct action movement. Matrix was formed for the 1981 Diablo blockade and thus adopted the consensus process, as did all other Abalone affinity groups. Consensus process, however, merely made explicit a somewhat vaguer process of consensus decision making that the members of Matrix were already practicing as part of the ethos of the Craft.

Matrix, and the Pagans generally, strongly distrusted authority, especially that exercised by the state. They saw their own contribution as the creation of group rituals that could give the movement cohesion and, they believed, link it with deeper powers. Like the Christians, the Pagans believed they were calling on a force whose power did not depend on the attention of the media, the public, or the people responsible for the arms race. Unlike the Christians, Matrix and the Pagans brought a spirit of irreverence to the movement, which helped to lighten the mood of actions that might otherwise have been as grim as the issues they addressed. Feminist witchcraft played a special role in LAG not only because so many of its values were widely shared, but also because the Pagan polytheism incorporated many cultural strands into a diverse and changing whole, in which there was no dogmatic insistence on identification with Pagan beliefs. Individuals who did not regard themselves as Pagans joined in Pagan rituals without feeling uncomfortable, in a way that would have been impossible if the Christians, for instance, had asserted cultural hegemony within the movement.

Some members of LAG wanted to play down Pagan rituals because they felt that extensive publicity about them was harmful to the movement. The Pagans themselves argued that turning their rituals into a public spectacle would undermine their power. The witches who conducted the rituals were at least as sensitive to the need for discretion as anyone else. Starhawk, a member of Matrix and a prominent LAG activist, told me that Matrix decided not to perform a ritual during an action in September 1982, a "tour of shame" of war-related industries in San Francisco. The march was to end at a large plaza between two corporate headquarters in the downtown area, which would have been a perfect space for a spiral dance of hundreds of demonstrators. Matrix was afraid that there would be too much press coverage and that a ritual of this sort might not be quite the way to reach a Financial District audience. But the members of Matrix happened to be walking at the end of the procession, and by the time they entered the plaza, the rest of the demonstrators were already engaged in a spiral dance.[8]

In spite of their acceptance of differences, the Pagans did have disagreements with other sections of the movement, perhaps the sharpest of which turned on the question of sacrifice. The Pagans did not believe in suffering or self-sacrifice unless it was unavoidable. At times their position brought them into conflict with some of the Christians over such issues as what kinds of jail sentences should be negotiated. Starhawk told me that she believed in doing as much damage to the state as possible, staying in jail as short a time as possible, and going out to do the same thing over again. She described the difference between the Pagans and the Christians in terms of feasting and fasting: the Pagans like to feast, the Christians like to fast. At a January 1983 demonstration at Vandenberg Air Force Base, after the arrests were made demonstrators were put in an empty school building to await arraignment. The clusters were placed in a separate schoolroom, where they waited for several hours. The Pagans spent this time playing a game called "truth or dare," in which people ask one another questions, usually of a sexual nature. (Often, I was told, liaisons within the cluster began out of such exchanges—one common question was, "Who in this cluster are you most attracted to?") A professor at a Bay Area university had just been asked to describe his most recent sexual fantasy when a U.S. attorney walked into the room. Without missing a beat, the professor responded, "I'd like to see everyone in this room licking and sucking and fucking all at the same time." Meanwhile, the Christians, in the next room, were spending the hours-long wait for arraignment in prayer.[9]

Christianity and Paganism were represented by relatively well-defined groups within LAG. By contrast, ecology, feminism, and to a lesser extent anarchism cut across LAG's various tendencies. Each of these perspectives was also at times represented by particular affinity groups and clusters. Ecology and feminism were espoused by virtually everyone in LAG, but there was little debate or discussion about what these perspectives meant for the direct action movement. Feminism in LAG tended to be identified with questions of internal process. Consensus decision making was referred to as "feminist process," and violations of it were likely to be regarded as antifeminist. The consensus process did in fact encourage the participation of the less self-confident and articulate, among whom many women found themselves, and often restrained those who might otherwise have dominated meetings. But the tendency to equate feminism with the consensus process gave to that process, as it was inherited from the Abalone (and earlier from the Clamshell), a moral weight that made it difficult to criticize or revise. In LAG, as in its predecessors, consensus process often involved a leveling, a denial of the experience, knowledge, or skills that some people possessed but not others. That denial was frequently an obstacle to learning within the movement, and the identification of consensus with feminism made the obstacle more formidable.

LAG was shaped by feminism and ecology because many participants in LAG had come out of these movements and because the thinking of virtually everyone in LAG was shaped by them. LAG members were usually careful not to use the generic "he" or other obvious forms of sexist language, and assumptions about men's and women's abilities that went more or less unchallenged in the New Left were at least considerably rarer in LAG. In the same way, most LAG people took for granted the view that concern for the environment is inseparable from concern for human life and that a rapacious, resource-squandering industrialism is inimical to the ideal society. Feminism and ecology formed the intellectual and cultural framework within which LAG functioned, but neither was an immediate focus of political attention.

Anarchism, like feminism and ecology, was widespread in LAG, but it was more contested and had more immediate implications for LAG's political work. Many people in LAG did not describe themselves as anarchists (which the anarchists accepted); nevertheless, even socialism and Marxism in LAG tended to have an anarchist or libertarian tinge. Those who called themselves anarchists meant a variety of things by the term: they favored some form of decentralized democracy, were suspicious not just of the United States government but of any state, and opposed hierarchies of authority of any sort. For most, collective action was entirely compatible with anarchism; a few took anarchism to mean the right of individuals to make their own decisions free of any collective restraint, but this attitude was not looked on with sympathy either by the other anarchists or the organization as a whole. The most extreme individual anarchists balked at the consensus process and generally did not participate in the organization except to join in large actions.

Those who called themselves anarchists were aware that anarchism generally means a rejection of the electoral process and leadership structures. But there was also a widespread appreciation within LAG of the pitfalls of such rejection. Even the anarchists I interviewed expressed some ambivalence on the question. One woman admitted that she did vote and was therefore perhaps not a very good anarchist. She appreciated the view that "voting only encourages them," but she felt it important to confront power wherever it might be, including in the electoral arena.

Whether LAG should have, or should acknowledge, leadership was an ongoing issue in the organization, intertwined with the question of whether anarchist values permit it. In the Santa Rita peace camp of June 1983, we regularly used the half hour or so after the guards gathered us into the tent and before the sheriff appeared to invite us to arraignment for a general meeting in which people made announcements and requests or shared their thoughts. On one such occasion, as she was describing the philosophy by which the camp was run, someone asked Starhawk in some confusion, "How *are* things run around here, anyway?" Starhawk replied: "The answer is that this camp is based on anarchy. That doesn't necessarily mean chaos, though that happens sometimes. It means that decisions aren't made by leaders because we don't have leaders. If you want something to happen, you find two or three people who agree with you, and you make it happen."[10]

Starhawk was right in the sense that there were certainly no leaders in the camp who stood above others and imposed decisions on us. Nevertheless, some people were looked to for guidance, especially Starhawk herself. No one else could command such rapt attention at general meetings. After we left jail, Starhawk said that although she had always believed that the movement was and should be leaderless, she had realized that there was an informal leadership in jail that had made an important contribution. The danger, she warned, was that an unacknowledged leadership was not accountable to its constituency and might abuse its authority. She had come to the conclusion that we should rethink the questions of leadership and of the form it should take. At a LAG meeting some months later, Starhawk suggested that we think of leadership as consisting of different roles that need to be filled in any group, that each of us identify the role for which we were best suited and try to develop our skills in that area. She proposed the following categories: the "graces," who welcome people into the group and extend themselves to potential allies; the "dragons," who guard the boundaries of the group, see that practical matters are taken care of, and ward off threats; the "crows," who maintain an overview, exercising the conventional analytical skills; and the "snakes," who maintain an "underview," saying the things that the group does not want to think about but needs to hear, keeping track of how people are feeling, and expressing unspoken feelings and thoughts within the group.[11]

Although there were some in LAG who tried to integrate anarchist values with a validation of leadership, others remained unconvinced that LAG or the direct action movement should have any formal leadership structures. Patrick Diehl, who worked in the LAG office and identified himself as an anarchist, told me that among other things anarchism meant a movement without leaders. When I pointed out that in jail I had not only seen an informal leadership operating but had observed nothing but appreciation for its efforts, he responded that what he opposed was a formal, institutionalized leadership. Certain people, he said, had leadership skills and should be encouraged to exercise them; problems emerged when people became entrenched in positions of authority and retained those positions regardless of their actual contributions. When I asked whether the unaccountability of an informal leadership structure might not also lead to problems, he maintained that as long as the movement remained vital such a thing would not happen.[12]

The group in LAG that distinguished itself most sharply from the anarchist perspective was the Overthrow Cluster, whose members considered themselves Marxists while being critical of orthodox Marxism. Ken Nightingale, a member of the cluster, told me that Marxists in LAG were more suspicious of importing ideas or forms of organization from abroad than Marxists generally have been. They also criticized Marxism, he said, for failing to make gender and the relation between humanity and the natural environment central to its analysis. Marxists, he argued, have not understood that the problem is not just capitalism but industrialism. Some people in LAG rejected Marxism entirely because of those weaknesses, but the Overthrow Cluster valued the Marxist understanding that economic forces and, in the international arena, imperialist drives are central to the shaping of power. The Overthrow Cluster did not hope or expect to turn LAG into a Marxist organization. They regarded LAG's diversity as one of its strengths, a model for a new kind of movement that would make room for differences. But they did want to bring the broader questions of analysis and strategy to LAG discussions.[13]

The dedicated and experienced organizers of the Overthrow Cluster played particularly important roles in holding LAG together and in guiding its development as an organization. The cluster also attracted unapologetic intellectuals with well-developed skills of political analysis. Members generally thought in political rather than in moral categories and regarded nonviolence as a matter of strategy rather than of fundamental principle. This view was acceptable in LAG and was also held in many other sectors of the organization. What set the Overthrow Cluster apart was its skepticism about consensus. Its decision to govern its own meetings by the vote was viewed with horror by other LAG members. That horror was compounded by the fact that the decision itself was arrived at by voting.[14]

In addition to the ideologically defined groups described, many affinity groups in LAG were not part of any particular tendency but helped to shape the politics of LAG by suggesting the range of possible constituencies LAG could attract and actions it could take. Some groups included many older people, such as Salt and Pepper in Santa Cruz, and Elders for Survival in the Bay Area. There were groups with particular skills, such as the Revolutionary Garden Party, a group of Bay Area gardeners. The Peace Navy, a group of Bay Area skippers, set up sea blockades of Port Chicago in their own small craft when ships departed with cargoes of arms for Central America. The Peace Navy outlasted LAG;

it has its own identity but considers itself part of the same movement. There were large numbers of rural groups in LAG, such as Turning Tide in Bolinas, the Cazadero Hill People, and the Mountain People from the Santa Barbara area. Few members of the rural groups participated actively in day-to-day affairs in the Bay Area, but they were an important part of the constituency for large actions. The groups seemed to have a special resilience, perhaps because they were often made up of neighbors who saw each other virtually every day.

The Communist Dupes illustrate an affinity group belonging to no particular tendency and taking little part in LAG meetings between actions, but nevertheless filling an important niche. The group took its name from Reagan's attacks on the peace movement as being composed of Soviet agents and Communist dupes. "We weren't being paid by anyone, so we figured we must be Communist dupes," one member told me. (For a time there was another affinity group called the Soviet Agents.) The Dupes, as they were affectionately called, specialized in small-scale actions that could be performed by one affinity group, sometimes with help from friends or other LAG people. Those actions were humorous and ironic, and their goal was to get people to think for themselves, never to preach at them.

One of the Dupes' earliest actions was to produce cardboard posters of the sort that government agencies sometimes put up in public places, which looked as if they had come from the Federal Emergency Management Agency, the agency in charge of civil defense. The posters were printed in government style, yellow with black lettering and black stick figures for illustration, with the headline "IN CASE OF NUCLEAR ATTACK." Instructions were given, beginning with "1. Remain Calm. 2. Avert Eyes from Flash." and ending with "7. Comfort the Dying. 8. Isolate Corpses to Prevent Spread of Disease." The posters were extremely convincing; one would not have thought, at first glance, that they had been issued by anyone other than the government.

About thirty Dupes and other LAG people spread out over the Bay Area Rapid Transit system early one morning, carrying posters in attaché cases constructed for the purpose. Car by car, they managed to cover about half of the system. Eleven people were apprehended, but the authorities let them go, unable to think of anything to charge them with. While some of the Dupes and their friends were putting up posters, others were riding the trains, pointing out the posters to other passengers and asking what they meant. One man said, "Well, it's a joke, but it's not really a joke." The two Dupes I interviewed said that this was exactly the kind of response they wanted.[15]

Another action of the Dupes involved an intervention in an Alameda County dispute over the salute to the flag. The Berkeley City Council had not been in the habit of pledging allegiance to the flag at its meetings. In early 1984, the Alameda County Board of Supervisors made an issue of this, threatening to punish the city of Berkeley in some way. On January 31, two dozen well-dressed Dupes and other LAG people arrived promptly at 9:00 A.M. for the regular meeting of the board of supervisors. After the pledge of allegiance, as the supervisors were sitting down, the audience burst into "The Star-Spangled Banner" and the supervisors again rose to their feet. They seemed pleased; one was observed singing along, and another was overheard saying to his neighbor that these seemed like his kind of people.

The concert, however, did not stop. "The Star-Spangled Banner" was followed by renditions, complete with every verse, of "My Country, 'Tis of Thee," "America, the Beautiful," and "It's a Grand Old Flag." Then "The Star-Spangled Banner" came around again, forcing the supervisors again to their feet. By this time the supervisors were becoming agitated. One ran nervously off and onto the stage where they were seated. After about twenty minutes of uninterrupted singing, the chairman seized a moment when the Dupes had stopped to catch their breath between songs, banged his gavel on the podium, and hurriedly adjourned the meeting. The supervisors fled into a back room while the Dupes exited, singing one last chorus of "The Star-Spangled Banner."

A supervisor interviewed by the press said he thought the singing took a good thing too far; it was "patriotic coercion." Another said he suspected a Berkeley conspiracy. The Dupes, also interviewed by the press on their way out of the building, explained that they were freedom-loving Americans who had come to praise the flag, and that they were not sure when they might return. "We never know," said one, "when the patriotic urge will hit us."[16]

From the Mainstream

If LAG could be described, in the words of one LAG activist, as a coalition of "hippies and Montclair housewives" (Montclair is an upper-middle-class Bay Area suburb), the groups I have described thus far in this tour of LAG's tendencies consisted chiefly of the hippies. Most were in their twenties and early thirties, though a substantial number were in their forties and some were even older. Most, though not all, were of middle-class origins; many were downwardly mobile, through various combinations of choice and necessity. Many had college degrees. Some, especially those in their late thirties or forties, had professional occupations, but most of those at the center of the movement had not gone beyond college and had found themselves thrown into the job market in the mid-seventies and later, when opportunities for college-educated young people were shrinking. Many had parents who had expected them to become professionals or to enter business. Instead, most of them found less stable jobs in the social services, as clerical workers, or in alternate businesses such as health food stores.

LAG tapped into a social world that, at least in the San Francisco Bay Area, was extensive in the early eighties. It was made up of people who, by the standards of white middle-class America, lived culturally unconventional and often economically marginal lives. Feminism, ecology, and antimilitarism were givens in this milieu, and there was a good deal of contempt for the consumerism of the mainstream middle class. The prevalent culture of personal life was consonant with LAG's values and contributed to the character of life within LAG. LAG's activist core was made up of couples or households of several people. People were not likely to live alone—most simply could not afford to. Even couples were likely to share housing with other people. Financial necessity was intertwined with the positive value of creating community beyond the confines of the nuclear family.

In the culture on which LAG drew, as in LAG itself, there were large numbers of lesbians and a fair number of gay men. (The smaller representation of gay men may have been due to the existence of a strong gay men's community in the Bay Area, with a political life of its own, as well as to the greater inclination of many lesbians, perhaps influenced by feminism, to become involved in issues beyond those of the gay and lesbian communities.) Nevertheless, lesbians and gays did not especially stand out in LAG because heterosexuality and the nuclear family were neither especially privileged nor disparaged: they were simply two ways, among many other possibilities, of organizing personal life. The term "partner" was more commonly used than "husband" or "wife" and could refer to someone of the same sex as easily as of the opposite sex. The marriages that did take place in LAG were likely to be explained as conciliatory gestures toward someone's parents or as a way of extending health insurance. It was more or less unthinkable for the woman to take the man's name. When Terry Messman and Darla Rucker married (before they joined LAG, when they were members of a nonviolent direct action group in Rocky Flats, Colorado), Terry added Rucker to his name. While they were married, he used the name Messman-Rucker for official purposes, Rucker more informally. Many LAG activists have remained childless, either out of uneasiness about bringing a child into the dangerous world we inhabit or because economic marginality and often precarious personal lives make it very difficult both to raise a child and to continue political activity.

What I found most striking about this culture of personal life was that it was taken for granted. Radicals of the sixties, especially in the women's movement, denounced marriage and family and theorized about alternate structures. But subsequently many former New Leftists resumed the professional careers that were interrupted by the movements of the sixties and formed families very similar to those in which they grew up, except that the women were more likely to work outside the home than their mothers had been. For the somewhat younger generation from which LAG drew much of its constituency, upward mobility was less often an option, and poverty had a less romantic glow. People in LAG formed their personal lives as they could, understanding the limits of the nuclear family and appreciating the community extending beyond it, but not regarding their personal arrangements as the key expression of their politics.

This "hippie" constituency gave LAG strength by providing a social base in which many people were available for political action. But it also imposed some limits on the movement. It stamped LAG with a cultural orientation that made it seem quite foreign to many people, and it infused LAG with an anti-intellectualism that was often an obstacle to political discussion and development. Not all of those who were part of LAG's core were equally identified with the counterculture. Some of the most influential people in LAG had come out of the movements of the sixties. In most cases they were closer to the counterculture than many others who had emerged from those movements; they were nevertheless aware of the problems facing a counterculturally oriented movement trying to broaden its constituency. Many of the people who staffed the office or joined LAG's working groups concerned with particular projects, such as relations with the media, came to feel a certain impatience with LAG's counterculture. Barbara Haber, an LAG activist who had been part of the movement for many years (and a founder of SDS) found LAG's countercultural orientation to be an obstacle in her efforts to draw other veterans of the New Left into the organization. LAG's few people of color often found the organization's countercultural emphasis an obstacle to involving other people of color.

In spite of these differences, people of different cultural orientations within LAG got along with one another surprisingly well. Common origins in the white middle class may help explain the alliance of hippies and Montclair housewives. In many cases, the hippies could have been the children or the grandchildren of the housewives. During my stay in jail, I saw a kind of family relationship develop among the various generations there. The "elders," the women over sixty, were especially valued for their experience and their stabilizing influence. During one general meeting, a woman in her early twenties indicated one of the elders and proudly announced that she had found her own "jail grandmother." When the judge gave us the choice of leaving and paying a fine or spending another four days in jail, a number of older women who could easily have paid the fine decided to stay in jail so that the young people would not have to face that experience by themselves.

Some of LAG's more respectable people (middle-aged or older, middle or upper middle class) were longtime participants in the peace movement and the left. Others had personal histories worlds apart from those of the hippies and radicals at LAG's core. Doris Bowles, for instance, was seventy-one years old when I interviewed her in 1984. Four years earlier, she told me, she had been a Republican. She lived in Montclair with her husband and attended the Montclair Presbyterian church. In 1979 she read about the Abalone Alliance. One day she drove to Rancho Seco, the site of one of the nuclear plants opposed by Abalone, and found a "little circle of friendly people sitting on the ground." She was impressed by what they had to say about the dangers of nuclear power and by the fact that they were doing something about it. Doris was a member of the Ploughshares Committee of her church, where, soon after retiring from her job as an analyst for a health insurance company, she heard an announcement for nonviolence training for a blockade of the Diablo Canyon plant. Doris decided to attend the training, knowing that it would probably lead to her own participation in the blockade and to her arrest.

At that training the Sunflower Brigade affinity group was formed, with Doris as a member. She went to jail at Diablo in 1981. After the Diablo blockade the Sunflower Brigade became involved with LAG, and Doris was arrested again in the course of two LAG blockades. In 1983 a member of the Sunflower Brigade, a minister, went to Nicaragua as part of Witness for Peace. His letters inspired Doris to learn more about Central America and become involved in opposition to U.S. intervention. In the summer of 1984 she went to Nicaragua with another woman from LAG to deliver medical supplies. On her return, Doris did a good deal of public speaking about the Nicaraguan revolution, with which she was very favorably impressed, and the danger of U.S. intervention.

Before she went to Nicaragua, Doris told me, she was still, in spite of her opposition to Reagan's pursuit of the Cold War, a vehement anti-Communist. Though she was aware that Nicaragua was not a Communist country, her visit there nevertheless led her to rethink her views: she told me that perhaps she was not an anti-Communist but an anti-Stalinist. In any event, if the Sandinistas thought highly of Karl Marx, she wanted to find out what he had to say. She set up a study group on Communism and the writings of Marx in her church, in which she remained quite active, and from which she found a good deal of support for her peace activism. I asked Doris how her family reacted to her political involvement. Her grown children, she reported, supported her, but her husband remained a staunch supporter of Reagan. She did not want to argue with him, she said; she believed that no one has a monopoly on the truth and found merit in some of her husband's views. Her husband thought she was turning into a Communist. "I don't think I am," she said, "but then, how would I know?"[17]

Doris told me that as she became involved in the direct action movement she encountered many shocks. The first one came at her nonviolence training. She arrived on time, the only person to do so, and sat in one of the few chairs in the room. "I always try to do things right and proper," she said. As the others came in, they sat in a circle on the floor. The training began, with Doris somewhat awkwardly remaining in her chair. Finally she joined the others on the floor. "That was one of the hardest things I had ever done. I had never sat on the floor in my life." There were other shocks: the lesbians in LAG, some of the inmates she has met in jail, some of the language and ideas that are bandied about in the direct action movement. Doris retained her own style, but she felt that others had the right to theirs as well and that involvement in LAG opened her eyes to many realities to which she had previously been oblivious.[18]

For Pat Daane, becoming part of the movement was an affirmation of faith. When I interviewed Pat she lived in Piedmont, an upper-middle-class East Bay town that is quite conservative by Bay Area standards. Pat was educated in a Catholic girls' school; she went on to spend three years in a convent. After leaving the convent she married, and moved to the Bay Area with her husband when he was offered a job as a bank executive. Pat was the mother of three children and until becoming involved with the direct action movement had been a member of the Junior League; she had also been the president of the parents' organization at her children's school. She was, and continued to be, a member of the Newman Center, an East Bay Catholic church.

Some time during the winter of 1982 a friend of Pat's asked her to view *The Last Epidemic*, a film that portrays the effects of a nuclear war on San Francisco. Pat saw the film, and when she described it to her family over dinner, her son, then six years old, asked "Does that mean that I'll never grow up?" "Not if I have anything to do with it," Pat answered—and then put the issue out of her mind. A few months later she saw an announcement in the Newman Center newsletter that there was to be a Mother's Day demonstration at the Livermore Laboratory, and she decided to go with some other women from the center.

Pat was taken aback by the way some of the demonstrators were dressed—in costumes representing death and in clown suits— but the morning passed uneventfully as she and several companions passed out leaflets at one of the subsidiary gates. Eventually they decided to look for the rest of their group, who had gone elsewhere. They were told that most of the demonstrators were at the main gate, where some women were committing civil disobedience. At the main gate they found six women sitting in the road waiting to be arrested. Pat was frightened; she felt that somehow she might be drawn into this scene and be arrested herself. She hid behind a police van and peered out from behind it.

One [of the women sitting in the road] had gray hair and was wearing a skirt—I could relate to skirts, right? and I thought, "That woman is laying down her life for my children." Then I knew that I would get arrested the next time there was an action; I would go to jail, and I knew I would fast the whole time. I didn't know why I knew that. We walked back to the car; I was in a sort of trance, I guess. I remember we prayed together, and I prayed out loud to have the courage to act on my responsibility. I knew at that moment that I would be getting arrested and I would be fasting. You don't turn back after that.[19]

Pat and others from her church organized an affinity group, the Newman Peacemakers, and Pat was subsequently arrested eight times. Pat's husband was not able to adjust to her involvement in the movement; their differences led to a divorce. Pat told me that maintaining her marriage was always very important to her, especially for the sake of the children, but that she could not forgo her involvement in the peace movement. "On anything else I would have compromised," she said, "but to me, this is a religious act. How could I renounce my faith?"[20]

For both Doris and Pat, entering LAG involved a sharp break with the past. Most of the more mainstream people who joined LAG actions, however, did so out of a history of involvement in the peace movement. Joan McIntyre, for instance, a Catholic and a member of the Mustard Seed affinity group, was the president of the board of the Ecumenical Peace Institute when she and others on the board decided to form an affinity group and become part of LAG. Joan had never before committed civil disobedience, and aspects of LAG's culture were alien to her, but she was by no means new to the peace movement. Joan, Doris, Pat, and others like them were able to influence many people whom LAG regulars would have had difficulty reaching. Doris spoke at her church after each of her arrests and after her trip to Nicaragua. Joan told me that when Mustard Seed decides to participate in an action, they make sure the Bay Area religious community knows about it. "That way," she said, "it's harder for them to dismiss the blockaders as a bunch of crazies."[21]

The Demise of LAG

After the blockade of the Livermore Laboratory in June 1983, LAG rapidly lost its momentum and focus. Though the blockade had been a clear success, the number committing civil disobedience had been smaller by several hundred than in the blockade of a year earlier, a fact which had not been missed by the press. That fact, in addition to the fear that the blockade could become no more than a yearly ritual, raised questions for many LAG members about whether the blockade should be repeated. Some, including a number of people on the office staff and in the working groups, believed that LAG could no longer go from one action to the next but needed a larger strategy within which to situate civil disobedience. A small group of people, including myself, proposed that LAG should choose a particular objective and orient all of its work toward this objective for a year, both civil disobedience and other forms of political action such as community organizing, education, and legal demonstrations in coalition with other organizations. It was assumed that the objective would be halting the deployment of first-strike nuclear weapons. What was controversial about this "campaign proposal" was not the campaign in question, but the idea that civil disobedience should be treated as only one among a number of tactics.

The campaign proposal did more harm than good. Most LAG

members saw it as an attack on civil disobedience, an attempt to destroy what made LAG unique and turn it into a more conventional organization. The strongest opposition to the proposal came from the affinity groups with the strongest links to the counterculture, from people who were part of communities that had come to revolve around civil disobedience. Many LAG members believed that strengthening the counterculture their affinity groups represented and extending its values beyond the present boundaries of the movement was crucial to creating a better, more peaceful world. The bitterness of the debate over the campaign proposal also reflected underlying antagonisms in LAG. The affinity groups defending the politics of civil disobedience saw the proposal as an attack on the counterculture by LAG's intellectuals. Though the campaign proposal was not passed, discussion of it dominated the conference held immediately after the June occupation; no clear alternative focus emerged from the discussion.

Robbie Osman, a core LAG activist who had strongly opposed the campaign proposal, subsequently argued that even though the proposal had not passed, great damage had been done by the debate, which dominated the July 1983 LAG conference, and by the support of LAG's informal leadership, which seemed to cast doubt on civil disobedience. Robbie argued that the people connected with the LAG office were tired of civil disobedience and, in many cases, skeptical of the counterculture associated with it, but that in trying to turn LAG away from a focus on CD they hurt the movement. "We had an incredible tool in the jail experience. It gave people a taste of the possibility of rebellion. Coming out of those fourteen days we had a dynamic that was vital and exciting and had great potential. I think the plug was pulled at that meeting."[22]

Other key LAG activists understood the conflict over the campaign proposal differently. Osha Neumann, for instance, agreed that this debate was a turning point in the history of LAG, but argued that what undermined LAG was not the campaign proposal but the rigidities of the movement, which stood in the way of finding new political directions. The main problems LAG faced, Osha suggested, were the limitations inherent in its structure and its focus on the tactic of civil disobedience. "The structure that we had evolved was enormously cumbersome and time-consuming; that itself limited participation. The process itself seemed to become arcane and exclusive. Also, many people were very committed to one kind of action; the people who were most devoted to CD simply weren't interested in any other approach. But it wasn't clear that if LAG had continued to do CD it would have stayed together. It's true that LAG wasn't able to change. But it's also true that it's not being able to change was one of the reasons for its demise."[23]

LAG continued to hold demonstrations, most of them sponsored by other organizations as well, mostly involving civil disobedience. In September, LAG participated in a protest at Port Chicago, a short distance north of Berkeley, against arms shipments to Central America. In October LAG joined with others in a week of demonstrations against the deployment of the Euromissiles. In April 1984, LAG again joined with other organizations in protesting a visit by Henry Kissinger to San Francisco, and in July many LAG people participated in a series of demonstrations outside the Democratic Convention.

LAG was an important participant in all of these demonstrations, but it did not set the tone for any of them, and in a number of cases the tone was quite different from that of the earlier LAG blockades. The Democratic Convention demonstrations, for example, drew large numbers of punks. Many LAG people were critical of the cat-and-mouse games some of the punks played with the police. In the following months a few LAG groups offered their services to organizations planning demonstrations. They served as trainers, preparing members of those organizations for political actions by leading discussions about what levels of militancy they would be comfortable with and what to do if those levels were exceeded. That was a far cry from the leading role LAG had recently played as the radical edge of the Bay Area peace movement. Many people who had once been central to LAG drifted out of the organization, in many cases to work with solidarity groups concerned with U.S. intervention in Central America. Much of the solidarity movement had a style that was quite different from that of the nonviolent direct action movement. Those organizations were less concerned with questions of internal process; they had no objections to hierarchy per se; and many of their activists idealized armed struggle and adopted the militant style they associated with Central American guerrilla organizations.

By June of 1984 the drain of activists from LAG had become so debilitating that a series of crisis meetings was called. The atmosphere of these meetings was one of willingness to reconsider almost everything, even the consensus process. The argument that LAG needed a more coherent structure of leadership found a more receptive audience than ever before. But most people did not think that LAG was likely to be revived by structural changes. Not just LAG, but the whole peace movement, was in decline; it was argued that the main causes of decline were external and had to do with more sophisticated policies on the part of the Reagan administration.

It was true that the peace movement as a whole had grown rapidly in the early eighties because many people had been alarmed by the belligerent tone Reagan had taken toward the Soviet Union, including loose talk of the possibility of nuclear war, in his early years in office. By the end of his first term Reagan had learned that language of this sort was likely to cost him votes. Reagan's "Star Wars" proposal did not convince activists that he had become less dangerous, but it did calm the fears of the public, thus detracting from the peace movement's audience. By 1984 the Reagan administration seemed to have concluded that it was not wise to challenge the Soviet Union on its own home ground, including Eastern Europe, because of the danger of triggering nuclear war. Although Reagan had been willing to use the threat of the bomb, he did not actually want a nuclear war; furthermore, it was becoming clear that the American public did not like nuclear brinksmanship. As a result the administration shifted the focus of its war against Communism to the Third World, especially to Central America.

Though LAG declined as its activists moved to anti-intervention work, no one proposed that the organization should shift its focus from the labs to some target relevant to the issue of intervention in Central America. LAG's religious wing did make this shift by establishing the Pledge of Resistance, where it promoted the politics of nonviolent direct action in relation to U.S. policy toward Central America. The Pagan anarchist community survived as a series of linked collective households, members of which participated in the occasional civil disobedience actions that were held over the following years. Many LAG people whose lives had been consumed by activism for several years took a break from politics.

LAG had introduced the ideas and techniques of nonviolent direct action and consensus decision making to a large proportion of a new generation of young activists and also to considerable numbers of older activists, especially women who entered the peace movement from the church. The direct action movement lost some of its visibility when LAG disappeared, because it was not immediately succeeded by another mass organization of the same kind as the Abalone had succeeded the Clamshell, and LAG the Abalone. But the ideas that these organizations had represented continued to circulate through the various movements of the mid- and late eighties.

LAG changed the culture of direct action by introducing spirituality as a major component. Though there were people in LAG who were entirely secular, the organization as a whole revolved around an alliance between Christians and Pagan anarchists. What these two wings of LAG had in common was a spiritually based approach to politics that gave LAG a broad appeal: many people who had never felt any affinity with the secular left could identify with a politics framed in religious terms. LAG's orientation toward spirituality also fostered a depth of commitment that probably would not have existed otherwise, because it made it possible to link politics with issues of fundamental meaning. LAG's concept of politics as exemplary action drew into the movement people who found ordinary politics repellent and also gave its actions a virtuous glow. LAG's orientation toward spirituality also reinforced community within the movement. Both the Christians and the Pagans saw doing politics and building community as inseparable, not only because they saw spiritual value in community, but also because they saw community as a necessary base for political action, especially political action involving sacrifice or risk. Spirituality built community in immediate ways, through the use of ritual. The Christian community in LAG was brought together largely around performing politicized versions of Christian rituals, and Pagan rituals played an important role in creating community in the movement as a whole.

The problem with a spiritual orientation was not just that it could, at least in the forms in which it entered LAG, be hostile to strategic thinking; it was also that LAG's politics of example rested on particular communities whose ways of life did not appeal to large numbers of people. People of very diverse backgrounds participated in LAG actions. Especially when actions were held, affinity groups representing a large cultural range coexisted. But over time it was the religious community (the term used by formally religious people, mainly Christians, to describe themselves) and the Pagan anarchists (closely linked to the world of feminist spirituality) that came to set the tone for the movement. These were the communities that served as bases for a politics of example. For most people, it was virtually impossible to engage in direct action over any extended period without being part of a supportive community; and for many people, the communities that presented themselves were not viable options.

Nevertheless, these two communities did make it possible for the politics of nonviolent direct action to flourish and to involve people in considerable numbers, and of considerable diversity. This was true not only in LAG but in the direct action movement as a whole. Beyond the specific issue-oriented organizations of the direct action movement, Pagan anarchism and religious pacifism were the two most important cultural/ideological currents woven through the whole. Pagan anarchism overlapped with feminist spirituality, a trend that encompassed sections of the women's movement, the lesbian movement, and the broad cultural arena surrounding both of these. Religious, mostly Christian, pacifism, had its roots in the Quakers and the small pacifist movement of the 1940s and 1950s, influenced by liberation theology and inspired by the example of the Latin American Base Communities. Both of these ideological currents gave the direct action movement links to important currents outside it and the ability to speak to large constituencies with great potential for political action. The question remained whether either feminist spirituality or religious pacifism could provide a sustainable political direction.

The Livermore Action Group (LAG): protesters at the nuclear-weapons-producing Lawrence Livermore Laboratory, Livermore, California, 1982. Photographer: Jessica Collett.

Above left: The Clamshell Alliance: the eighteen protesters who made up the first occupation of the Seabrook plant, walking down the railroad tracks toward the proposed site. Seabrook, New Hampshire, August 1, 1976. Photographer: Lionel J-M Delevingne. *Opposite:* The Clamshell Alliance: the mass occupation of Seabrook, April 30, 1977. Photographer: Lionel J-M Delevingne. *Above:* The "tent city" set up during the Seabrook occupation, April 30, 1977. Photographer: Lionel J-M Delevingne.

The Abalone Alliance: an affinity group blockading the main gate to
the Diablo nuclear plant during the mass occupation of September
1981. Photographer: Steve Stallone.

The Mother Bear Brigade, an Abalone Alliance affinity group, blockading the main entrance to the Diablo plant during the occupation of 1981. Photographer: Steve Stallone.

The Abalone Alliance blockade of Diablo, 1981: an arrest at sea.
Photographer: Paul Orbuch.

The "backcountry" occupation of Diablo, 1981: an affinity group looks down on the plant. Photographer: Roy King.

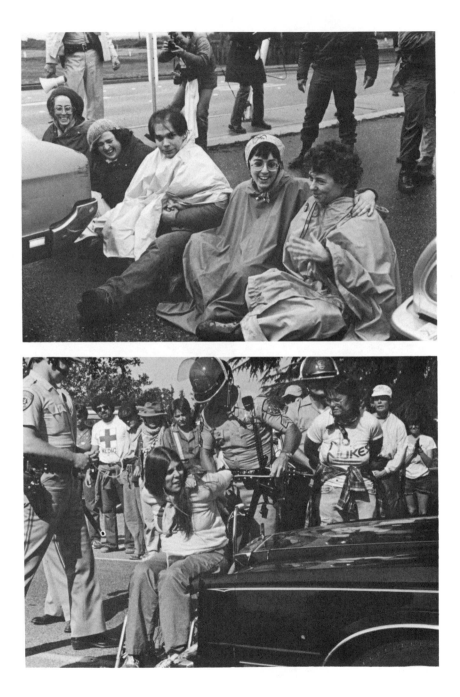

Above left: The LAG occupation of the Vandenberg, California, nuclear test site, 1982. An affinity group blocking the road to the site. Marcy Darnovsky is at the left end of the line of protesters; Barbara Haber is at the right end. Photographer: Bob van Scoy. *Opposite:* The June 1982 LAG blockade of the Livermore Laboratory. Darla Rucker (in wheelchair) and Pamela Osgood, members of the Girl Scouts, an all-women affinity group, being arrested. Photographer: Steve Stallone. *Above:* The women's tents at Santa Rita, where protesters were held following the June 1983 LAG blockade of the Livermore Laboratory. Photographer: Bill Knowland. Reprinted by kind permission of the *Oakland Tribune.*

CAN YOU RECOGNIZE A
TERRORIST?

KNOW THE DIFFERENCE BETWEEN:

 A TERRORIST,

and...

A FREEDOM-FIGHTER

 HOSTAGES,

and...

POLITICAL PRISONERS

BOMBING AN EMBASSY,

and...

MINING A FOREIGN HARBOR

 NATIONALIST FANATICS,

and...

PATRIOTIC CITIZENS

For More Information, Contact the Terrorist Hotline (415) 986-0145

A poster produced by the Communist Dupes, a LAG affinity group, and put up in the San Francisco and Oakland airports. The phone number for a "terrorist hotline" was the local number for the CIA.

IN CASE OF NUCLEAR ATTACK

 1. REMAIN CALM

 2. AVERT EYES FROM FLASH

 3. BRACE FOR BLAST

 4. DUCK AND COVER/ PLACE NEWSPAPER OVER HEAD

 5. RESERVE MEDICAL ATTENTION FOR HIGH PRIORITY EVACUEES

 6. HAVE FOOD AND WATER FOR SEVERAL WEEKS OF ISOLATION

 7. COMFORT THE DYING

 8. ISOLATE CORPSES TO PREVENT SPREAD OF DISEASE

For More Information Contact the Federal Emergency Management Agency

A poster produced by the Communist Dupes and distributed through the Bay Area Rapid Transit system.

Above left: The spiral dance in the San Francisco financial district that concluded LAG's "Hall of Shame" protest against banks and corporations with military connections. Osha Neumann (gray hair, black jacket) is second from the left, third line in. Photographer: Roy King. *Opposite:* A May Day ritual by Reclaiming, the Pagan/witches' community some of whose members formed Matrix, a witches' affinity group affiliated with LAG. Photographer: Roy King. *Above:* The second Women's Pentagon Action, 1981. The march to the Pentagon carrying puppets. The white puppet symbolized defiance. Photographer: Joan E. Biren.

Above left: The second Women's Pentagon Action, 1981. A drummer and flute player leading the march to the Pentagon. Photographer: Joan E. Biren. *Opposite:* The second Women's Pentagon Action. Women planting cardboard gravestones for women who died as a result of war or other violence. Photographer: Joan E. Biren. *Above:* The second Women's Pentagon Action. The web around the Pentagon. Photographer: Joan E. Biren.

Seneca Falls, 1983. Women going over the fence to the nuclear test site. Photographer: Joan E. Biren.

Chapter Five

Feminist Spirituality and Magical Politics

Few of the ideological currents that have run through the direct action movement have been universally accepted in the movement. Not everyone has claimed to be an anarchist. Nonviolence has been interpreted differently by different groups and has occasionally been challenged by those who think the movement should be more confrontational. Even in its more spiritually oriented phases the movement has included many people who are firmly secular. In each of its major organizations there have been critics of the consensus process, many of whom have argued that political efficacy requires some degree of hierarchy.

Feminism and an environmental sensibility are the only "ideologies" that have never been disavowed or challenged by any significant group within the movement. Though both feminism and environmentalism have been important aspects of the movement, they have played different roles. Feminism has also had an organized presence within the movement, in the form of women's affinity groups, women's clusters, and women's actions, taking place within and outside the framework of the existing "mixed" organizations of the movement. Because it has been accepted by the whole movement and has also had an organized presence within the movement, it has been able to play a dynamic role in shaping ideology.

Activists in the movement have tended to speak as if "feminism" had only one possible meaning. In fact there are many varieties. The cluster of feminisms that have been most important

157

in the direct action movement have common roots in the late 1960s
and early 1970s, when contemporary feminism was taking shape.
The term "radical feminism" had two somewhat different meanings: on the one hand it referred to the radical sector of the
women's movement as a whole, which called for fundamental social
change, as distinct from liberal organizations such as the National
Organization for Women, which called for women's equality within
the existing system. Within the radical sector the term—often
capitalized to distinguish it—referred to specific organizations
that saw the oppression of women by men as the basis of all social
hierarchy, believed that the transformation of consciousness and
culture was crucial to reordering these relations, and was often
linked to an argument for separate women's organizations and
for female separatism as a strategy and a social aim.

Radical feminism (in this more specific sense) was engaged in
debate with socialist feminism, the other side of the radical sector
of the women's movement. Socialist feminists were engaged in
the effort to find some meeting ground between socialism and
feminism; they believed that class was as important as gender,
that changing economic and political structures was at least as
important as transforming consciousness, and rejected separatism
as a goal of the women's movement. The sharpest debates were
over the most immediate organizational questions: socialist feminists remained part of a movement, sometimes part of organizations, that included men; radical feminists could not see this as
feminist practice. In the late seventies and eighties these debates
faded. Separatism seemed less viable, at least as a political strategy, and the importance of consciousness and culture was increasingly apparent. Radical feminism was transformed into a
broad arena of alternative women's culture and politics.

The role of feminism in the nonviolent direct action movement has been remarkable. The movement, made up of more or
less equal numbers of men and women, has made feminism a
central element of its politics. Moreover, the feminism the movement has adopted, which took the form of militant separatism
less than a decade earlier, has become an important element in
the glue holding the direct action movement together. This evolution has been possible because the direct action movement has
had a different understanding of politics from earlier move-

ments. Its affinity with forms of feminism rooted in radical feminism is due to a common emphasis on the role of consciousness and culture in revolutionary change and also to a common belief that building alternative community is in itself a political act.

The feminist tendencies in the direct action movement—anarcha-feminism, ecofeminism, and feminist spirituality—share a conception of revolution that revolves around creating new kinds of community and transforming culture and consciousness rather than seizing power. The view of revolution as an ongoing process of social and personal transformation, rather than an event that takes place at a particular moment, is a feminist contribution to the movement. Feminism has played a large part also in shaping the movement's utopian concept of democracy and its commitment to absolute egalitarianism and to a prefigurative political practice in which those values are acted upon in the present.

Feminism has shaped the practice of the movement as well as its ideology, particularly in creating community. Though consensus decision making came to the direct action movement from the countercultural left and was modeled on Quaker practice, it eventually became synonymous with feminist process. Feminism has also been the main source of the symbolism, ritual, and political theater that have been used to affirm and create bonds among movement participants, to project the movement's vision of community, and to dramatize particular political issues. Feminism has reinforced the concepts of cultural revolution, utopian democracy, and prefigurative community, all of which are also elements of anarchism and radical pacifism. But feminism has probably been the most important force in assuring that these concepts are lived out and shaping their content in practice.

Feminism has also reinforced the movement's orientation toward spirituality and its antistrategic bias. Feminist spirituality was barely present in the Clamshell, where it was represented by rural affinity groups based in lesbian communities. It was not salient in the Abalone until the Diablo blockade, one of the constituencies for which was alternative women's culture and Paganism. In LAG and the direct action disarmament movement generally women's spirituality became a major presence and virtually overwhelmed secular forms of feminism. At the same time, Christians were also a significant presence in the movement; shared religiosity made it possible for these groups to coexist and even to appreciate one another in spite of very different cultural and political styles. The fact that feminist spirituality and Paganism on the one hand and Christianity on the other became polar forces in the direct action movement directed the movement inexorably toward a politics of example. For the Pagans and feminists, the example was a countercultural alternative community; for the Christians, it was moral witness. The movement's spirituality has taken it to a wide audience. The question remains whether it is possible for the movement to sustain constituencies beyond these two communities.

Women's Actions

The influence of feminism in the direct action movement has grown with the prominence of women's groups and actions, some of them within the existing direct action organizations, some of them organized autonomously but understood to be part of the direct action movement as a whole. The structure of the direct action movement has made it easy for a feminist presence to develop. From the Clamshell on there have been all-women affinity groups; in LAG feminism was strengthened by a feminist cluster that carried out a number of women's actions. Feminism became significant when the direct action movement turned to the arms race; it was in that context that the women organized autonomous large actions as their part of the nonviolent direct action movement.

The largest of these separate actions have been the Women's Pentagon Actions in 1980 and 1981, which brought thousands of women to Washington to encircle the Pentagon and to express their opposition to war through theater and ritual; the Seneca Women's Peace Camp of the summer of 1983, which paralleled the British Greenham Common encampment by a massive women's presence adjacent to the Seneca Army Depot in upstate New York, a facility used by the Department of Defense to store nuclear weapons; and a Mother's Day action at the Department of Energy's Nevada Nuclear Test Site, north of Las Vegas, in 1987, which drew thousands of women from around the country, many of them linked indirectly if at all to the countercultural core of the direct action movement. There have been countless smaller women's actions linked with the direct action movement, some on occasions such as Mother's Day and some simply part of the on-going efforts of groups of women associated with the movement.

The first Women's Pentagon Action came out of a conference entitled "Women and Life on Earth: Ecofeminism in the 1980s," held early in 1980 and supported by anarchist philosopher Murray Bookchin's Institute for Social Ecology, which brought together the women of the antinuclear and environmental movements and women who, with the decline of organized radical feminism in the mid-1970s, had become involved in women's spirituality. For many the conference represented a reentry into politics, this time into a women's enclave that was part of a larger mixed movement. Ynestra King of the Institute for Social Ecology, an important figure in the development of ecofeminism, coordinated the conference; Anna Gyorgy and other women from the Clamshell contributed experience in organizing; and the author Grace Paley and others from the War Resister's League in New York strengthened the pacifist orientation of the meeting. The conference attempted to bridge political and spiritual concerns through a politics that would link militarism to patriarchy and other forms of oppression and would rely on direct personal expression, drawing power from symbolism and drama. The first Women's Pentagon Action, planned to embody the vision expressed by the conference, was called for November.

On Sunday, November 17, 2,000 women gathered in Washington. Workshops on a range of feminist topics were held before the action. Monday morning began with a march through Arlington Cemetery. As the women approached the Pentagon they were joined by drummers and by four women carrying large puppets in the form of women, each symbolizing a different stage of the demonstration: one was in black, for mourning; another in red, for rage; a third was yellow, for empowerment; and the fourth puppet, in white, symbolized defiance. In the first phase of the demonstration, some women planted cardboard tombstones, made the previous day, on the Pentagon lawn. Some carried very personal inscriptions ("my mother, who died during an abortion," "three Vietnamese women killed by my son"), some were dedicated to well-known figures such as Karen Silkwood and Anne Frank, and some bore more general inscriptions (such as "victims of Love Canal" and "raped women"). As some of the women placed the tombstones on the lawn, the rest stood in a circle around them, wailing in grief. The red puppet was brought to the center of the circle, the women shouted, crowded together, and began to chant, yell, and bang on cans. The yellow and white puppets then became the beginning and end of the chain of women linked and extended by the ribbons they held in their hands. When the two puppets met, the women had encircled the Pentagon.

At this point the defiant stage of the demonstration began. Women who had prepared to do civil disobedience left the circle; some wove the doors to the Pentagon shut with brightly colored yarn while others sat in the doorways. As arrests began, the women not participating in civil disobedience went back to the lawn and formed a closing circle. Women were encouraged to express whatever thoughts or feelings they might have, and selections from women's history were read. When rain and sleet made it difficult to continue, the women dispersed.[1]

The striking effects of the action were not attributable to its numbers, which were only moderate, but to its esthetics, which broke away from the traditional rally format of speakers and audience and allowed greater participation and personal expression. Some of the ideas employed at the Women's Pentagon Action were adopted by women's groups elsewhere in the country. The most popular was weaving as a metaphor of women's power against hated institutions (and as a way of injecting color into actions), which had first been used by a Vermont affinity group, the Weavers, at demonstrations against a local nuclear plant. The Women's Pentagon Action inspired events in various parts of the country; in San Francisco, 300 women calling themselves "Women's Pentagon Action West" gathered outside the San Francisco Bohemian Club, whose members are men in positions of corporate and governmental power. The women set up cardboard tombstones inscribed with names of women who were victims of violence. In response to the Shakespearean motto of the Bohemian club, "Weaving spiders come not here" (and reflecting the influence of Paganism, witchcraft, and women's spirituality) they chanted,

We are the flow, we are the ebb
We are the weavers, we are the web.[2]

The next Women's Pentagon Action attracted about four thousand women and took a similar form. Plans to hold a Women's Pentagon Action every year were derailed both by the massive demonstration at the United Nations in 1983, which included a large civil disobedience action by women and absorbed the energy of many who had participated in the Pentagon actions, and also by a dispute within the Women's Pentagon Action grouping. Some women argued that the actions had overwhelmingly drawn white women because economic issues had not been emphasized sufficiently. In deference to this view a women's action was held on Wall Street in December 1984. That action was considerably smaller than the earlier Pentagon actions had been, and it drew an equally white group of demonstrators.

Meanwhile, feminists in the Finger Lakes area of upstate New York had discovered that the cruise missiles destined for the Greenham Common Air Force Base in England were being sent from the Seneca Army Depot in Seneca Falls. As the site of the first feminist convention in the United States in 1848, Seneca Falls seemed an ideal place to establish a women's peace camp, a sister presence to the women's encampment at Greenham Common. Money was raised and a piece of land adjacent to the Army Depot was bought; ownership was placed in the hands of the thousand or so women who participated in organizing the camp. The encampment itself began at the end of May 1983. Over the course of the summer about 15,000 women came through the camp at one point or another. Many affinity groups conducted actions on their own, not all of which involved civil disobedience. One group entered the depot at night, painted messages and symbols, wove webs, and left undetected; others held candlelight vigils at the front gate; another planted rosebushes at the front gate (which were uprooted several days later); another placed mementos and banners on the fence and released helium-filled balloons with messages of peace. Most of the actions, however, led to arrest— for climbing the fence, for stepping over the yellow line at the front gate, for painting shadows representing those killed in Hiroshima in front of the gate.

Many of the women in the camp were lesbians, and the camp had a pronounced countercultural tone. It met with considerable hostility in that conservative rural area, and the local police acted to protect the rights of those connected with the camp only with reluctance. In late July, roughly a hundred women embarked on a fifteen-mile "walk for peace" for which a permit had been obtained, from the historical home of Elizabeth Cady Stanton in Seneca Falls to the encampment. The group included both members of the encampment and others who had come for the day to show their support. In the town of Waterloo the women found an angry crowd of several hundred people, many of them waving American flags, blocking the way. The marchers sat down in the road; the townspeople began to threaten violence. The sheriff ordered the crowd to disperse and arrested the fifty-four women who were still sitting in the road, charging them with disorderly conduct. Most refused bail on the ground that their arrests were illegal; they remained in jail for several days until their trial, at which charges were dismissed. Meanwhile, another group of women from the camp held a vigil outside the schoolhouse where the marchers were being held. The demonstrators were trapped in the schoolyard and assaulted by an angry crowd as a group of deputy sheriffs looked on, unwilling to intervene. Another walk was planned; Bella Abzug came to the camp and issued an appeal to governor Mario Cuomo, who called out the National Guard. The second walk, under the protection of the National Guard, was peaceful, culminating with civil disobedience at the gate.

On August 1, two days after the arrests at Waterloo, more than a thousand women converged on the camp from New York and elsewhere for the largest action of the summer. Early in the morning, fourteen women climbed the fence and entered the depot's airfield; thirteen were given "ban and bar" letters, one was arrested as a second offender. Later, 2,500 women marched to the gate used by trucks carrying weapons. Two hundred and forty-four women were detained after climbing over the fence by the gate; ten were arrested as second offenders. Smaller actions continued through the month of August. By the beginning of September the activist population was beginning to disperse, and the camp was in danger of becoming a refuge for women whose main interest was finding a place to live, a problem that had been largely avoided throughout the summer by the requirement that every woman at the camp belong to an affinity group. In early September, the encampment was officially ended, although a small group maintained a presence.[3]

In the late 1980s, the appeal of direct action expanded to groups of women closer to the mainstream. In 1987 a Mother's Day Action was held at the Nevada Test Site, a stretch of Nevada desert in which the United States tests the majority of its nuclear weapons. The action was organized largely by the women of the American Peace Test, a group that started out as the direct action committee of the Nuclear Freeze but left that organization, amicably, when it became clear that the Freeze would not sponsor direct action. The action was also sponsored by the Nevada Desert Experience, a Catholic antiwar group that has maintained a presence at the test site for many years. Because of the cost of traveling to the site and the relatively mainstream sponsorship of the action, the roughly 2,000 women who came to the first action were older and straighter than participants in previous women's actions had been. The counterculture was present but not dominant. About 700 women were arrested in the course of the first action, after having climbed over the fence to the test site. A larger number of women than usual were willing to be arrested because sentences for demonstrators at the Nevada Test Site had been light in the recent past. Nye County lacked the jail facilities to hold large numbers of people, and Nye County officials made it clear that they wanted the federal government to take responsibility for dealing with civil disobedience at the site.

Lesbians played a particularly salient role in the two Women's Pentagon Actions, at Seneca, and increasingly in the direct action movement as a whole. Groups of lesbians, mostly from the country, participated in the Clamshell. In LAG, the Feminist Cluster of all-woman affinity groups, mostly lesbian, many from rural areas, gave feminism a strong presence. Lesbians have been a numerically significant element in the movement. About a third of the women in jail at Santa Rita in 1983 were lesbians, probably about the same proportion as the year before. Lesbians have made up a much larger proportion of those participating in women-only actions; they were a large majority of those participating in the two Women's Pentagon Actions and in the Seneca Peace Camp.

Their presence in the direct action movement has been much more important than that of gay men. Though gay direct action groups have begun to organize around the issue of AIDS, there have been no men's actions paralleling the women's peace actions.

Lesbians have also been increasingly prominent as leaders of the direct action movement, and not only of its women's component. This tendency has been especially visible in the rural and semirural areas where lesbians from the movements of the sixties and seventies have congregated. In northern New England, particularly Vermont and Western Massachusetts, lesbians have played a major role in antinuclear actions. In Key West, a group of lesbians brought together chiefly through the efforts of feminist pacifist writer Barbara Deming have been the core of ongoing actions at the Key West Naval Base and at Cape Canaveral. In St. Augustine, Florida, lesbians who collectively own and inhabit several adjacent houses have organized a group called Seeds for Peace, which has been the moving force in local peace and environmental actions.

In the late 1970s the influence of lesbians within the direct action movement was felt largely in rural areas. In the 1980s, lesbians played a larger role in the cities and on a national level. In Boston, a group of women, mainly lesbians, has provided leadership for the Pledge of Resistance in particular and for antiwar direct action more generally. When a large demonstration was held in Washington, D.C., against the CIA in April 1986, it was mainly lesbians who organized and led its direct action component, in which 600 men and women were arrested. The 1987 march on Washington for gay and lesbian rights and attention to the issue of AIDS drew on the entire gay community, but it was lesbians from the direct action movement who provided the nonviolence training for civil disobedience. Lesbians say they are not surprised to find themselves in positions of leadership in regard to nonviolent direct action. Once they have come out of the closet, taking other kinds of risks is easy; their marginality gives them a stake in fundamental social change; and their grounding in feminism gives them an understanding of the interconnectedness of many issues that is less developed among gay men. Some point out that lesbians and gays have played important roles in the peace movement, the left, and the civil rights movement. But in earlier movements lesbians and gays have been prominent as individuals. In the direct action movement, and to some extent in the peace and social justice movement that surrounds the direct action movement, networks of lesbians are increasingly important at every level.

Feminist Ideologies
in the Direct Action Movement

The activists who founded the Clamshell, the Abalone, and LAG were committed to feminism as part of a broad radical politics; each of these organizations attracted women whose main political identity was feminist and groups of men and women whose theoretical perspectives influenced their understanding of feminism. The first specifically feminist theory to be introduced to the movement was anarcha-feminism, contributed by anarchists who had been student activists at Stanford, subsequently fanned out to Santa Cruz and San Francisco, and collectively joined the Abalone Alliance in time to become a significant presence at the Diablo blockade of 1981. Part of a national and international network of New Left- and feminist-inspired anarchists, they were persuaded by the radical feminist view that men's oppression of women was the basic form of social oppression and that the family was the central instrument of oppression. It followed that a feminist critique and vision must be at the center of anarchist politics.

The Stanford group was influenced by the writings of anarchist philosopher Murray Bookchin, especially *Post-Scarcity Anarchism,*[4] and also by a series of pamphlets written by women anarchists with roots in radical feminism. Bookchin argued that post-scarcity conditions transformed the nature of revolution, making a classless, stateless, ecologically balanced society attainable for the first time. Bookchin's utopian politics and his contention that the working class had been replaced by youth and the counterculture as the leading edge of revolution provided a theoretical framework for the political intuitions of those whose outlook was shaped by the movements of the early seventies.

The theoretical framework Bookchin laid out was compatible

with a radical feminist critique of domination by gender and of the family as an institution of oppression. A number of women anarchists, influenced both by radical feminism with its separatist strategy and by the more inclusive vision of Bookchin and other anarchists, brought the two together in the argument that anarchism could realize its own potential only by recognizing its need for a feminist politics and accepting direction from women. Peggy Kornegger, author of an influential anarcha-feminist piece, argued that radical feminism and anarchism were natural allies. Both perspectives, she pointed out, were based on critiques of dominance; both sought to replace power relations with equality. She argued that women's consciousness-raising groups—small, leaderless groups based on face-to-face relations—embodied anarchist principles, and that women were readily drawn to anarchist philosophy by their history of powerlessness and delegitimation. Quoting another anarcha-feminist, Kornegger said that "women often practice Anarchism and do not know it, while some men call themselves Anarchists and do not practice it." She asserted that "women are in the unique position of being the bearers of a subsurface anarchist consciousness" and that only by incorporating this consciousness can the anarchist movement be true to its own principles.[5]

Other anarcha-feminist authors echoed and developed these themes. Carol Ehrlich wrote that the fundamental goals of anarchism and radical feminism were the same: "Not to 'seize' power, as the socialists are fond of urging, but to abolish power."[6] Kytha Kurin argued that in order to achieve its own goals, the radical feminist perspective must move beyond separatism and, with an ecological perspective, become the guiding philosophy of a movement of men as well as women.[7]

By the end of the 1970s, many feminists regarded separatism as an inadequate strategy. Part of anarcha-feminism's attraction was that it addressed this problem without rejecting the radical feminist analysis that had been associated with separatism. But anarcha-feminism was not equipped to address another problem of the women's movement, described in the title of a widely read essay as "The Tyranny of Structurelessness." That essay argued that every group has leaders, that informal leaders are less accountable and therefore more dangerous than formally recognized ones, and that antileadership ideology weakened the women's movement by permitting crippling attacks on the very activists who had helped the movement find its direction.[8]

The flexibility the anarcha-feminists demonstrated in handling the question of separatism abandoned them when they addressed the question of leadership. Here they could only reiterate the original radical feminist (and anarchist) view that hierarchies of any kind were necessarily oppressive. Carol Ehrlich argued in a widely read piece that socialist feminism should be rejected in favor of a radical feminist and anarchist perspective and acknowledged that some feminists had come under attack within the movement simply because they had taken on leading roles. The only antidote lay in paying greater attention to anarchist principles.[9]

Anarcha-feminism came to direct action through the Abalone Alliance and was an important element in the variety of anarchism that shaped that organization. Anarcha-feminism also influenced the feminist wing of the Pagan movement and, to a lesser degree, the broader women's spirituality movement. But anarcha-feminism relied on a commitment to ongoing political practice, to the intellectual effort of understanding anarchist theory and the Marxist precepts that anarcha-feminism built upon and criticized. Though many anarcha-feminists did not identify with women's spirituality, and some criticized it for its apolitical tendency, that movement was nevertheless the largest coherent constituency receptive to the general approach of anarcha-feminism. Thus its anti-intellectualism and ambivalence toward politics impeded the further development of anarcha-feminist theory.

Paganism entered the direct action movement along with anarcha-feminism. Anarcha-feminism existed as a set of networks only peripherally connected to the women's spirituality movement in which Paganism is anchored, and some anarcha-feminists were too firmly secular to be drawn to Paganism. But most of the anarcha-feminist households that were part of the direct action movement considered themselves Pagans and held Pagan rituals. Pagans and witches were not as prominent in the Abalone as the anarcha-feminists, but they were present at the 1981 Diablo blockade, where the two groups overlapped and reinforced each others' concern for constructing a prefigurative community. It was in LAG and more generally in the movement against nuclear arms that Pagans and witches were to become a significant factor in the direct action movement. Pagan rituals became a routine feature of actions and were often helpful in breaking down barriers and drawing people together. Those rituals emphasize the power of human collectivity, and the human bond with the natural environment, and acceptance of the unconscious and irrational in human personality and experience.

Paganism, witchcraft, and women's spirituality all look to a tradition of pre-Christian spirituality and attempt to draw out its feminist implications. Groups of people practicing a religion based on pre-Christian European traditions and calling themselves witches have existed in the United States and England for decades. They may well have been inspired by anthropologist Margaret Murray's 1921 book *The Witch Cult in Western Europe*, which examined a variety of early European cults and called them all witchcraft. Feminists were drawn to witchcraft by its association with goddess figures, its antihierarchical implications, and its respect for nature. They wanted a religious tradition that did not revolve around a transcendent male god; and they saw its theatrical potential and its shock value. Margot Adler's *Drawing Down the Moon* and Starhawk's *Dreaming the Dark* were both expressions of the growing interest of radical feminists in witchcraft and Paganism; both helped to politicize the Craft by emphasizing its radical and feminist dimensions, thus drawing many young radical feminists into its orbit.[10] Older groupings within what is called the Craft remain apolitical and uninterested in feminism, but the feminist and radical branch of the movement, which also uses the term Neo-Paganism to describe itself, is the fastest growing sector of the movement.

The looseness of these movements is reflected in their imprecise, often confusing terminology. Witches consider themselves Pagans, but not all Pagans are witches. The Craft is more tightly organized than Paganism or the women's spirituality movement; generally speaking, a woman (or man) must be a member of a coven in order to consider herself or himself a witch (though there are increasing numbers of witches unconnected to covens). Covens are held together by large networking organizations such as the Covenant of the Goddess and the Circle. It is estimated that there are upward of 100,000 witches and Pagans in the United States.[11] The movement intersects with the much larger New Age phenomenon, but Neo-Paganism at least has a much closer connection with feminism and radical politics. Neo-Pagan feminism identifies closely with the direct action movement, and Neo-Pagan groups have often held rituals coinciding with antinuclear actions. The Livermore blockade of June 1983, for instance, was held on the solstice; at a Neo-Pagan festival in Wisconsin celebrating the solstice, some sixty women got up at 6:00 A.M. to conduct a ritual in support of the blockade.

Neo-Paganism and feminist spirituality appeal to women largely because they give women powerful figures with whom to identify and because they challenge alienation by constructing rituals that stress the connections among human beings and between humanity and nature. Margot Adler believes that her attraction to witchcraft began when she was a twelve-year-old studying ancient Greece. "I came in contact with Artemis and Athena and took to them in a very powerful way. I wasn't worshipping them, I was *becoming* them. I saw them as stronger role models than anything around in the society at the time." Many years later, she learned of a coven in England, which sent her a tape of their rituals. The first was called "Drawing Down the Moon," in which a woman took on the role of Artemis. "This was what I had locked up in a closet years earlier," Margot said. "This woman was becoming Artemis in ritual."[12]

The polytheism of Paganism has been attractive to anarchists and others around the direct action movement as an alternative to cultural imperialism. It accepts and incorporates new cultures, new goddesses and gods, rather than attempts to fit them in a preexisting mold. Pre-Christian Paganism consisted of many different religious traditions. The multiplicity of local gods and goddesses made conversion irrelevant; groups could simply incorporate new deities as they encountered others who worshipped them. "You can't imagine religious wars in this context," Adler pointed out. "Pagan religions work according to ecological principles: spiritual diversity is like ecological diversity." This acceptance of difference, she argued, was possible because Pagan religions were fundamentally rooted in practices rather than in ideologies. Rituals expressed peoples' relation to what they did: planting crops, taking cows to pasture, menstruating. They did not rest upon assertions of creed.

In contemporary industrialized society, Adler argues, Paganism speaks to unmet needs by addressing experiences that cannot be explained in material terms and by asserting the connections among human beings and between humans and nature. "Most of us live in a world very much bounded by separation and alienation. What all the chanting and so forth does is it breaks down the barriers that make you think you are a separate being. It brings you back to the reality, which is that you are connected; it allows people to feel what reconnecting with the earth and with other people means."[13]

Paganism and women's spirituality have fostered belief in a prehistoric matriarchal Golden Age. Many women in the direct action movement, especially those influenced by women's spirituality, believe that in the earliest human societies, goddesses were worshipped and women held positions of power. In these peaceful societies people lived harmoniously with one another and with their neighbors and treated the natural environment with respect. According to this account, this Golden Age was followed by patriarchy, which attempted to uproot earlier earth-based goddess religions in favor of various monotheisms that justified competing cultural imperialisms, each worshipping a single, transcendent male god. Patriarchy and monotheism are thus linked with war and the domination of nature as well as women. The patriarchal stage of development may have been necessary as a spur to certain kinds of technological development, but it has outlived its usefulness and become a threat to the human race and to the earth. This view of world history suggests that survival rests on the ability of the human race to proceed to the next stage of development, which will be neither matriarchal nor patriarchal but based on equality between men and women and the abolition of all social hierarchies. It suggests that such a society would honor many of the qualities traditionally associated with women, such as nurturance, intimacy, and sensual pleasure, and would devalue militarism, competition, and the love of power, which developed in the patriarchal context.

The idea of a Golden Age of matriarchy was presented as the dominant position in Charlene Spretnak's *Politics of Women's Spir-*

ituality. It has also been encouraged by Merlin Stone in *When God Was a Woman* and Riane Eisler in *The Chalice and the Blade*.[14] Matriarchy here means a social system organized around matriliny and goddess worship in which women have positions of power. These books present evidence that such societies have existed, that they were not destructive of their natural environments and lived in peace with their neighbors. The idea of matriarchy as a stage in social development associated with primitive communism goes back to Friedrich Engels. In the twentieth century, this view has been opposed by the dominant trend in anthropology, on the ground that the goddess worship or matrilocality that evidently existed in many paleolithic societies was not necessarily associated with matriarchy in the sense of women's power over men. Many societies can be found that exhibit those qualities along with female subordination. Furthermore, militarism, destruction of the natural environment, and hierarchical social structures can be found in societies in which goddess worship, matrilocality, or matriliny exist.

Mainstream anthropologists charge the theorists of matriarchy with reading data through the lens of their own political preferences and projecting feminism and primitive communism onto early human experience. The theorists of matriarchy have some basis, however, for accusing their opponents, in turn, of an ideologically charged reading of evidence. Bronislaw Malinowski, a leading opponent of the theory of matriarchy, based his critique on his own study of the Trobriand Islands, where he found a matrilineal structure of inheritance coexisting with the subordination of women.[15] Malinowski argued that anthropology should orient itself toward fieldwork to ensure the accuracy of its claims. The problem is that fieldwork consists of studying "primitive" societies in the modern era that have inevitably been changed by the modern societies that now surround them. The fact that in India, for instance, long-standing goddess worship exists side by side with extreme subordination of women does not prove that a matriarchy including both goddess worship and women's power never existed there. Goddess worship might well have survived the destruction of women's power. Moreover, fieldwork is not a foolproof antidote to ideological bias. A feminist anthropologist reexamining the Trobriand Islands claims that Malinowski did not report evidence of women's playing powerful roles in that society.[16] In a 1930 debate over matriarchy between Malinowski and Robert Briffault, the ideological stakes on both sides were clear. Briffault, a radical, profeminist anthropologist, argued that matriarchy had been the predominant form of early social organization. Malinowski, arguing that the nuclear family had always been the dominant social form, made clear his opposition to feminism and to primitive (and presumably modern) communism.[17]

The direct action movement is not a society of anthropologists, and it is not necessary for activists who identify with women's spirituality to follow the literature on this debate in detail; nor is there necessarily anything wrong with reading somewhat popularized accounts of these issues. Popular movements often construct Golden Age stories to reinforce the legitimacy of their aims. Such stories are usually a complex mixture of valid and not-so-valid accounts of the past; their main purpose is to undermine the claims of existing authorities and provide a historical basis for alternate visions. By emphasizing the historical transiency of patriarchy and the existence of societies organized differently, an account of a matriarchal past inspires confidence that patriarchy can be dismantled. By linking women's power with peace, ecology, spirituality, and egalitarianism, the theory of matriarchy gives women a special role in movements for peace and social change and provides a ground for the values held by the cultural wing of feminism.[18]

The influence of the matriarchy theory within women's spirituality, and thus in the direct action movement, has not been completely benign, however. The association of matriarchy with peace and other good things and of patriarchy with war and other bad things, in addition to ignoring bad things associated with early societies and the good things in later ones, also flattens the transition from one stage of social development to the next and reinforces some of the politically problematic aspects of women's spirituality. By romanticizing primitive societies, the matriarchy theory justifies the hostility toward rationality and science and the blanket rejection of technology that pervade women's spirituality and the direct action movement. The belief that rationality, science, and especially technology are evil regardless of the uses to which they are put is widespread within the alternative culture. This attitude produces a politics that is not very helpful in dealing with the problems posed by advanced technology and makes it easy for outsiders to dismiss the movement as naive.

The formula matriarchy-peace/patriarchy-war further implies that what went wrong was just that men gained power and ignores the relationship between gender hierarchies and other kinds of hierarchies. The matriarchy theory is questioned by many feminist and left anthropologists, who see more evidence for equality between men and women than for matriarchy in early human societies. In their more moderate view, very early kinship societies, which generally lived at peace with their neighbors, tended to lack hierarchies of gender and of class; with the increase of trade and warfare internal stratification emerged, and men asserted power over women.[19]

To describe a transition from egalitarian to hierarchical societies as a passage from matriarchy to patriarchy presents men as the enemy, gives women a monopoly on positive qualities, and reinforces the traditional association of men with rationality and women with nurturance and emotion. These attitudes have in fact had a good deal of influence within the direct action movement, in large part contributions of women's spirituality. Attempts by women or men to engage in political debate or to assert leadership, especially intellectual leadership, are likely to be attacked as "male." However, not everyone who identifies with women's spirituality takes the matriarchy thesis literally. Both Starhawk and Margot Adler regard it primarily as a metaphor, an alternative to the stories about the origins of human society told within the mainstream culture. Furthermore, women's spirituality, with its tendency to reinforce traditional definitions of gender, coexists with currents within the direct action movement that also define themselves as feminist but take different approaches to gender. Marge Piercy's *Woman on the Edge of Time*, a novel about a future in which the boundaries between male and female roles have been largely erased and masculinity and femininity are no longer recognizable categories, has played a large role in shaping the way Pagan anarchists and others imagine a utopian future.

Ecofeminism, which from its inception was more theoretical than either anarcha-feminism or Paganism, has provided an arena for the development of more flexible and sophisticated approaches. Like anarcha-feminists, ecofeminists saw a common ground in anarchist and feminist philosophies and sought to underline the relationship of an ecological perspective to both of these. Ecofeminism was influenced by women's spirituality as well, both theoretically and in the political actions through which it found expression. But at the same time it provided a basis for addressing some of the theoretical and political problems raised by women's spirituality, especially its separatist implications.

The term "ecofeminism" was first used by the French author Françoise d'Eaubonne in *La Feminisme ou la mort*.[20] It was adopted in 1980 by women organizing a conference they called "Women and Life on Earth: Ecofeminism in the 1980s," which led to the first Women's Pentagon Action. Ynestra King, a coordinator of the conference, and others from Murray Bookchin's Institute for Social Ecology helped shape the further development of ecofeminism as a politics and a theoretical perspective.

In the late 1970s a number of books attempted to combine radical feminist and ecological concerns, including Susan Griffin's *Woman and Nature* and Mary Daly's *Gyn/Ecology*. In the 1980s many more works appeared that identified themselves with ecofeminism, in particular Carolyn Merchant's *Death of Nature,* Charlene Spretnak's collection, *Politics of Women's Spirituality,* and an issue of *Heresies* devoted to feminism and ecology. Margot Adler's account of witchcraft in the United States, *Drawing Down the Moon,* and Starhawk's *Dreaming the Dark: Magic, Sex and Politics* straddle the worlds of Paganism, feminist spirituality, and ecofeminism.[21] In 1986, a conference entitled "Ecofeminist Perspectives" in Los Angeles attracted roughly 1,500 activists and scholars; the turnout suggests that the audience for this approach is growing.

Ecofeminists argue that patriarchy, the domination of women by men, is associated with the attempt to dominate nature. To justify their exploitation, both women and nature are objectified by placing them in the category of "the other"; the human connection with the natural world and the feminine in men's natures are denied. Ecofeminists regard the despoliation of the environment and violence and militarism as rooted in the culture of domination; they argue that both have become serious threats to the human race and must be overcome. Patriarchy must be replaced with an egalitarian social organization in which men and women have equal power and a social ecology in which the natural environment is cultivated rather than manipulated and destroyed. Ecofeminists also believe that capitalism is linked to domination and must be replaced by some form of socialism; they envision small-scale economies and local grass roots democracy, rather than the large-scale, state-directed social economies of existing socialist nations.

Ecofeminism has been strongly influenced by anarchism, especially by Murray Bookchin. Like him, ecofeminists reject the Marxist tendency to privilege the economic realm over the cultural; they reject the Leninist concept of the revolutionary party; and they put forward a concept of nonviolent revolution that would dismantle rather than seize state power. But, like Bookchin's work, ecofeminism also has roots in Marxist theory, especially the concept of alienation and the vision of a socialist or communist society that would liberate human potential. Ecofeminism has also adopted some of the critical theory of the Frankfurt School; Max Horkheimer's *Eclipse of Reason,* with its argument that social repression requires the repression of human nature (and the natural environment), has been particularly influential.[22] Ecofeminism has attempted to develop a holistic theory of domination that can address race and class as well as gender and ecology. It has paid less attention to specific questions of organization, movement building, or strategy.

Though such early writers in the ecofeminist line as Mary Daly and Susan Griffin were closely associated with separatist radical feminism, arguing that women should identify with nature against men, ecofeminism has developed some distance from the radical feminist perspective. Ynestra King, for instance, has taken a stance somewhere between radical feminism and traditional Marxism. She has criticized Marxism and the socialist feminist tradition for excessive emphasis on the economic, a tendency to subordinate questions of gender to those of class, a "rationalist severance of the woman/nature connection [in] advocating the integration of women into production, [its failure to] challenge the culture-versus-nature formulation itself." But instead of aligning herself with radical feminism, King has criticized the radical feminist/socialist feminist split and attempted to transcend it. This split reflects the historical division between rationalism and romanticism, a manifestation of the nature/culture dichotomy in which women's oppression is rooted.

If the nature/culture antagonism is the primary contradiction of our time, it is also what weds feminism and ecology and makes woman the historic subject. Without an ecological perspective which asserts the interdependence of living things, feminism is disembodied. . . . Ecological feminism . . . is about connectedness and wholeness and the return of all that has been denigrated and denied to build this hierarchical civilization with its multiple systems of dominance. It is the potential voice of the denied, the ugly and the speechless—all those things called "feminine." It is no accident that the feminist movement rose again in the same decade as the ecological crisis. The implications of feminism extend to issues of the meaning, purpose and survival of life.[23]

The Lesbian Contribution
to the Direct Action Movement

Countercultural lesbian communities have provided the most consistent organized base for the feminist wing of the direct action movement and especially for feminist spirituality. The feminism that has prevailed in the direct action movement has always had a close association with lesbianism; in the late 1960s and early 1970s, the tensions between radical feminism and socialist feminism partly had to do with the fact that radical feminist organizations were generally hospitable to lesbians, whereas socialist feminist organizations were dominated by heterosexual women. At the time, socialist feminists accused radical feminists of being more interested in consciousness raising and the creation of a women's culture than in political action. Ironically, in the eighties radical feminism (or its ideological successors) has been much more significant as a basis for feminist activism in the women's movement, the peace movement, and elsewhere than has socialist feminism.

To some extent the increased prominence in the movements of the eighties of the descendants of radical feminism reflects the movement of socialist feminism in the 1970s from activist politics into academia, where it is the foundation of Women's Studies programs and feminist analysis in several disciplines. The socialist feminist tendency of the women's movement, at its height in the early seventies, was made up largely of graduate students; by the late seventies many of these women were pursuing teaching and research that, although usually feminist in character, was often remote from ongoing political movements. Radical feminists, generally less academic, were more likely to remain involved in politics and thus were able to pass their ideas on to a younger generation of feminist activists. The political differences between radical and socialist feminism were compounded by the heterosexual orientation of most socialist feminists, many of whom had families by the early eighties. The preponderance of lesbians within radical feminism made for more marginal life-styles, a more urgent need for community, and a greater openness to political activity, especially in a movement with a strong flavor of marginality.

Though radical feminism was much more militantly separatist than socialist feminism, in the late sixties and through the seventies both were sustained by an autonomous women's movement. They shared a culture in which political alliances and personal relationships with men were to be apologized for, if not rejected. The separatist orientation of the women's movement was partly a reaction to the misogyny of the New Left and the antiwar movement; only autonomous women's organizations could effectively challenge the male-dominated structures and political agendas of those movements. Feminist separatism also had more personal roots. In the sixties and early seventies, higher education was available to large numbers of women, job opportunities for college-educated women were expanding, birth control was readily available, and prosperity seemed to open many options. A generation of young women could afford to put off marriage and family to make a radical critique of those institutions. The generation that constructed the politics of the sixties and seventies was furthermore extremely large, and its cultures, including the culture of radical feminism, had an influence unprecedented in American social history.

By the late seventies the radical wing of the women's movement as a whole was severely strained by the tightening of the economy. This wing of the movement had been created by women in their twenties and thirties, although some were older; after a decade this cohort faced longer-range decisions—about having families, for instance, or pursuing careers. Socialist feminism, losing its organized constituency and lacking a political strategy, virtually collapsed as a political tendency. Radical feminism, with its large lesbian constituency, found it easier to sustain a politics based on a critique of the family. But harsher political realities also undermined the strategy of feminist revolution based on a separate women's culture, and as a result many radical feminist organizations collapsed as well. In more general terms, however, a radical feminist perspective continued to appeal to a community of women who were still leading unconventional lives largely outside the university. This community, in which lesbianism was influential if not predominant, overlapped with the similarly unconventional community of men and women who formed the base for the antinuclear movements of the late seventies and eighties. The two groups thus came together in the same alternative political culture, which by that time included affinity for a predominantly non-Christian spirituality.

Radical feminism has been able to enter the direct action movement and exert a strong influence because the community that sustains this perspective has matured and has proved capable of a flexibility that the basic texts of radical feminism, written in the late sixties and early seventies, did not demonstrate. The shrillness of the lesbian feminism of the mid-seventies accomplished the purpose of creating space for lesbianism within a broader radical community. It was part of a larger process by which homosexuality was gaining greater acceptance in American society. That process enabled lesbian feminists to apply a feminist perspective to broader issues and to work with mixed organizations. By the early eighties, when the issue of nuclear war became the main focus of the radical community, the lesbian feminist community was ready to become a significant part of that movement.

Lesbian feminists were attracted to the direct action movement by the overlap of values and cultural orientation between the two communities. The lesbian groups from rural New England who played an important role in the Women's Pentagon Action and Seneca had been part of the women's movement in the early seventies and moved to the country to create autonomous lives. Many of these women built houses together and supported themselves by such basic skills as carpentry and farming. The ecofeminist perspective allowed them to reenter politics, which they in turn infused with their strong spirituality.

In the cities, lesbian feminists were drawn to the direct action movement's commitment to feminism and anarchist structure. Urban lesbians, less spiritually oriented than their rural counterparts, were drawn to direct action because it provided a purposeful community and an arena in which the broader implications of feminist politics could be explored, and because the battle for the acceptance was so nearly won that some lesbians were willing to join broader movements. Susan Cavin, a lesbian feminist who was once a militant separatist, later an activist in the New York City peace movement, argued that lesbians are moving into positions of leadership in the peace and other movements partly because the lesbian community benefits from alliances with other social change groups, and partly because they take pleasure in exercising leadership. "There is a certain group of lesbians," Cavin said, "who have almost been socialized to be boys. They see themselves as equal to men, and they are dying for the chance to compete and run organizations. Some want to do it on Wall Street; if you have radical politics, you go into the peace movement. For lesbians, that's mainstream; it's moving out of the feminist ghetto." [24]

The lesbian feminist community has shown a special affinity with the direct action movement. The informal leadership of all of the major direct action organizations, except for those specifically concerned with all-women actions, was predominantly heterosexual until the second half of the eighties, when lesbians expanded their role in the leadership of peace and anti-intervention groups. Through the 1980s lesbian affinity groups were a major part of actions and of the ongoing life of the direct action movement: they have stayed with the movement when others have disappeared.

The prominent role of lesbians in the movement may be explained in part by the stability and resilience of the friendship networks that are usually the basis of lesbian affinity groups. When a lesbian couple separates, there is a good chance that they will retain a strong relationship. Lesbians, their lovers, and their former lovers often make up what amount to family groupings. Ynestra King described this experience in her own life:

My former lover is like family to me and my current lover. My current lover understands that she has no one else, you can't abandon someone just because you don't want to be in a sexual relationship anymore. It's not negotiable. It's not that there aren't certain tensions. But my ex-lover wants to see me alone sometimes, she needs support, and my current lover has to understand that, it's a necessity of life. And my former lover has been very supportive of my current lover, who's just coming out. This kind of experience runs through the movement.[25]

Networks of this sort can give a political community stability, especially when the lesbian component of the movement is so large that political work begins to merge with social life. Heterosexual women in the direct action movement often feel some tension between their political and social lives. The nuclear family, with its strong ties to mainstream culture, exerts a pull away from the marginal politics of direct action. Single heterosexual women often have strong ties with other women, but the likelihood that their sexual relationships with men will end in estrangement undermines the stability of affinity and other working groups. Among heterosexuals, the ideology of marriage and family undercuts the construction of community by devaluing relationships that do not fit its mold. Pagan affinity groups have shown some ability to absorb and survive shifting sexual relationships, perhaps because the Pagan community, like the lesbian community, has constructed an alternative culture in which everyone is expected to have many valued ties. Though there are Pagan families, the family is not privileged to the degree it is in mainstream society. Furthermore, many Pagans, like many lesbians, find themselves cut off from their own families; the Pagan community assumes a place in their lives that has no parallel in the lives of straight heterosexual women.

Lesbians, as we have seen, have played a much larger role in the direct action movement than gay men. The reasons, Susan Cavin argues, are partly that the pacifist perspective generally appeals more to women than to men, and partly that although gay men have considerable political experience within their own community, they do not feel the same solidarity with other groups or understand the connections between a range of social issues as lesbians do. The gay movement includes direct action groups, especially around the issue of AIDS, some of whom see themselves as linked to the direct action movement as a whole. Act Up, a New York group of about two hundred gay men, conducts actions against the medical establishment. At a national conference on AIDS, they distributed themselves through the audience, wearing white lab coats. When vice president George Bush took the podium, they rose and turned their backs, showing the pink triangles homosexuals had been forced to wear in Nazi Germany. Lesbians with experience in the direct action movement at first provided the leadership for civil disobedience in the gay community; as AIDS-related protests have grown, gay men have gained experience in this area and are joining lesbians as nonviolence trainers.

Feminism and Magical Politics

Radical feminism and feminist spirituality have brought to the direct action movement a conception of politics as magic in two senses, one naive and the other sophisticated. Feminist spirituality has encouraged the already substantial streak of anti-intellectualism and intellectual laziness in the movement—the tendency to avoid theory, history, and political economy and to substitute magical thinking for strategic analysis. Some Pagans believe that there is a real Goddess whose help can be invoked through ritual; at least they are willing to entertain the idea. Groups of Pagans have held private rituals designed to cause nuclear plants to close down and missile tests to fail. The privacy of these rituals suggests that they were not meant as political theater or community-building, but to have a practical effect. A similar assumption is that collective action based on passionately held ethical beliefs will necessarily bring about practical results. Each of the large-scale actions conducted by the organizations I have looked at has been accompanied by the unexamined (and unrealistic) expectation that the action itself would bring about the plant closure or some other objective. At the same time there is a very sophisticated side to the magical politics feminists and Pagans have brought to the direct action movement. This is its grasp of the importance of symbolism and ritual on the way people think and of the enormous power of collective action proceeding from a positive vision—not to close down a plant, but to transform the consciousness and perhaps even the lives of participants, and to introduce new ideas into the broader culture. Collective action based on a shared vision opens critical questions, helps to define the views of people outside the movement, and spurs political pressure in other arenas. The fact that the naive and the sophisticated versions of magical politics are so closely linked makes it difficult for participants to distinguish between the two and to remember that the impact of visionary collective action is on consciousness rather than directly on its institutional targets.

Many Pagans simultaneously believe in the Goddess as reality and the Goddess as metaphor for the power of human collectivity and human bonds with nature. In the same way, many participants in the direct action movement have simultaneously held naive and sophisticated concepts of magical politics. The Abalone activists who organized the 1981 blockade of Diablo were able temporarily to put everything else in their lives aside out of the implicit expectation that the blockade would shut the plant down. This assumption, which no one could reasonably have defended, was nevertheless so deep that no thought was put into ending the blockade if it did not succeed in closing the plant. Nevertheless, organizers and participants in the blockade regarded it as a success, even though it did not accomplish its aim. The fact that the faulty construction of the plant was made public in the immediate wake of the action helped to give the protesters a sense of accomplishment. But it was also possible to see the action as a success because it was a turning point in changing public attitudes toward nuclear power. In a discussion of what the direct action movement means by victory, Starhawk wrote that the success of the Diablo blockade was less contingent on

physically stopping the workers [than on] changing the reality, the consciousness, of the society in which the plant exists. Not the blockade alone, but the years of effort and organizing that preceded the blockade, created that victory. The ritual, the magic, spins the bond that can sustain us to continue the work over years, over lifetimes.

Transforming culture is a long-term project. . . . Though power-from-within can burst forth in an instant, its rising is mostly a process slow as the turning wheels of generations. If we cannot live to see the completion of that revolution, we can plant its seeds in our circles, we can dream its shape in our visions, and our rituals can feed its growing power.[26]

Magical politics means not only finding new ways of exerting power, outside the boundaries of conventional politics, but also redistributing power, giving everyone an equal voice, with a conviction that all voices are or at least will become equally worthwhile. Feminism has placed the concepts of empowerment and personal transformation at the center of the direct action movement's concept of its mission. Many women have been drawn into the movement by consensus and radical egalitarianism, generally referred to as feminist process, which assures those with little political experience or intellectual self-confidence that they will be heard. Charlotte Davis, for instance, who had been a medical technologist in a hospital in San Francisco, contrasted working with Abalone with the job that she had left, where her superior would call a meeting, announce the agenda, and proceed to talk at the technicians present. In Abalone, Charlotte said, there were no superiors; everyone's input was sought and valued.

For me, the most important thing was that in almost every meeting I was in, we went around in a circle and everyone said what they had to say. As we went around and people said what they really thought and felt, it became clear to me that every person in the world thinks well, if you give them enough time and space. If one person came up with an objection that made sense, we all listened to it. We were not forced to vote. That's how I think ideas should develop. That kind of feeling of all of us working together on a problem was real important to me. And bullies were exposed immediately, because they couldn't bear to sit and listen.[27]

The direct action movement encourages changes beyond playing an equal role in decision making. Many have been spurred to make the way they lead their lives more consonant with their vision of how society should be organized. Nina Swaim, for instance, a member of the Weavers affinity group in rural Vermont that initiated the practice of weaving brightly colored yarn across

the doors of nuclear plants, said that she and the others attempted to put their vision into practice in their daily lives as well
as in their political work.

A lot of us did a lot of life-style evaluation. We started recycling, not
using electricity. We began thinking about what we had become used
to. We couldn't really eat bananas if we were serious about being
against imperialism. We took it a lot further than Seabrook. We tried
to find ways to live that were much simpler, that didn't need things
like [the Seabrook plant]. The vision was not just feminist. It was
about how are we going to live, how are we going to eat, how are we
going to raise our children, in a way that won't end up the way it is
now. It was an extraordinary experience. It was easier then, because
I thought there really was hope; I now think it's going to take a lot
longer than I thought then.[28]

The relationship of feminism to nonviolence is ambivalent in
the direct action movement. There is a strong implicit connection
between nonviolence and the feminist perspective of a more hu-
mane community. Nevertheless, at times women in the movement have been reluctant to give up a militance that stretches the
nonviolence code to its limits or openly violates it. It is understood that men who enter the movement must often learn to respond to provocation nonviolently. During the Diablo blockade,
for example, the Spartacists, a Marxist-Leninist sect, violated the
Abalone's agreement with the owner of the land on which the
camp was held by selling their literature. When they refused to
put their pamphlets away, the rest of the campers encircled them,
argued with them, and moved them out of the camp without violence. In the course of this maneuver, a number of men threatened to strike the Spartacists; groups of women talked them
around. But the most heated challenge to the nonviolence code
has come from women who view pacifism as acquiescence to violence and feel no responsibility to be "open, friendly and respectful" toward rapists, batterers, or men who engage in more subtle
forms of violence against women. The tactic of sitting in the road
(as opposed to standing) was first used in LAG at a Mother's Day
action organized by the Feminist Cluster; it was met with a degree of police violence. Two members of the Feminist Cluster
burned pages of the Bible that had been distributed to the protesters held in jail after the 1982 blockade of the labs. This act

brought a harsh response from the authorities and was seen by many protesters as a violation of the code.

Although some feminists continue to associate militance with a willingness to engage in or at least contemplate violence, women's experience as victims or potential victims of violence also produces a profound commitment to nonviolence. A young woman activist, overhearing an argument in the Abalone office that the movement should be willing to resort to violence, interrupted to protest. "My childhood was really violent and I don't want any more violence in my life," she said. She had grown up responding to violence in kind; at the Diablo blockade, her first major movement experience, she doubted that she could maintain the nonviolence code. But talking with a woman nonviolence trainer began to show her the roots of violence in her personal history and the possibility of change:

I started to learn that a lot of how I would respond to cops was based on my responses to parents, teachers. There was a lot of stored anger. As I began to deal with some of that personally, I've been able to have more control over what I do. I used to have fantasies of retributive murder; they have guns, we have to get guns. Now I'm starting to learn other things. If I'm hassled I'll still scream. But I've seen so much success in terms of human vulnerability. There's a lot of power there, in nonviolence; it can be incredibly moving. I don't trust the pig in myself.[29]

On balance, feminism has been a strong influence for nonviolence within the direct action movement. The movement's commitment to nonviolence has been reassuring to many, especially women, who would not join if actions were likely to turn violent. Anarcha-feminism and ecofeminism provide a theoretical basis for this stance by arguing that militarism is an expression of patriarchy and that both can be transcended only by nonviolent revolution. Though radical feminism has at times included an assumption that abstaining from violence means a softening of militance, it also contains countervailing currents. The view that men are by nature more violent than women has long had currency in the radical or cultural feminist wing of the movement; the belief that women have a natural affinity for nonviolence often colors discussion of the issue in the direct action movement. But the anarcha-feminist or ecofeminist theoretical stance presents a more sophisticated argument: women can play a special role in the construction of a nonviolent movement because they are more likely to be victims than perpetrators of violence and because they are acculturated to deal with conflict in nonviolent ways.

Nonviolence, the ecofeminists argue, is the logical conclusion of a feminist and ecological politics. "If you maintain a consistent critique of domination, if you are concerned about peace, ecology, and gender," Ynestra King said, "you have to have a politics with a cultural base, one that calls into question old ways of living. The politics of nonviolence is the only thing that makes sense, in terms of thinking about militarism as a manifestation of dominance, and advancing an intentional feminist strategy."[30]

Because of its emphasis on self-transformation and the building of community, its association with spirituality and its support for nonviolence, the specifically feminist current in the direct action movement has often had a particular affinity for the religious wing of the movement. At times the feminist and Christian wings of the movement have been sharply at odds. But as impatience with the nonviolence code has dwindled, feminism and the faith-based wing of the movement, primarily Christian, have in many areas been drawn to one another.[31]

In Boston, for instance, the Pledge of Resistance, which has come to be the organizational center of the direct action movement, is based on an alliance between Christian and feminist activists. The affinity group structure and consensus process were attractive to both Christians and feminists, and over several years of activity the two groups have developed a great deal of respect for one another. Kate Hoffman, a coordinator of the Pledge with a background in the lesbian feminist movement, points out that they share a concern with building community, an emphasis on personal experience, and the search for a politics that avoids hard rhetorical stances. "One thing the faith-based and the women's movements have in common," Kate said, "is rejecting a sharp ideological perspective, a softer politics that uses words like vision and truth and self-determination rather than phrases like 'smash the state' or 'burn it to the ground.'" Both groups are moved by the Nicaraguans' attempt to create a genuinely democratic society against heavy odds; the role of liberation theology gives many

Christians, especially Catholics, a special sense of affinity with the Nicaraguan revolution; feminists are impressed by attempts to create more egalitarian relations between men and women. It has been easier for both feminists and Christians to identify with Nicaragua than with the Salvadoran opposition, because the Nicaraguan movement seems more nonviolent and less "macho."[32]

The experience of the Boston Pledge of Resistance illustrates two aspects of the role of feminism in the direct action movement. Feminists, perhaps more than any other group within the movement, have shown the ability to reach out, to extend direct action beyond a narrow countercultural community. At the same time, they are based in a community that remains narrow and exclusive, consisting of countercultural and lesbian networks. The feminists who joined with radical Christians to form the Boston Pledge of Resistance worked together well because they already knew one another well: all had been involved in the women's movement at Brown University; they had moved to Boston more or less as a group after graduation; almost all were lesbians. In Boston they gravitated toward collective political effort, in the direct action rather than the women's movement. The ties they had built between them over years made it easy for them to exert leadership.

That the lesbian/feminists of the Boston Pledge were not particularly identified with Paganism may have strengthened their position. In some parts of the country Christians in the movement have been reluctant to become too closely associated with Pagans, for fear of losing their access to the mainstream churches. But Pagan feminism has also shown a surprising ability to reach beyond its own community and to speak to culturally mainstream audiences. Margot Adler, a witch and a reporter for National Public Radio, argues that Pagan feminist anarchism is able to speak to many people despite its dissonance with the prevailing culture because it acknowledges and strengthens the bonds among people and between people and nature, something that many people crave. Because Pagan spirituality affirms the search for meaning and for human connection, Margot argues, it can reach far beyond its origins in the counterculture.

To illustrate her point Margot tells a story. In 1982 she was invited to Harvard as a Niemann Fellow, to take part in a months-long program for established journalists. Although her book *Drawing Down the Moon,* an insider's account of witchcraft in the United States, had made her witchcraft public knowledge, Margot was shy about discussing this aspect of her life with her mostly conventional fellow students. But as the program drew to a close, she felt the need to acknowledge this side of herself; so she invited the other members of her class to a ritual in the garden of the Niemann Center. More than half came, including a number of straight middle-aged men. Margot conducted a ritual around the theme of protection from danger, because several members of the class were headed for crisis spots around the globe. She served her fellow students glasses of wine, had them stand in a circle holding hands, and taught them a few songs. It was her impression that many of them had never had an experience like this before, but they seemed to enjoy it and thanked her when they left. A few weeks later, at the final banquet, to Margot's surprise the class stood up, held hands, and sang one of the songs that she had taught them. Two of the men cried, one of them the crustiest journalist in the class. Since that time members of this class have remained in closer touch than any previous group of Niemann Fellows, and a number of them have told Margot that it was her ritual that allowed them to acknowledge the ties they had developed.[33]

The Limits of Magical Politics

Margot Adler argues that Pagan anarchist feminism provides tools for reaching beyond the present boundaries of direct action. It is certainly true that much of what is most appealing about the movement has been contributed or at least greatly reinforced by Pagan anarchist feminism: its playfulness, its concept of politics as theater, its insistence on a strictly egalitarian internal process, its utopian vision. But the prominence of Pagan feminism is problematic for the effort to expand the movement. It is one thing to participate in a Pagan feminist ritual occasionally, but to become part of a movement in which Paganism is a major strand requires either considerable alienation from traditional, mainstream American culture or an unusual degree of open-mindedness.

The movement's Paganism intersects with the many existing forms of unconventional spirituality, especially among those who consider themselves part of the New Age, and could help to introduce at least some of these people to politics. Nevertheless, Paganism and feminist spirituality put many people off. Even some people in the movement find them hard to take, including those who are themselves part of the broader counterculture. The Seneca Peace Camp, for instance, became a magnet for lesbian spiritual feminists who were more interested in finding a place to stay where they would feel culturally at home than in the issue of disarmament. In midsummer, after the Michigan Women's Music Festival, there was an influx of women who regarded Seneca as the next stop. One of the Seneca organizers, a lesbian feminist, described some of the problems, such as the women who refused to help maintain the camp because their job was communing with nature, or women who climbed trees and howled at the moon. Kate Hoffman, also a lesbian feminist, did civil disobedience at Seneca but was not comfortable there. "I found the rituals bizarre," she said. "The camp was there to challenge the base. But it became a refuge for mentally ill people, and a lot of energy had to go into that." When a dialogue opened up between the women at the camp and the Seneca Falls townspeople, the main issue local residents raised was lesbianism. Although women at the camp welcomed an opportunity to challenge homophobia, the culture that pervaded the camp added to the difficulties involved in bridging already sharp differences.[34]

In conceiving of politics largely as exemplary action, the direct action movement puts itself forward as a model: the question is whether the communities on which the movement is based are viable models for people outside those communities. In its early stages the direct action movement revolved largely around communities of young people who were located somewhere between the traditional left and the counterculture, many of whom left the movement after several years of intense political activity. As their influence declined, that of newer groups increased. In its later stages the direct action movement has revolved largely around the Pagan feminist community on the one hand and the "religious community," made up largely of radical Christians, on the other.

The Pagan feminist community has a genuine capacity for outreach, but as a model of political community of men and women it has flaws. The feminist component of the movement has been the most dedicated to community. By conceiving of community building as politics, however, it has undermined strategy. Community building and politics in fact are not the same thing: they can sustain one another but they can also contradict. A movement that makes political impact its only goal must sacrifice community: an egalitarian internal process, for instance, is often an obstacle to effective action against the existing system. After 1983, LAG members saw that repeated blockades would not expand the movement or its influence. The direct action focus was retained because LAG's affinity groups revolved around civil disobedience, and a different focus would disrupt the organization's existing community and internal culture. Choosing community over politics in the end does not serve the community: movement communities that lack political purpose tend to fall apart. But maintaining political direction requires a willingness to rethink accepted ideas and structures, which threatens internal unity. In the short run feminism's emphasis on maintaining community may preserve an alternative community, but in the long run it weakens the movement.

Feminism, especially radical feminism, is problematic as a basis for community in a movement made up of men and women because of its bias toward political and cultural separatism. In the direct action movement this bias has been considerably more muted than in the women's movement. Nevertheless, feminism continues to be understood as women's politics. In a movement that questions the separation between personal and political, feminism is most fully represented not only by separate women's actions but also by separate, mostly lesbian, women's communities. On the one hand feminism has made community possible in the direct action movement: without a movement-wide acceptance of the lessons of feminism there would be no hope of egalitarianism in the movement or in its vision. But the question of what feminism means in the context of a mixed movement has not been worked out. There is something disingenuous, inauthentic, and ultimately unconvincing about men's claiming feminism as their own political identity. Furthermore, feminism as a guiding political principle involves a pull toward separatism on both personal and political levels. Lesbian communities have provided the most solid social base for the feminist wing of the movement and have played an important role in the movement as a whole. But the lesbian model is limited. The relationship of heterosexual women to separatism is more mixed: separatism can be liberatory, but because it is only one side of social reality it, too, is limited, even inauthentic.

Many intellectuals who have adopted a postmodernist perspective identify (usually from a distance) with the direct action movement, especially the side of it that is shaped by anarcha-feminism, Paganism, and feminist spirituality. Postmodernism appreciates play, theater, a sense of the absurd and the incongruous, the substitution of irony for a search for value. It also has involved a celebration of consciousness and a rejection of the idea that there are objective forces that limit the ability of human consciousness to shape social reality. The slogan of the French radicals of 1968 was "All power to the imagination!" Radicalism rejecting any limits to social imagination expresses one side of the politics of postmodernism. The other side is an extreme relativism that merges with nihilism: there is no basis for universal values, no dynamic relationship between consciousness and a reality even partially external to it, therefore no basis for effective political action.

The magical politics of the direct action movement make it seem a vehicle for the postmodern sensibility. Magical politics makes sense to a generation of political activists who are fascinated by a popular culture that glorifies alienation and casts doubts on any concept of meaningful or effective action. Postmodernist analysis helps explain why the culture of the direct action movement is so different from earlier mass movements, how politics as theater and magic, as experience and example rather than a social force engaged with other social forces, has come to be so appealing.

But the direct action movement, fortunately for the possibility of sustained and effective political activity, is not merely an expression of postmodernism. It is ultimately based on a powerful and passionate conviction, utterly alien to the spirit of postmodernism, that meaning and values exist and that politics is the attempt to define and act upon them. Feminist spirituality contains the conviction that a fundamental reality exists in the bonds among people and between people and the natural environment. The politics of the direct action movement's religious community are even more explicitly based on a rejection of relativism and nihilism, an assertion of meaning in faith and in history. The opposite of nihilism, a fixed conviction that one knows what is true or good, is also dangerous and has often been the rationale for a movement's attempt to impose its views on others. Perhaps one of the virtues of the movement is that although it believes that there are meaningful objectives to political action, it refuses to settle on any narrow or final formula for the good society but insists that definition lies in the process of its construction.

Chapter Six

The Religious Community

Mass Politics and Moral Witness

Unlike the feminist strand within the direct action movement, which is so enmeshed with the movement as a whole that it is difficult to define its boundaries, the religious, primarily Christian, wing of the movement is a distinct community with its own organizations, which base their politics on traditions that others in the movement are not expected to share, practice rituals in which others are not expected to participate, and employ symbolism that others are not expected to understand. Members of the movement's religious community are not necessarily uninterested in communication. The community is made up of practicing Christians, Catholic and Protestant, and smaller but increasing numbers of religious Jews, some of whom are members of regular congregations. For others, the primary or only religious affiliation is with alternative, often ecumenical, groups identified with the peace movement rather than with any mainstream church or synagogue. In either case, members of the religious community are able to speak to enormous numbers of people whom the rest of the direct action movement has little ability to reach.

Perhaps because of its access to such large and powerful audiences, the religious community has a sense of its own actual and potential power that other sections of the direct action movement sometimes lack. The organizations the religious people create within the movement are more long-lived than others; the religious people themselves, once they become part of the movement, are likely to stick with it through thick and thin. Many are

195

older than those who make up the more counterculturally oriented sections of the movement; many of them have rearranged their lives to make movement activism central; they have found ways to reconcile activism with work and family pressures. The religious community provides a considerable degree of stability for its members; it brings a continuity and steady dedication to the movement that no other community has been able to achieve.

Like the feminist community, the religious community espouses a politics of example rather than one primarily of strategic intervention or efficacy. But unlike the feminists, who come out of a mass movement and a tradition of thinking about politics in social terms, the Christians, who make up the core of the religious community, come out of a tradition that political or moral action is the expression of an individual's responsibility to his or her own conscience. Feminism sees political action as a way of changing people's ideas or social institutions; a substantial current within Christian pacifism sees political action primarily as a form of communication between the individual and God. The tradition of Christian pacifism is one of small groups of highly dedicated people engaging in acts of conscience that have not been tailored to the needs of mass movements. There are religious, especially Christian, direct action groups who are willing to make great sacrifices and are not interested in the needs of a mass movement. But the religious groups that have entered the mainstream of the direct action movement have done so out of the conviction that a mass movement is required for the kind of social change they want—that such a movement can be built around a morally charged vision.

The religious community has found common ground with the rest of the movement in its commitment to a politics of example, but it defines that politics quite differently from others in the movement. For the Pagan-influenced feminist community and many others, exemplary politics is prefigurative politics: it means living, insofar as possible, as one would in the envisioned society. It means self-realization through reconstructing the bonds among people and between people and their natural environment. The power of such a politics comes from the vision it projects and the hope that it might be possible in the present collectively to construct a more whole and fulfilling life. Christian pacifism also involves prefigurative politics, but of a different kind: here the goal is not so much self-realization, at least as Pagans and other non-Christians think about it, as self-abnegation, self-transformation through sacrifice. Sacrifice can also be a path to self-realization and to the creation of bonds with others, especially in a society in which materialism tends to drown out values and destroy genuine human connections. For this reason and also because of its deep roots in Christian tradition and its association with spirituality, self-sacrifice has a genuine appeal. But it leads to a very different kind of politics from that implied by the Pagan feminist perspective.

Nonviolence and the Christian Peace Movement

The roots of the Christian direct action movement lie in the Christian peace movement of the 1950s. The peace movement as a whole, which flourished in the years immediately after World War Two with the widespread hope of world government engendered by the defeat of fascism, suffered a sharp decline in the early 1950s with the onset of the Cold War. Peace activism began to revive in the late fifties because of growing popular disaffection with Cold War policies, the lessening of the hold of McCarthyism over U.S. politics, and signs that the Soviet Union, under Khrushchev, might be open to a less hostile relationship with the United States. The passage of time was also a factor in the reemergence of the peace movement. A new generation of young people who had not lived through World War Two, at least not as adults, who were not committed to finding a new enemy that could take the place of fascism, and to whom the Cold War and anti-Communism did not make a great deal of sense was the constituency for a new peace movement.[1]

The peace movement of the late fifties consisted on the one hand of organizations such as the Committee for a Sane Nuclear Policy (Sane), which relied largely on legal pressure tactics such as demonstrations and newspaper ads, and a radical pacifist wing, largely religiously based, which emphasized civil disobedience. The most prominent of the radical pacifist organizations was the Committee for Non-Violent Action (CNVA), which sponsored the 1958

voyage of the *Golden Rule* with a crew of four Quakers into a
nuclear testing zone in the South Pacific. In 1959 and 1960 this
act was followed by direct action campaigns against an ICBM base
near Omaha, Nebraska, and against the Polaris submarines stationed in New London, Connecticut. Meanwhile the Fellowship
of Reconciliation, another radical pacifist organization, held a two-
year long vigil at the Fort Detrick, Maryland, research center for
chemical, bacteriological, and radiological weapons. From 1955
on, a number of Catholic Workers and other radical pacifists stood
in front of City Hall, in downtown New York, during each annual air raid drill, protesting the program by refusing to take
shelter as the sirens sounded.

Though the radical pacifist organizations remained very small
in comparison with the growing numbers attracted to the legally
oriented wing of the movement, its tactics appealed to young
people throughout the peace movement and were carried into
organizations such as Sane in spite of the protests of the more cautious adult leadership. In 1958 and 1959, high school Sane chapters throughout the New York school system encouraged students
to refuse to follow their teachers to basements and other "protected" areas during the annual air raid drill; so many of these
protests took place in 1959 that in 1960 the city held the annual
air raid drill after high school hours. That year, high school and
college Sane groups held a demonstration in front of City Hall,
during which 2,000 protesters refused to take shelter; the city
had not provided enough police vans to arrest and jail more than
a fraction of those present. It was the last of New York's air raid
drills.[2]

In spite of the appeal of civil disobedience, no attempt was
made to build a mass peace movement around it. The early civil
rights movement first brought the philosophy of nonviolence and
the tactics of direct action to the building of a mass movement.
From the first sit-in, in Greensboro, North Carolina, in February
of 1960, until Black Power in 1965 and 1966, the civil rights
movement relied primarily on nonviolent civil disobedience and
demonstrated the power of this approach for mass organizing.
By the mid-sixties, however, large sections of the movement began to renounce nonviolence in favor of greater militance. Though
the religious pacifist current in the North continued its work and

served to remind many of the values underlying protest, its influence within the movement as a whole declined. The visibility of the nonviolent wing of the movement decreased in part because the media focus turned to more sensational currents, in part because the antiwar movement was attracting large numbers of young people who were angry about the war in Vietnam and uninterested in a politics of nonviolence. The antiwar movement rarely engaged in violence, but it tended to identify militance with violent rhetoric and tactics likely to provoke violence from the other side. Groups such as the War Resister's League and the Fellowship of Reconciliation maintained their nonviolent protest against the war, but the tone of the antiwar movement was set by a student movement that was rapidly escalating its tactics and its language.[3]

Many organizers of the initial antinuclear groups were refugees from the antiwar movement, which by the early seventies was largely burnt out by its own anger. Former antiwar activists, many with ties to the counterculture, who were disappointed in a movement that seemed to have lost touch with its own vision of a better society, readily turned to the Quaker tradition for the articulation of a politics that could be the basis for community. They found allies in two of the most radical offices of the American Friends Service Committee—in Cambridge, Massachusetts, and San Francisco. The early antinuclear groups, especially the Clamshell Alliance, were also assisted by the Movement for a New Society (MNS), a Philadelphia-based group with origins in A Quaker Action Group (AQAG), formed in 1966. AQAG had been centrally involved in the southern civil rights movement; AQAG and later MNS took consensus decision making, nonviolence, and direct action, as they had been practiced in the civil rights movement, as the building blocks of an envisioned nonviolent revolution. Convinced that antinuclear protest had mass potential, MNS activists devoted themselves to building the antinuclear movement and instructing its activists in consensus decision making and the techniques of nonviolent action.[4]

The Quakers thus had a formative influence within the nonviolent direct action movement. But although small numbers of Quakers played an important role in shaping the movement, in numerical terms Quakers never became an important component. And although the Quakers' commitment to nonviolence is based on religion, their influence in the movement has not been experienced as particularly religious; their style has been much more secular than that of the Christian groups that were to join the movement later, as it turned toward the arms race and then Central America.

Some of the religious groupings in the direct action movement originated in protest against the war in Vietnam. In May 1968, Daniel and Philip Berrigan, both Catholic priests, along with a group of Catholic peace activists, destroyed draft files in Catonsville, Maryland, with napalm made according to directions they found in the U.S. Special Forces Handbook. The sense of community among those who had participated in this action was strengthened over the course of several years in jail; they continued civil disobedience against the war on being freed, and by the mid-seventies were making a transition to protest against nuclear weapons.

A number of those involved in these actions, including Philip Berrigan and his wife, Elizabeth MacAllister, a former nun, established Jonah House in Baltimore, where an occasionally shifting community of about ten adults and, more recently, the two Berrigan-MacAllister children have lived ever since. Berrigan and MacAllister, meanwhile, announced their marriage and were formally expelled from the Catholic church. Jonah House has served as a basis for ongoing civil disobedience actions, as a model to other groups of Christian protesters attempting to establish "under-the-roof" communities, and as a focal point for the larger Christian pacifist movement, especially the several East Coast groups that together make up the Atlantic Life Community. In addition to strengthening the bonds among protesters, communal living has had the advantage of being relatively inexpensive and providing the children with care when their parents are in jail.

In 1980, the people from Jonah House, along with others, began a year-long campaign against the Pentagon, coming from around the country to take part in the regular tours led by Pentagon staff. During these tours, protesters poured blood over models of weapons systems, knelt, prayed, and were then arrested. Some were able to leave the tour long enough to enter offices closed to the public and pour blood over files. The idea of holding "Isaiah actions," that is, of attempting literally to beat swords into ploughshares, came from the Pentagon campaign and from the experience of another Christian pacifist group, the Brandywine Peace Community, which had held a witness against the Mark 12A missile. Several of the Brandywine people, along with several people from Jonah House, formed the nucleus of a group that conducted the first of what would eventually be eleven Ploughshares actions in September 1980. Ten activists entered the King of Prussia, Pennsylvania, nuclear weapons plant, severely damaged two missiles, and were subsequently given sentences ranging from eighteen months to ten years.[5]

Meanwhile, Christian or Christian-based protest groups were forming elsewhere in the country. The Atlantic Life Community, which contributed participants to the Pentagon campaign and the Ploughshares actions, consisted of an ongoing under-the-roof community in New Haven, Connecticut, and a number of extended communities elsewhere. On the West Coast, Robert Aldrich, a nuclear engineer, resigned from his job in 1973, charging that the Trident missile he had been working on was a first-strike weapon and therefore in violation of international law. Aldrich persuaded Jim and Shelley Douglass, Catholics and former civil rights and antiwar activists, that the Trident base at Bangor, Washington, should be the focus of a campaign. In 1975, the Douglasses, along with thirteen others, came together to form the Pacific Life Community, committed to nonviolent opposition to the Trident and to self-transformation. Most came from a Christian background, all had been repelled by the rhetoric and style of the antiwar movement in its last days and were convinced that something different was needed. Looking to Gandhi, Martin Luther King, and the Catholic Worker movement for guidance, they organized a public education campaign against the Trident and conducted civil disobedience actions in which, at their height, six to eight thousand people climbed the fence and were arrested.[6]

Though the Douglasses and others hoped to attract large numbers of people to protest nuclear weapons, they also believed that action must originate in a core community in which self-education and self-transformation would be combined with politics. Seven members of the Pacific Life Community moved into a house together, and the whole community held regular meetings in which members examined their personal implications in the system of violence. For men, this examination often meant dealing with sexism and with insensitivity to feelings; for women, it could mean confronting a failure to take responsibility. After about three years, personality clashes and the departure of some members from the area led to a split. Those who remained decided to establish a permanent presence at the base. In 1978, calling itself Ground Zero, the group moved to Poulsbo, Washington, and found a building from which actions at the base have since been conducted. (The Bangor base is immediately to the west of Poulsbo; the plot of land on which Ground Zero has its headquarters lies on the boundary between town and base.) Some of these actions have drawn large numbers of people from the Seattle and Vancouver areas, some have drawn peace activists from further away. But Ground Zero itself has remained a small group of religiously inspired activists who live more or less at subsistence level and who, although they do not share a house, form a tightly knit community that shares resources and helps members with child care and other responsibilities.

Ground Zero then turned toward the creation of a broader community of nonviolent protest. Jim and Shelley Douglass bought a house overlooking the railroad tracks leading to the base, an ideal spot for observing the delivery of weapons components. In 1981, Ground Zero began to contact people living in towns and cities along the railroad tracks linking the Bangor base with other nuclear weapons facilities. Names were provided by Sojourners, a Christian peace ministry coming out of the evangelical churches, and other peace and justice groups in the Christian community, providing the basis for a network called the Agape Community. Members included housewives, some pastors in churches near the tracks, and others who could keep an eye on the tracks during daytime hours, monitor train movements, and organize vigils along the tracks. Most of these trains carried missile motors. In December of 1982, a reporter in Seattle called Jim Douglass to ask if he knew anything about a train probably bearing nuclear warheads going toward the base from Everett, Washington. Jim Douglass walked out of his house and saw a train painted entirely white coming into the train yard, carrying heavily armed men in turrets on top of the cars. The markings indicated that the cars came from Texas; when the train left Bangor, members of the Agape Community traced its route back to the Pantex nuclear-weapons-producing plant in Amarillo. Meanwhile, research into documents from the Washington Utilities and Transportation Commission confirmed that trains with the marking observed on the white train did carry nuclear warheads.

The Agape Community now began to grow rapidly and to focus its attention on white trains. Several months after the first train had been spotted, a new member of the community, a woman in a small town in Colorado, called to say that a letter she sent out to all the members of her church had brought a response from a woman whose husband had been ordered by the railroad to go to Oklahoma to work on a special government train, painted white, with the same markings Jim Douglass had seen on the train entering the base. Vigils were organized in thirty-five towns and cities along the tracks; at Fort Collins, Colorado, and at Bangor, people blocked the train's progress by sitting on the tracks and were arrested. This action required enormous courage, because no one could be sure that the trains would stop. Since that time thirteen white trains have been tracked and protested with vigils and civil disobedience. The Agape Community, meanwhile, grew to encompass groups in roughly three hundred towns and cities across the country.[7]

Liberation Theology and Direct Action

The Christian wing of the direct action movement has origins in the tradition and influence of liberation theology, as well as in the tradition of radical Christian pacifism. By the late seventies, the radical theology that had swept Latin America over the preceding decade was finding a receptive audience among Christians in the United States, especially Catholics, including many who had been unaffected by the largely secular protest movements of the sixties. The growing influence of the Third World in both Catholic and Protestant churches, and the growing emphasis on questions of peace and justice at successive meetings of the World Council of Churches, gave legitimacy to a radical interpretation of Christianity. The murder of Archbishop Romero and then of four American nuns and religious women in El Salvador in 1981 led many American Catholics to feel a personal connection to El Salvador and a personal responsibility for U.S. policy in Central America.

In November of 1983, in the wake of the U.S. invasion of Grenada the month before, fifty-three peace and justice activists from the religious community held a retreat at the Kirkridge Center in Pennsylvania to talk about how to respond if the United States should invade Nicaragua. They committed themselves to travel to Nicaragua in order to stand in the way of U.S.-sponsored violence, whether in the form of an invasion or of attacks by the Contras. The following April, a group of Northern California church people visited the Nicaraguan border town of Jalapa, which had recently suffered attacks by the Contras; some townspeople suggested that the presence of Americans might provide some protection. A larger group of American church people then went to Managua to persuade the Sandinista leadership to give them permission to send Americans to Nicaraguan war zones, to bear witness and to serve as protection to the people living there.

In the United States, a group representing many sections of the Christian peace and justice community (generally called "the religious community" by those within it) decided to establish an ongoing witness in Nicaragua and to call the effort Witness for Peace. The two major centers for this effort were Washington, D.C., and Northern California, especially the San Francisco Bay Area and Santa Cruz. In Washington, the leadership role was taken by Sojourners, an organization founded in 1971 by evangelical Protestants concerned first with the war in Vietnam and then with the arms race. In California a leading role was played by people associated with the radically oriented Graduate Theological Union in Berkeley, many of them connected with the existing direct action movement. Though the initial plan of Witness for Peace was that small numbers of Christians would maintain a long-term witness in war zones, the organization soon decided that more Americans would be educated and more pressure put on the U.S. government by shorter-term visits of larger groups of people. Witness for Peace has sent between 2,500 and 3,000 people to Nicaragua for relatively short stays in the war zones.

The Catholic and Protestant churches have provided the bases for organizing these visits, and the majority of visitors have been adults of all ages from mainstream communities and churches whose lifestyles are far removed from that of the radical peace movement.[8]

The religious community in the United States, while organizing Americans to go to Nicaragua to put themselves between the Contras and their potential Nicaraguan victims, also took on the task of organizing supporters in the United States to commit themselves to civil disobedience in the event of an invasion of Nicaragua. Members of Sojourners and some from the Quaker peace movement in Philadelphia, recalling the decision at the retreat at Kirkridge, called for a pledge of civil disobedience in the event of an invasion of Nicaragua, to be circulated as widely as possible. Meanwhile, religious activists in the Bay Area were thinking along the same lines. In July of 1984 a pledge was agreed upon and the Pledge of Resistance was established to circulate it, to support actions designed to discourage U.S. aid to the Contras, and to pressure the United States to back off from its hostile stance toward Nicaragua. On both sides of the country the religious community was drawn into this effort; like Witness for Peace, it allowed religious radicals to speak to people in mainstream religious communities. In three months, 40,000 people around the country had signed the pledge. The Pledge also encouraged people to set up "solidarity crosses," painted with the names and ages of Nicaraguans killed by the Contras, in front of their houses. Large numbers of these crosses began to appear in cities with radical communities. The Witness for Peace office in the Bay Area began receiving letters from people in places like Elkhorn, Nevada, saying that they had put crosses in their front yards.

The Sanctuary movement is also part of the community of religious activists, and it bears a relation to the direct action movement, though a more distant one than either Witness for Peace or the Pledge of Resistance. Both Witness for Peace and the Pledge appeal to constituencies in the churches, but both have at their core groups of activists who tend to be marginal to their churches and to regard the peace movement and in particular its religious community as their real church. The Pledge of Resistance, which is based on civil disobedience, came out of the radical end of the religious community, which was also very important in the formation of Witness for Peace. The two groups participate in more or less the same culture, and both insist on the use of consensus decision-making process.

The Sanctuary movement, while including religious radicals, comes out of a firmly church-based constituency, and is shaped by a somewhat different culture. Consensus process is not necessarily used, and many in the movement differentiate themselves from the direct action movement, arguing that according to their interpretation of the law, providing sanctuary to refugees is entirely legal. This argument is made most strongly by the wing of the Sanctuary movement that is located in the Southwest. People are more vulnerable there to prosecution than the sanctuary workers in the movement's two other centers, Chicago and the San Francisco Bay Area. Furthermore, by emphasizing the humanitarian side of sanctuary and downplaying its radical political implications, they are able to gain more support in the largely conservative communities of the Southwest. The Chicago group in particular argues strongly for a more explicitly radical approach; not only the Chicago people but many elsewhere in the movement acknowledge that a decisive legal ruling against sanctuary would not persuade them to stop. Nevertheless, the Sanctuary movement is fairly remote from the anarchist feminist philosophy that pervades the direct action movement. There are middle-aged, professionally established people throughout the activist religious community, but in the Sanctuary movement these people set the tone; in Witness for Peace and especially in the Pledge of Resistance, the tone is set more by a younger, more culturally radical group.[9]

The Diversity of Religious Direct Action

In addition to these large organizations, the religious community includes a large number of small groupings; those most involved in the direct action movement tend to call themselves affinity groups, others call themselves communities or, following the Latin American example, base communities. In the San Francisco Bay Area, Spirit, organized by a group of seminary students, and Bardemaeus, also formed by young activists, were the foci of the most radical wing of the religious community and have tended to engage in the highest-risk actions, such as entering offices to destroy files and pouring blood. Mustard Seed, organized by members of the board of the Ecumenical Peace Institute, an umbrella organization for the Bay Area Christian peace movement, is composed of older people and has been more cautious, for the most part simply participating in the civil disobedience of the religious community and the direct action movement generally.

The religious community has primarily been based on ecumenical Christian groups outside the organized churches, but there are some instances of congregations as such participating in the movement; San Francisco's Dolores Street Baptist Church, for instance, which is affiliated with the quite conservative Southern Baptist Convention, was represented by large numbers of its congregation in both of the major blockades of the Livermore Laboratory. More than any other wing of the direct action movement, the religious community has a political life of its own. In the Bay Area, where the religious community is strongest, it has held Good Friday services at the Livermore Laboratory every year since 1981. The first of these was organized by Spirit; since then the entire religious community has become involved in planning and conducting them. As the service has changed over time the distinction between Catholic and Protestant ritual has largely dissolved. The traditional stations of the cross are presented in such a way that Christ's suffering becomes a very broad metaphor for the sufferings of the poor and the politically oppressed. The service is always concluded with civil disobedience.

Though the activist religious community is overwhelmingly Christian, it also includes increasing numbers of Jews, and in a sense the Pagans and witches are part of this community as well. From the beginning there have been many Jews in the direct action movement, but for the most part they have been secularly oriented and have not participated *as* Jews. The large numbers of Jews who participated in the movements of the sixties were caught up in the same rebellion against their upbringing that shaped the movement as a whole; for most, this rebellion meant a dissociation from any Jewish identification. The revival of Judaism that has swept the present generation has touched many on the left, resulting in *chavurot* (religious study groups), *kehilot* (informal religious communities), and even a few radical synagogues oriented toward political activity. For many of these groups, the Sanctuary movement has been the main point of entry into radical politics because it is organized by congregations and has welcomed Jewish participation, and also because of the parallels between repression in Central America and in Hitler's Germany.

Although the Sanctuary movement and the activist religious community are overwhelmingly Christian, radical Jewish groups have been welcomed more wholeheartedly there than in the organized Jewish community, which has, over the last decades, come to represent the center-to-right of American Jews, who identify closely with Israel and are very resistant to criticism of its foreign policies, such as its support for repressive regimes in Central America. Like the radical Christian community, which has enough legitimacy to at least make itself heard in the churches, the Jewish left at least has the credentials to speak to synagogues and within the largely hostile world of the major Jewish organizations. The difference is that the Jewish left has a smaller constituency to draw upon, because traditionally Jewish radicals have been secular. In its early stages, the Zionist movement provided a point of contact between radical and mainstream Jews. As Israel has increasingly identified itself with the right, Zionism has almost entirely lost its appeal to radical Jews. Religion has become the main vehicle of Jewish identification, but the depth of the tradition of secularism among American Jews, especially left Jews, creates special problems for those who are trying to organize a self-consciously Jewish left.

The Pagans, along with the subcategory of witches, should be mentioned in any discussion of the religious sector of the direct action movement, although they are not included in "the religious community" and are different from it in many ways. The orientation the Pagans and witches bring to the movement is genuinely religious. The spiritual tone of the direct action movement as a whole results more from their involvement than that of the Christians. There are more Pagans, in the large actions if not in the ongoing work of the movement, and they have thoroughly incorporated themselves, creating rituals appropriate for the movement as a whole, whereas the Christians have tended to re-

main within their own community and have been more concerned with reaching outward to the churches than in exerting
influence over the direct action movement.

A shared spiritual orientation has been the basis for informal
cooperation between Christians and Pagans. On an individual level
many Christians in the movement become quite sympathetic to
the Pagans, often accepting Paganism and witchcraft as legitimate
religious expression and even participating in Pagan rituals out
of a shared veneration for nature. At times individual Christians
and Pagans have been brought together by their common attraction to metaphor and symbolism and their shared willingness to
take risks. In the early morning hours, before LAG's September
1984 blockade of the Livermore labs, four women, three Pagans
and a Christian, poured blood in front of the Livermore-affili-
ated Sandia Laboratory. These women knew each other from the
Feminist Cluster.

A common spiritual orientation, however, has not eradicated
the differences between Christians and Pagans. On a number of
occasions feminism has bridged what might have been explosive
differences between the two wings of the movement. In the wake
of LAG's two major blockades, when civil disobedience had gained
a certain legitimacy in Berkeley, members of a church in a poor
area of the city began an antiprostitution campaign in which groups
of church members approached prostitutes on the street, surrounded them, and tried to dissuade them from continuing their
work. The priest, who was both the organizer of the campaign
and a member of one of LAG's affinity groups, told the press that
he was applying the technique of civil disobedience he had learned
in his peace movement activities. Many women in LAG were hor-
rified by what they saw as harassment of prostitutes. A group was
organized to urge him to stop; there were threats of civil disobedience at his church. The woman who had called this group together was one of LAG's most prominent Christian activists; though
Pagans and witches attended the meeting, they allowed others to
take the lead and refrained from joining the delegation, afraid
that their presence would turn the discussion into a confrontation
with highly charged historical connotations. As one of the women
said, it would probably not have helped if she were to accompany
the delegation and address the priest with something like, "Hi,

I'm a witch, and I don't like the way you Christians are treating these prostitutes." As it turned out, the priest listened to the objections raised by the delegation and the campaign was called off.

Though Pagans and Christians have cooperated at many points, the religious community as a whole has not tried to establish ties with the Pagan community, partly out of the fear that the mainstream church members they hope to reach would not understand but would be even more hesitant to join the services and actions held by the religious community. Furthermore, even though the Christians and the Pagans share a spiritual orientation to political action, beyond that point their perspectives are diametrically opposed. The spirituality of the Christians is very much tied to suffering, which they invest with religious and political value. The spirituality of the Pagans is based on a celebration of life; they see suffering as something that should be kept to a minimum. To some extent this replays, on a new terrain, old cultural differences between Christians and Jews, who make up a substantial component of the Pagan movement. Within the direct action movement, the sharpest disagreements between the Christians and the Pagans have been over whether long jail sentences should be seen as valuable in and of themselves. Though this debate is mainly about the value of suffering, it also reflects different attitudes toward authority; many of the Christians are willing to grant the state, and social authorities more generally, a legitimacy the Pagans do not concede. The Christians are often uncomfortable with the earthiness and rowdy antiauthoritarianism of the Pagan anarchists, particularly the movement's feminist community. As a result of the tensions and differences between the two groups, Christians and Pagans have for the most part stood at different ends of the direct action movement.

Faith, Politics, and History

The religious community brings to the direct action movement an ability to articulate the large questions of meaning that drew them into the movement and sustain their political activity. The connection they feel between faith and political work was described by Ken Butigan, a former member of Spirit, now a staff worker for the Pledge of Resistance. Ken went with Spirit to Seattle not as a participant in the blockade against the Trident but to support those who did. For two weeks, the blockaders went out in boats each morning, not knowing whether the Trident would come in that day, and not entirely sure that they would return. The Trident might stop when it saw them, or it might plough right through their boats. Darla Rucker and Terry Messman were both participants in the blockade; Darla, who uses a wheelchair, needed special assistance getting on and off the boat each day. Ken recalled,

Each morning I would go down to the water with Darla and Terry, I would carry Darla down to the *Zodiac*, one of the boats that Greenpeace had provided. Each time I did that I realized I might never see them again. There was the possibility they both might be killed. Then, after they floated out, there was the waiting, a contemplative vigil on the shore. That letting go, then receiving back again did more to create a sense of community than I've ever experienced before. By the time the sub actually came, I was reconciled to it. We are given our lives by the Spirit, for justice, for creating community; we offer our lives back. Sometimes our lives are taken, sometimes they're given back, a kind of continuous ballet with the universe, reciprocating, breathing in and out. Sometimes it takes a lot of courage, sometimes it takes putting up with boredom, or attention to details, so we can get the work done. That doesn't make it any less religious.[10]

The religious community tends to bring to the movement a historical perspective that other sectors lack. The Pagans, the witches, and the anarchists have adopted their beliefs rather than grown up in them, and the traditions with which they have come to identify lack the solid continuity of organized religion. For both the Christians and the religious Jews who are increasingly being drawn into the movement, the Holocaust, and to a lesser extent Hiroshima, are the reference points that transformed the nature of both religion and social action, having set problems for humanity that require a new kind of response. Spiritually informed, nonviolent direct action, members of the religious community argue, is a step toward such a response, because it addresses the problem of violence, it focuses on individual responsibility for personal and social transformation, and it provides the basis for a prefigurative community that can sustain activism and serve as a model of a better society.

Jim Rice, a staff member of Sojourners, in Washington, D.C., told me that the Holocaust is the central image that guides his political work; over the last few years he has read many books on it, drawn over and over to the questions of why it happened and why the German Christians failed to stop it. For him the Holocaust is a metaphor for the depravity of which human beings are capable. "It teaches an important lesson about the nuclear arms race. One of our defenses is, it can't happen; but it can, people have done that. The 'never again' image is important, and not just for Jews. I think a lot about that: what would I have done if I had been in Germany? Because of Hiroshima, because of the escalation of violence in World War Two, Hitler won. The good guys dropped the bomb."[11]

For many of the Christians in the movement, the central lesson of the Holocaust is that the churches did little if anything to stop it. "The Holocaust has been an important symbol for the religious community," Ron Stief, former chair of Witness for Peace, points out.

People are aware that the Holocaust happened with the full support of the churches. There were notable exceptions, Bonhoffer and others, but basically the people who knew it was happening said, there's nothing we can do about it. Hitler got away with murdering the Jews because the churches sat there and didn't do anything. Are we going to sit here and let Reagan get away with murdering people in Central America, or are we going to do something about it?[12]

The Holocaust also shapes the outlook of religious Jewish activists, though for them the issues that it raises are posed somewhat differently. David Cooper, organizer and lay leader of the movement-oriented Kehilah Synagogue in Berkeley and a Sanctuary activist, points out that if Jews are going to criticize Christians for not having come to their aid in Nazi Germany, they must come to the aid of equally helpless people in Central America. On a broader level, he argues, the Holocaust sets the background for all social action in our time—especially for Jews but for others as well. Whether or not activists are consciously aware of it, he claims, the Holocaust has posed the questions that social movements must now address.

The Holocaust told us that as human beings we are capable of anything given sufficient technology. It applies to Hiroshima and the future holocaust of the planet as well. Hiroshima tells us that the bomb is destructive and Auschwitz tells us that we are potentially destructive. Earlier generations could rely on God's intervention; now we have to rely on our own intervention. Perhaps that's how God acts. For the generation before us, these were things that happened in their lifetime; to confront these things, a new generation had to grow to maturity. As in the Bible—you would think that the generation that had known slavery would know it was not good to go back to, but in fact it was those people who were nostalgic when they came to the desert. After forty years in the desert, it is possible that a new generation can lead the way out.[13]

Liberation theology and the example of Christianity as a revolutionary force in Central America have greatly influenced the way both Christianity and social activism are viewed within the religious community. Through the mid-seventies, liberation theology was accessible to an English-speaking audience primarily through the theological works of Gustavo Gutierrez, Leonardo Boff, and others; by the late seventies and early eighties, it was being popularized by articles in *Sojourners* magazine and by theologian Robert McAfee Brown. Brown's *Theology in a New Key: Responding to Liberation Themes* and *Unexpected News: Reading the Bible with Third World Eyes* brought liberation theology to American Christians in terms that they could understand.[14] Many of those who are now part of the activist religious community were untouched by the movement against the war in Vietnam, which largely bypassed the churches, and were introduced to social protest by events in Central America in the late seventies and early eighties. Marilyn Chilcote, the pastor of St. John's Presbyterian in Berkeley and the chairwoman of the East Bay Sanctuary Covenant, grew up in a conservative family and community and was, she says, "asleep in the sixties." As a seminary student, through contact with Central American activists, she came to believe that they had a much clearer understanding of the Bible than Americans, one that Americans urgently needed to hear. "Third world people," Chilcote said, "are much more like the people the Bible was written for than we are. When the Central Americans talked about discipleship, about faithfulness, it had a ring of integrity, of validity. I was grasped by a vision of what the church at its best can be."[15]

Radical Christianity and Marxism

Introduced to Marxism by liberation theology, the religious community has found it a powerful tool for understanding social conflict and outlining a vision of a just society. Many Christian activists are attracted to Marxism because they see it as compatible with Biblical social criticism. American churchgoers, they claim, will often accept a radical viewpoint if it is presented in Biblical terms. Ron Stief of Witness for Peace points out that protest against oppression and the injunction to take the side of the poor and the powerless are recurrent themes in the Bible.

In a presentation to a church, I will say, Jesus talked about commitment to the poor, changing society to one that would be just to the widow, to the poor. Everyone in the congregation knows that's in the Bible. Then I say, in the Old Testament, if the king gets out of hand, a prophet will come and say no. I make a connection to what's happening in Nicaragua. I talk about it at a human level, at the level of justice. The Bible says, you should not oppress people. When you point that out, people feel like they're getting ripped off by our government. Marxist analysis is very close to the analysis of the [Biblical] Jesus movement. The conditions then were very much like the conditions in Nicaragua under Somoza. So there's a close affinity in language between the two.[16]

Ironically, the religious community has gravitated toward terms of class and oppression associated with Marxism just as the secular left has begun to lose confidence in those categories and in Marxist analysis generally. In a sense, the traditional, secular left has lost its faith in the future: existing socialism no longer offers a compelling vision, and few on the left believe that it is likely, much less inevitable, that a socialist revolution will take place in time to halt the drift toward catastrophe. One reason that the Christian left is now able to espouse Marxism with an enthusiasm the secular left lacks is that Christians have in faith what secular

Marxists once had in dialectical materialism. The combination of Marxist analysis and Christian faith, an identification with an international Christian revolutionary movement, gives American Christian radicals the strength to continue their work even when it does not seem to be having much immediate effect.

The religious community has turned to Marxism for an analysis of oppression and class struggle, but it understands those terms somewhat differently from secular Marxists. Traditionally, Marxists have looked for groups that not only are oppressed but have as yet unrecognized access to a power that will transform them into agents of revolution. The working class is at the center of Marxist theory not only because it is exploited, but also because it is so situated in capitalist society that when it becomes self-conscious and mobilized, it will be capable of creating a revolution. Marxism has identified other oppressed groupings, such as women and racial and ethnic minorities; but because potential revolutionary power is assumed to lie with the working class, Marxists have concentrated on the linkages between oppressed groups and the working class.

The radical Christians are much more interested in oppression itself than in how a group is situated to exert power. They are relatively uninterested in the working class as such: they seek to organize the abused and powerless. The categories the Christians are drawn to are, not surprisingly, fundamentally moral. The religious community has, for instance, taken up the issue of homelessness. Terry Messman has turned to full-time organizing of the homeless in Oakland, California, and he tries to develop ties between the people he is organizing and the religious community by efforts such as bringing busloads of them to the Good Friday services at the Livermore labs. There is a very thin line between taking the side of the poor and taking on their burdens; within the religious community there is a good deal of respect for those who have voluntarily given up middle-class existence in order to live in poverty.

The Christians' emphasis on identifying with the oppressed is closely related to the value they place on suffering and the moral power they believe it confers. Going to jail, for the Christians, is often a religious experience in itself. Terry Messman illustrates this view with a story about how he joined the movement. As a journalism student at the University of Montana, he interviewed members of the Mountain Life Community, a radical Christian group in Missoula that was planning to hold a worship service at the gates of the Malmster Air Force Base, an ICBM command and control center, and then to carry wooden crosses into the base and be arrested. Terry was particularly moved by his interview with John Lemnitzer, a Lutheran minister.

On the day of the action, I watched John walk across the white line with his cross and be surrounded by military guards. It was a moment of conversion for me. I stopped being a journalist. I laid down my pen and notebook in the road, joined John, and was arrested. We spent Easter night in jail. That night my faith became real to me. I worshipped the God of peace and love for the first time. I understood what being part of the body of Christ meant; we are to risk our freedom and eventually our lives.[17]

Going to jail can be a spiritual experience not only because it is a form of sacrifice but also because it forces a coming to terms with issues that are at the root of both religious faith and political commitment. Ken Butigan, another member of Spirit, was arrested along with two others for pouring blood at the San Francisco Federal Building to protest U.S. aid to the Contras; he was given a forty-five day sentence. He was separated from the others and during his internment was sent to four different prisons, with long periods of travel from one to the next.

When you're in transit you're totally cut off. By the time I got to Terminal Island [Prison] it was the end of fifteen days of isolation, and it all caught up with me. I remember sitting on my bunk, and even though this wasn't the gulag, or even what people experience in Salvador, I felt the void. I felt abandoned by God, by my community. My rational side wasn't there. I sat with that feeling of nothingness for about half an hour. Then this sense came: you will never be abandoned. I started to cry, quietly, because I had a cell mate. I realized that I was a lot stronger for having gone through that sense of abandonment. After that it was OK.[18]

The willingness of many radical Christians to act on their consciences and suffer the consequences gives them a certain preeminence in the movement but also makes them leery of attention to political strategy. Many argue that their responsibility is to offer witness; the results are in God's hands. This approach leads groups such as Jonah House to ignore the question of building a mass movement and concentrate on actions that bring long jail sentences and are restricted to a small group of activists. Philip Berrigan argued in defense of this approach that "jail witness is a long-term testimony of what is being done to the best people in this country. It is a consistent reminder of what this society is really about. The movement is strongest when it has the greatest number of sisters and brothers in jail, because of the tremendous appeal to conscience." Suffering, for the radical Christians, is also of value because of the role that it plays in self-transformation. Jail, Berrigan argues, matures and strengthens people, deepens spirituality and commitment to nonviolence, and helps to create a movement that embodies the values it professes.[19]

Although many people in the movement are not Christians and even enter with an entrenched aversion to Christianity's history of intolerance and imperialism, the Christian activists have readily found a place in the movement. They are widely respected for their willingness to take exemplary action, and their emphasis on moral witness overlaps significantly with the anarchist, feminist, and Pagan orientation toward what I have called a politics of experience. Both are forms of magical politics, in the sense that they rely heavily on symbol and ritual to transform consciousness, and in the sense also that they easily slide over into forms of magical thinking. Believing in a connection between the degree of self-sacrifice an action requires and its political impact is like believing in the literal efficacy of prayer, which is also very much like believing that a Pagan ritual can summon the power of the Goddess and thus have an immediate effect on material reality, or that a sufficiently massive direct action will close a plant, regardless of the social forces arrayed behind the nuclear industry or the arms race.

Though all forms of Christian activism in the movement emphasize moral witness, only a minority of the movement's Christians understand moral witness primarily in terms of actions by individuals or small groups. The Christian radicals in the mainstream of the direct action movement are much more concerned with building a mass movement on the streets than are the Jonah House people. Many of the former also see a need to balance

moral witness and political efficacy. Carolyn Scarr of the Mustard
Seed affinity group, who calls herself a "Unitarian mystic," pointed
out that actions designed only to offer witness can become ritual-
ized. The police are informed in advance that a group of Christians will, say, hold a service and then sit in the road in front of
the Livermore labs; the police know that the action will involve a
small group of well-behaved people, and they are likely to be co-
operative and even friendly. Actions of moral witness can become
just as safe as conventional political activity.

It's easy to get pushed into a little place of permitted dissent carried
out within the system, while the system rolls on unimpeded. Either
way your actions are stymied. What you're left with is the uneasy
middle ground of tension between the two, and uncertainty. And
that's the only place where anything can get done, I think.[20]

Within the religious community, there are great variations in
willingness to go to jail for extended periods and take other risks;
generally the younger people, those who are part of the counterculture or in other ways have radically cut themselves off from
mainstream American society, are willing to risk the most for their
principles. The religious community, however, is united by the
sense of political activity as an expression of faith and of the
peace movement—in particular the religious community of
the peace movement—as church. The interdenominational character of most religious groups strengthens their members' sense
of the religious community as a "saving remnant," a seed of spirituality within a corrupted establishment.

Some members of the community have found a great deal of
sympathy and support for their political activity within their
churches; others have gone through difficult trials. Lee Williamson, for instance, a member of Mustard Seed, was the pastor of
the Methodist church in Pleasanton, California, close to Livermore; a number of his parishioners were employees of the labs.
Williamson joined LAG and was arrested and went to jail in June
of 1983; these events set off a bitter conflict in his church between those who wanted the church to take on the role of a peace
church and those who disapproved of Williamson's action. His
opponents were able to obtain his removal; he is now the pastor
of an inner-city church in San Francisco with an older congrega-

tion and considerably less opportunity for innovative work.[21] Carolyn Scarr remembers a meeting of Mustard Seed at which, for the benefit of a visitor, each member identified his or her church. Williamson said that he worshipped at Mustard Seed.

Ken Butigan echoes this sense of the movement as church from the more radical wing of the community. He recalls Shelley Douglass of Ground Zero telling him about her participation in the march on Selma for civil rights in 1965, in which she saw

a community gathered together, casting out fear, participating in a movement for peace and justice—that was her first real experience of church. I don't want to say that the peace movement is a religion, but for those of us who are open to it there are elements of initiation, of sacramentality, of transformation, of tradition. If I were to die I feel that what I've been involved in will carry the torch, that the work will go on.[22]

Spirituality and Community

The ideal of community shapes daily life for the Christian activists to a greater extent than it does for most people in the direct action movement, with the exception of some of the Pagan anarchists. The members of Mustard Seed provide support for one another in a variety of ways: when members of the group are arrested, there is a bail kitty to call upon; and when they go to jail, others take care of their children and look after the details of daily life. There is a sense of extended family among the members; children regard the adults more or less as aunts and uncles. The group meets monthly for worship and political discussion; every summer there is a camping trip, and other events—such as wine tasting before a meeting at the house of a Sonoma County member—are organized spontaneously. Members of Mustard Seed see it as a permanent fixture in their lives.

Many of the more radical Christian affinity groups have been shorter-lived, partly because members are younger and less settled, and partly because not everyone can meet the high level of expectations. While these groups last, however, the sense of community is even stronger. Spirit was formed out of about ten students at the Union Theological Seminary in Berkeley who came together through a Christian action at the Livermore labs. When the affinity group was formed, they all lived within a two-block radius, close to the school. Darla Rucker and Terry Messman were the only married couple in the group; they were also the only couple with children. Their house became the center where meetings were held, leaflets were produced, and anyone who temporarily needed a place to live was likely to stay; and on most days at least a few members of the group passed through the house on one errand or another. Darla Rucker remembers,

There was always a group you knew you were going to act with, there was always support, always people to pick you up when you got out of jail. After one action, Pat got out before we expected her to. She called our house. Someone ran and got a cake, someone got champagne, we all got in a car, when she came out she was greeted by all of us. Every event that was important to one of us, we were all there; when my son was born every single person was in the room with me. We celebrated holidays together. People would sleep on our floor so they would be there on Christmas morning when the kids woke up. It was the most wonderful experience of my life.[23]

Spirit lasted for about three years. It broke up primarily because of its inability to absorb different levels of political commitment; some people saw political work as their central life commitment, while others wanted to find room to pursue other goals. Darla, Terry, and Ken, who organized Spirit and were central to it while it lasted, have continued to be mainstays of the direct action movement and of the radical wing of the religious community. Darla pointed out that many of the radical religious groups consist of a core that lasts more or less indefinitely and a periphery that comes and goes; this is true of Jonah House and of many of the Catholic Worker households around the country.

Communities such as Jonah House, which operate mostly on their own, avoid some of the pressures faced by groups like Spirit that have tried to carve out a role for Christian radicalism within a mass movement. One of Spirit's problems was that some of its members were not, in the long run, willing to make the higher commitment or take the risks. The differences within the group over individual levels of commitment came to the surface as many members approached graduation and began to plan their future lives. But those were probably not the only factors in Spirit's demise. Another radical Christian group in the Bay Area, Bardemaeus, broke up over similar issues at about the same time, even though it was not made up of students. Both of these groups were formed as the larger movement was growing in the early eighties; both fell apart when the movement as a whole declined several years later. In any cycle of the direct action movement, differences are easily tolerated or, in the heady atmosphere of political enthusiasm, not seen in the early period of growth. When the movement becomes stronger and is forced to deal seriously with issues of strategy, differences are likely to surface; as the movement declines, a general feeling of disappointment makes those differences appear stark and insurmountable. This pattern is particularly pronounced among the religious activists because they hold each other to such high standards. But even when affinity groups fall apart and the movement as a whole declines, many of the religious activists find ways of continuing their political work.

Radical Christianity and the Politics of Moral Witness

The religious community has been a more stable base for ongoing direct action than any other part of the movement because it draws inspiration from a powerful international movement. Its ties to churches and other religious organizations in the United States give it resources other sections of the movement lack; it has access to a broad constituency. Most religious activists are members of churches; some of them are pastors or are very active in church affairs. The fact that their radicalism is rooted in religion tends to give it a certain legitimacy in the eyes of other religious people. Sherry Beville, for instance, who for years has been, along with her husband, one of the most active members of St. Leander's in the Bay Area city of San Leandro, was introduced to religious radicalism through the Catholic Crucillo movement. At a series of Crucillo meetings she saw films about conditions in Latin America and the responsibility of the multinational corporations; she began reading on the Third World, attending other films and workshops, and making a connection between militarism and hunger. After about two years of this exploration she attended a retreat at an ecumenical religious center where

she made a pledge to take nonviolence training and do civil disobedience at the Livermore Laboratory. She took the training with
members of the Ecumenical Peace Institute, and with them formed
Mustard Seed. Since then she has been involved in political work
around the questions of disarmament and U.S. involvement in
Central America and has been jailed a number of times.

Sherry continues to be an active member of her church, where
she is listened to with respect ("I'm seen as a nice middle-class
person, raising a family," she says) and in a variety of ways she
and her husband have been able to bring others in the church to
support the movement. At first Sherry was taken aback by the
lesbians, witches, and Pagans she met in the movement, but she
says that she has learned a great deal from getting to know lesbians. She has gained respect for the Pagans and acknowledges
that they, too, are deeply spiritual and that the religion they practice is as genuine as hers. As they have become involved in the
direct action movement, Sherry and her husband have increased
their involvement in their own church, where Frank has now become a deacon, and Sherry's role as a deacon's wife enhances her
leadership. Sherry, Frank, and others like them play a crucial role
in bridging the direct action movement and a constituency in which
many people are open to its aims.[24]

In addition to having access to a clearly defined and often receptive constituency, the religious activists have more access to
institutional support than do other sections of the direct action
movement. The religious community is particularly large in the
San Francisco Bay Area, partly because there are many churches
in the area sympathetic to the peace movement, and partly because the Graduate Theological Union attracts students from all
areas of the country by its orientation toward a radical form of
Christianity. The Graduate Theological Union provides ongoing
support for religious activism by sponsoring projects, seminars,
and lectures. The churches in the Bay Area, and in Northern
California, both Protestant and Catholic, provide a base for social
activism that often overlaps or merges with the direct action
movement.

Of the roughly two hundred churches that have declared sanctuary nationwide, about a hundred are in Northern California
and about twenty-five in the Bay Area. Because of the legitimacy

the churches provide for such activities, and widespread public support, it would be very difficult for the authorities to arrest sanctuary workers as they have in the Southwest. An Alameda County sheriff, asked by the press what he intended to do about churches providing sanctuary, said that if he knew of a church engaged in such activities he would have to make an arrest, but that he knew of no such church.

The indirect support the churches provide for the movement is perhaps most apparent in the Bay Area, but it is significant throughout the country. Organizations such as Pax Christi, the Center of Concern, and the Christic Institute directly or indirectly nourish the radical strand within the Catholic church; Clergy and Laity Concerned does the same for the Protestant churches. While these groups have no organizational link with the direct action movement, they help build an atmosphere of support that encourages some church members to join the movement or to support it in other ways. The network of Christian activist organizations provides some members of the direct action religious community with jobs, gives them access to contacts nationwide, and also often makes it easier for them to organize their lives around political activity. In the sixties and early seventies, the influence of the left was sustained in large part by a similar network of organizations. As the organized strength of the secular left has declined, the left wing of the churches has in a sense taken its place.

The religious community has also strengthened the direct action movement by emphasizing a direct, immediate humanitarianism that is not as prominent in nonreligious activism and that broadens the movement's appeal. Witness for Peace delegations protect specific Nicaraguan villages by placing themselves between the Contras and their intended victims. Sanctuary workers risk their own freedom to keep Central American refugees from being returned to repression and possibly death. Nonreligious activists contribute to the same aims, but usually focus on broad political change rather than on the lives of particular people.

The religious community's emphasis on helping those in need appeals not only to religious people but to many others whose first concern is to make the world a better place in some concrete way. Will Lotter, who along with his wife Jane is a key Sanctuary worker in Davis, California, said that he was attracted to the movement because "it was one thing you could do that would actually make a difference in a refugee's life. This was something I could actually do to visibly say no to our government's policy. It has given me a real sense of satisfaction. We've met lots of refugees; it's been neat. You have some real substance to your activity." In the Bay Area, many people have joined or rejoined churches in large part to be able to work with the Sanctuary movement. Will Lotter, who is a member of a church that voted to declare sanctuary, came to the movement from a humanitarian rather than a religious perspective, but he says that those differences do not matter within the movement: the spirit is the same. Thus far the Sanctuary movement has not fully confronted the issue of civil disobedience, because it argues that its activity is legal. If providing sanctuary to refugees were finally declared illegal, Will Lotter said, many in the movement would continue their work on grounds of prior obedience to a higher religious law. He would break the law in order to defend someone's life.[25]

At a time of religious revival in the United States and for that matter in much of the world, the direct action movement's orientation toward spirituality is an important part of its appeal, and the ability of the religious community to link the movement to broader religious constituencies is crucial to the movement's vitality and growth. But the Christian perspective reinforces some problems of the direct action movement that have arisen from other sources and introduces problems of its own. Many people in the religious community regard strategic thinking as incompatible with a spiritual approach to politics, which, they argue, means acting on the basis of one's conscience, not calculating effects. In fact the influence of the religious activists is enhanced by their obvious sincerity, their lack of interest in tailoring their actions and statements to what the public might be comfortable with. Small groups can afford to disregard strategy, and so can a mass movement, at least for a limited time, especially if it coexists with other movements that are willing to devote more attention to strategic thinking. If it were to become a larger component of protest generally, the direct action movement, including its religious community, would have to address the question of strategy more seriously.

Radical Christianity creates problems also for the development of a prefigurative and radically democratic movement. A politics that emphasizes self-sacrifice may command respect, but it is likely to have trouble attracting large numbers of participants. Liberation theology, which places the same emphasis on self-sacrifice as American radical Christianity, is the basis for massive popular movements. But in Latin America this politics takes place in a context of pervasive poverty and political repression: there it is more a matter of honoring the suffering that fills most people's lives than of calling upon them to give things up. For Latin American priests and intellectuals, liberation theology implies forgoing a certain level of comfort and security, but it also brings incorporation into a powerful and inspiring mass movement, which has its own rewards. Radical Christians like to point out that poor people in the Third World understand the message of the Bible easily because it is about oppression and resistance in a society very much like those they live in. Biblical politics may require more reinterpretation to provide a basis for a mass movement in the United States. The Pagan anarchists lack the cultural legitimacy that the Christian activists can call upon, but it may be that their concept of prefigurative politics, which rejects the language of self-sacrifice and tries to create the basis for a whole and fulfilling life in the present, may be a better basis for a mass movement.

The most serious problem with the Christian perspective, for the direct action movement, is that its moral elitism leads to some ambivalence about egalitarian democracy. Like the feminists, the radical Christians believe in leadership by example; but for the Christians example is tinged with a heroism that is often incompatible with collective action. In believing that faith and willingness to take special risks give them a special claim to morality, the radical Christians implicitly set up moral hierarchies that are antithetical to the spirit of grass roots democracy and that coexist uneasily with the consensus process. Debates in jail about whether or not to accept relatively lengthy sentences often turn into debates about moral superiority and inferiority. There are some differences on these issues within the religious community: the Catholics are likelier to take risky action and also more willing to abandon democratic process. One Catholic priest, for instance, who has been to jail many times and who is supported in his activity by only a minority of his congregation declared his church a sanctuary for Central American refugees. He was condemned for not consulting the congregation first. He did not regret his action. "You don't vote on morality," he said. "Morality will lose every time."

Chapter Seven

Radical Politics in Late Capitalist Society

This book is directed toward two sometimes overlapping audiences: students of social movements, especially those who want to understand why the movements of the postwar era have taken forms so different from those of earlier times, and movement activists, especially those who want to make these movements broader and more effective. Both audiences are, or should be, concerned about the inadequacies of social movement theory and more broadly about the crisis in the theory of social change. Traditional Marxism looked to the emergence of a revolutionary working class that would be able to overthrow capitalism and establish socialism. At least through the 1930s this perspective provided a framework for understanding the movements of the advanced capitalist nations, in which working-class struggles were central. Marxism also provided a theory for understanding the structure of society and a guide to strategy.

In the postwar era, the working class can no longer be described as likely to play the guiding role in movements for social change. Although it is true that an expanded definition of the working class allows the claim that the constituencies of postwar social movements are drawn largely from that class, those movements have not for the most part identified themselves in terms of class or addressed class issues. The crisis of Marxism has become particularly apparent in the 1970s and 1980s; nonviolent direct action is a striking example of a movement that has had little use for Marxism and that cannot be explained within the traditional Marxist framework. The question for the movement is, If Marxism does not provide a guide to strategy, what theory, or theories, can be put in its place? The movement has not found an answer. Anarchism, spirituality, feminism, and nonviolence all provide standpoints for the development of a critique and an alternative vision, but none in itself addresses the question of strategy. Strategic thinking is lacking in the movement no doubt partly because there has been no coherent intellectual framework within which it could take place.

The crisis of Marxism has spurred students of social movements to find new ways of understanding the sources of protest. Among scholars in the United States, the approach to this question has been circuitous. Before asking why the nature of protest has changed, it was first necessary to cast off the pluralist perspective that dominated the social sciences in the fifties, which was more interested in condemning oppositional movements as "irrational" than in understanding what motivated them. In the seventies, social scientists who supported protest made a case for the political rationality of protest movements and also developed analytical tools those movements could use in pursuing their aims. But this literature is not very useful for understanding why protest as a whole has changed, nor does it explain movements such as the direct action movement that reject conventional ideas of political rationality.

It is the scholars collectively known as New Social Movement theorists, mostly Western Europeans, who have made the greatest contributions to these questions. Building on twentieth-century developments in Marxism, they have put forward a framework for understanding late capitalism that explains much of what is new about the movements of the postwar era. This effort has been related to the postmodern attempt to understand the transformation of culture in the postwar era, and the literature has contributed important insights into late capitalist protest movements. But New Social Movement theory and postmodernism have nevertheless fallen short of providing a satisfactory guide to understanding the movements of the postwar era. In different ways, these perspectives help to explain the diffuse and fragmentary nature of these movements, but fail to address their striving toward coherence and universality, a striving that is present throughout the new movements but is especially strong in the direct action movement. New Social Movement theory has had little influence within the direct action movement, at least in the United States, partly because of the anti-intellectual tendency within the movement, partly because the theory is mostly European and often abstract and obscure, even when translated into English. But the same could be said of the writings of Karl Marx and other Marxists.

The unfortunate fact is that New Social Movement theory is by and large academic in a way that Marxism, at its best, was not. The theory has provided some tools for understanding the new movements but virtually none for advancing movement strategy. Though the New Social Movement theorists have generally been supporters of the new movements, in some cases actively engaged, the theory has not identified itself with those movements and their prospects as Marxism did in relation to the movement of the working class. The result has been a gain in modesty but a loss in theoretical power. In this chapter, I will trace the efforts to develop a framework for understanding the movements of the postwar era, in the United States and especially in Europe, using the experience of the direct action movement as a point of reference. If what is helpful about these theories can be distinguished from what is not, it may be possible to find a more satisfactory approach, one capable of combining the analytic and the strategic.

The pluralist perspective that dominated the study of social movements in the United States in the 1950s and into the 1960s was shaped by a distrust of social movements and a desire to show that the United States was fundamentally different from Europe. Whereas the histories of European nations might produce class conflict and a need for social change, in the United States such things were unnecessary—were based on personal or social pathology and politically irrational.[1] Many of the liberal intellectuals who identified with this view had once been sympathetic to radicalism and to movements for social change, but the emergence of fascism and Stalinism on the other side of the Atlantic had led them to fear the power of popular movements and to hope that the United States was indeed different. Many of them regarded McCarthyism as a milder example of what could go wrong when established political institutions were disrupted, and educated elites challenged, by popular forces.[2]

One of the most salient elements of the social movements of the postwar era has been the claim that established political institutions are obstacles to social change and that radical social movements, though they may participate in the political arena, must have a base outside it and a critique of it. Because this claim was not comprehensible to pluralism, the pluralist perspective has not been a resource for the study of postwar social movements, least of all the direct action movement, which defines itself by the effort to create a politics outside the electoral arena. The one virtue of the pluralist perspective, in relation to the study of the new social movements, is its insistence on emotion and irrationality as an element of politics. Emerging in the 1950s, pluralism was infused with a Freudian perspective that recognized the unconscious but unfortunately (though very much in the Freudian tradition) viewed it as a danger to civilized rationality. Pluralist accounts of social movements have almost universally used psychological analysis as a way of discrediting the movements they have studied.

The new social movements call for a theory that recognizes the psychological, particularly the direct action movement, which rests so much of its appeal on ritual and the construction of community. But what is called for is a theory that goes beyond the view that rationality is inherently positive and irrationality inherently negative. The conscious and the unconscious are intertwined in all forms of political life, not just in social movements. A theory capable of understanding the relationship between the two and developing it in a constructive way would have to recognize that both levels are not only necessarily present but equally legitimate.

The Rationality of Collective Action: Resource Mobilization Theory

Those who had participated in or had been inspired by the movements of the 1960s and began to write about contemporary and past movements in the late sixties and seventies understandably were not persuaded by the pluralist perspective. Those who came to be known as the Resource Mobilization School rejected the pluralists' assumption that protest was irrational; they saw protest as a rational response to inequality and injustice. The pluralists located themselves as external critics of movements for social change; the Resource Mobilization analysts identified with the aims of the movements they studied and asked how these movements attracted particular constituencies, how they achieved their influence, and why some were more effective than others.

Resource Mobilization theory argued that a movement's success or failure could be explained by its ability to mobilize resources, including a mass base, funds and equipment, and leverage in relation to those in power; it emphasized the importance of exploiting political differences within ruling elites in order to gain support from elements of the elite. This approach made possible rich accounts of the experiences of particular social movements, by enabling students of those movements to step intellectually inside the object of study, to look at the problems the movements faced and their solutions from a point of view very close to that of the people actually involved.[3] Resource Mobilization theorists also drew from their work conclusions with practical value for an audience of movement activists. For instance, William Gamson, a prominent Resource Mobilization analyst, argued that successful movement recruitment tends to be based on appeals to preexisting networks rather than to unrelated individuals; this argument has been of interest to organizers looking for ways of rebuilding the peace movement in the 1980s.[4]

The Resource Mobilization School was an important step forward in the study of social movements, but it was more useful for the study of some movements than others. The direct action movement is a particularly bad candidate for the Resource Mobilization approach, the strength of which was its sympathetic identification with the movements it studied and its ability to take their goals and their efforts to achieve those goals seriously. Its weakness was its assumption that movement success must be measurable in terms of the achievement of concrete goals or concessions from those in power. It left little room for the transformation of consciousness, in society or in the movement, or the building of community as a significant movement goal.[5] Resource Mobilization analysis took the rules of existing democratic politics for granted and asked how movements for social change could op-

erate most effectively within that system. Its assertion of the rationality of protest made it a good tool for assessing effectiveness
but a poor tool for understanding the sources of political engagement.

Resource Mobilization theory could help in explaining why the
movements of the sixties failed or succeeded in achieving specific
aims, but it did not go very far toward explaining the origins of
the particular passions that shaped those movements.[6] The usefulness of Resource Mobilization theory diminishes as movements
that operate outside this arena and emphasize the transformation
of consciousness become more widespread. In the context of the
late 1970s and the 1980s, the Nuclear Freeze would be a good
candidate for Resource Mobilization analysis. But the direct action movement, with its emphasis on personal transformation and
community, its lack of interest in political power, is either incomprehensible or a failure in terms of this theory.

In Western Europe, the study of social movements has taken a
different path, resulting in a different set of problems. Because
of the historically closer connections between European intellectuals, the left, and Marxism, in Europe the legitimacy of social
movements has largely been taken for granted. There has been
no parallel, among European intellectuals or in European universities, to the American battle between the pluralists and their critics. The terrain of debate about social movements in the postwar
period has been the legacy of Marxism; the issues have been how
that legacy should be reinterpreted and whether it should be retained or rejected. The New Social Movement theorists have addressed the questions of why the movements of the postwar era
have been in many ways different from movements of the past
and what the answers suggest about Marxism's continued utility
and how Marxism might be transformed. The New Social Movement theorists are linked to others, especially the Fordist (or post-
Fordist) political economists, who have been concerned with the
question of the transformation of Western capitalism in the twentieth century. In this arena also most of the leading voices are
Western European, though some American political economists
have contributed to this perspective.

Because the Western European discussion of new social movements has taken place in the context of debates about the trans-

formation of capitalist political economy in the postwar period, the Western European social movement literature has a much greater theoretical sophistication than the parallel literature from the United States. The problem is that the literature of the Western European New Social Movement is in a sense not really about the new social movements. Though they support and identify with the movements they discuss, the intellectual interest of these scholars is less in the movements themselves than in a series of debates about Marxism. As a result, their literature addresses some aspects of these movements but neglects others. Its grounding in twentieth-century developments in and critiques of Marxist political economy allows it to raise much broader questions than those raised by Resource Mobilization theorists, questions that are of relevance to the study of social movements in the United States as well as Europe, including the direct action movement. But the New Social Movement theorists have produced few concrete studies of the movements to which they refer in the course of theoretical debate. The absence of a vital intellectual connection to the new social movements, the fact that these theorists understand themselves as developing theory *about* rather than *for* the movements, gives New Social Movement theory certain blind spots and, overall, an academic cast. It is thus less accessible to activists, and less helpful as a resource for formulating strategy, than it could be.

Because the New Social Movement theorists have opened up ways of thinking about the differences between movements of the postwar era and those of previous periods and what their significance may be in a changing social context, it is worth examining their work and its theoretical bases in some detail. Because that work has emerged out of a large network of theoretical and political groupings, each with its own history and its own multiple connections, the story of how a new perspective on social movements emerged could be told in many different ways. I tell it in a way that highlights the theoretical developments that seem to me most useful for an understanding of the direct action movement and the movements that surrounded it in the late 1970s and the 1980s. My synthesis of New Social Movement theory and my account of its immediate intellectual lineage leave out many elements of the theory and many schools of thought that have influenced it.

Constituencies of the New Movements:
Agents of Change in the Postwar Era

The story begins with Antonio Gramsci, who, in the 1920s and 1930s, put forward a revised account of the structure of capitalism, suggesting the need for different political strategies from those envisioned by more traditional versions of Marxism. Gramsci argued that in the United States, and to some degree in Western Europe as well, the construction of basic industry had been accomplished and capitalism was driven by the production of consumer goods. Such economies, Gramsci argued, required a more highly trained and motivated working class and new patterns of mass consumption. The need for workers who would apply themselves to their tasks and for a population that would sustain economic growth by consumption implied that force was no longer an adequate means of social control: the working class must be made to identify and cooperate with the system; and therefore education, culture, and consciousness were increasingly important terrains of struggle. The structural complexity of the working class and its overlapping interests with other sectors of the population suggested to Gramsci that revolutionary struggle would be led not by a unified working class but by a coalition of forces led by particular sectors of the working class. Gramsci called this phase of capitalist development "Fordism," drawing the term from Henry Ford's role in the development of assembly line production and Taylorist attempts at the scientific regulation of work.[7]

Gramsci's formulation retained the idea of the working class or some part of it at the center of a revolutionary movement, but it opened up the possibilities of including new groups within the category "working class," of the creation of alliances between elements of the working class and other groups, and of emphasizing the transformation of consciousness as a part of the revolutionary process. The movements of the sixties, in both Europe and the United States, did not fit the patterns predicted by traditional Marxism; Gramsci's approach, however, opened up new ways of thinking about the revolutionary process. The first, which came to be called New Working Class theory, took somewhat different forms in Europe and in the United States. In the United States, blue-collar workers, traditionally thought of as the center of the working class, were not involved in the new movements and were in fact hostile to them. New Left intellectuals responded by expanding their definition of the working class. In Europe, where working-class elements continued to play an important role in protest movements, New Working Class theory led to a shift in the emphasis from the working class as a whole to the elements playing the largest role in the movements of the time.

In the United States, a group of people in and around SDS put forward the notion that sectors of the middle class were being drawn into the working class by the extension of corporate influence into new areas of society. According to this account, the universities had become the training ground for the new working class. No longer dedicated to the pursuit of knowledge for its own sake, the universities had become bureaucracies producing intellectually skilled workers who would serve the interests of the corporations and maintain the system. Student radicalism, accordingly, could be understood as a response to a new process of proletarianization and alienation.[8] The impulse to make the student movement legitimate within the existing categories of Marxism was later extended to other sections of the movement. It was not difficult to place the movements of blacks and other people of color within this context, because in the United States the vast majority of people of color fall within even the narrowest definition of the working class. Incorporating the women's movement into this model was more difficult, but some early Marxist Feminists argued that housework and child care, though unpaid, should nevertheless be considered productive labor and that the great majority of women should thus be counted as part of the working class.[9]

In Europe, where substantial numbers especially of highly skilled workers exhibited militancy throughout the sixties, Alain Touraine, in *Post-Industrial Society*, argued that capitalism had entered a stage in which the industrial working class would no longer serve as the decisive revolutionary agent, but that sections of the working class might play a key role in revolution, along with other sectors of society.[10] Along similar lines, André Gorz argued that immiseration could no longer be seen as the basis of working-class revolutionary consciousness, that more emphasis should be placed on the alienation brought about by a system that channeled workers into white-collar areas of work that raised hopes for creativity and then disappointed them.[11] Serge Mallet suggested that revolutionary expectations should be focused on the highly trained workers whose skills greatly outdistanced any opportunity to exercise them. Along with Alain Touraine, he suggested that skilled workers in crucial integrated industries, especially the nuclear power and other energy-producing industries, would be in a position to play the role in reorganizing the political economy that Marx had ascribed to the working class as a whole.[12] The participation of militant, highly skilled young workers in the events of May 1968 seemed to confirm this analysis, and encouraged this approach. European New Working Class theory, especially Gorz's *New Strategy for Labor,* was widely read within SDS in the United States and influenced thinking about the question of working-class organizing.

Both varieties of New Working Class theory were ultimately inadequate to an understanding of the movements of the sixties. They were eventually put aside, and have not been revived, because they are no more useful for understanding the movements of the seventies and eighties. Redefining students and women as workers came to seem strained. It did not answer the question of how the existing movements of the sixties could lead a revolution without the support of the traditional working class. It also did not address the real weaknesses in Marxist theory in relation to the movements of the sixties and beyond, namely, its difficulty in explaining generational revolt, its failure to address the question of gender, its inadequacy in relation to race, and its lack of a theory of cultural crisis.

Nevertheless, New Working Class theories made important contributions to theoretical development. They provided a way of thinking about the changing structure of work and of the working classes in Europe and the United States, and also the breakdown of boundaries between the working class and the "middle class," never adequately theorized in the Marxist framework, but increasingly large and significant as a base of social movements. New Working Class theories also stimulated a theoretically useful response. While New Working Class theorists were trying to explain how new constituencies came to be at the center of efforts for social change, others, also looking to Gramsci, tried to understand the conservatism of the labor movement and of the sections of the working class it represented. In the late seventies, a group of French Marxists who came to be called the Regulation School put forward an interpretation of advanced capitalism that incorporated Gramsci's analysis of Fordism into Marxist categories of political economy. Regulation School theory implied that if the traditional working classes had become conservative, other sections of that class or other social groups altogether might retain the potential for revolutionary activity. A version of this approach was the basis, in the seventies and eighties, for New Social Movement theory.

Traditional Marxist political economy mainly addressed large categories: feudalism, capitalism, socialism, how they operate, how societies make the transition from one to the next. Michel Aglietta and others who made up the Regulation School wanted to explain the various stages of development that have taken place within capitalism. Aglietta argued that every phase of capitalist development has two aspects, a "regime of accumulation," that is, a particular strategy of economic development, and a "mode of regulation," a particular set of economic policies and class relationships that enable a particular strategy of accumulation to function smoothly. The Fordist stage of capitalism, Aglietta argued, was based on Keynesian policies of growth and an accord between capital and labor that freed capital from the fear of radicalism by promising labor high wages and substantial benefits. Aglietta and others suggested that economic expansion based on Fordism reached its limits in the mid-sixties. Declining productivity and other signs of trouble were masked, especially in the United States, by spending on the war in Vietnam. The full impact of the crisis of Fordism was not felt until the mid-seventies.[13]

In the United States, radical political economists pursued closely related ideas under the rubric of "the Social Structure of Accumulation." Like the Regulation School, they argued that to function smoothly, capitalism must integrate particular strategies of accumulation with particular institutions of social and political control. The difference between the two groups was that the Regulation School took a structuralist approach that focused on the internal dynamics of capitalism. The American radical economists emphasized the role of class struggle in the changing strategies of capital. In *Beyond the Wasteland,* Samuel Bowles, David Gordon, and Tom Weisskopf argued that the class struggles of the thirties had forced capital to reach an accommodation with labor, that the need to contain radicalism rather than inherent characteristics of capitalism produced the welfare state and the structures of Fordism generally.[14] According to this account, Fordism began to break down in the sixties not because it had reached its limits as a strategy of accumulation but because after twenty years or so of prosperity labor had become dissatisfied with the deal it had made. Strikes increased in number and became more militant; the capital-labor accord began to break down, forcing capital to search for new forms of control.

Neither French Regulation theory nor American analysis of the social structure of accumulation directly addressed the question why movements of the postwar era might be different from those that had preceded them, but they suggested that the movements of the thirties were associated with the construction of Fordism and those of the sixties and later with its degeneration. The problem with this approach was that the movements of the sixties appeared and reached their height before the crisis of Fordism had had any measurable impact on daily life. Nevertheless, the concepts of Fordism and post-Fordism (the term that some used to refer to the era of Fordism's degeneration) provided a suggestive framework for thinking about the new kinds of movements that had appeared in the postwar era.

The Regulation School and the American Social Structure of Accumulation theorists had seen themselves as extending or refining Marxist theory, adding concepts compatible with a Marxist perspective that made it a better tool for understanding the postwar era. Meanwhile, another group of social scientists, mostly Germans and Italians, began to outline New Social Movement theory, linking Fordist and post-Fordist political economy with an analysis of the state, culture, and ideology and naming the construction of community and collective identities as important terrains of struggle.[15] Because they emphasized culture as a terrain of struggle equal in importance to politics and the economy, and because they rejected the Marxist concept of broadly predetermined stages of history, New Social Movement theorists see their work as an alternative to Marxism rather than a helpful revision. Regulation School and Social Structure of Accumulation theorists had not meant to suggest, by their account of the capital-labor accord, that the working class no longer had an interest in socialism or that the labor movement had ceased to be an agent of social change. Much of New Social Movement theory has adapted those assumptions.

The movements of the postwar era, especially the women's, environmental/ecology, and peace movements of the seventies and eighties, seemed to provide evidence for the view that the working class was no longer an important source of social change. Of course many of the people in those movements could be called working-class, especially broadly defined; but the movements did not put themselves forward as specifically representing the working class or its interests. New Social Movement theory, inspired by the wave of protest that swept Western Europe in the late seventies and eighties, presented itself as both analyst and protagonist of those movements. Some analysts have used the term "new social movements" to refer specifically to the movements of that period; others have included the civil rights, antiwar, and other movements of the sixties. New Social Movement theory has had less impact in the United States than in Europe, partly because much of it remains untranslated, partly because it is framed in terms of Marxist theory, which is much less familiar to American academics than to Europeans. But for anyone concerned with understanding the direct action movement or the movements that have surrounded it, New Social Movement theory is worth taking seriously. It provides much better tools for understanding those movements than the Mobilization Resource theory that continues to dominate thinking among American students of social movements.

New Social Movement theorists have argued that in the postwar period stability has been ensured largely by the apparatus of a "security state."[16] This term is double-edged: state-supported welfare and other benefits have provided a certain security for large sections of the population; at the same time widespread dependence on the state or entanglement with it gives the state a ready means of constraining impulses to revolt. In this context social control takes new forms: it spreads its tentacles into social life and culture, which consequently lose even the limited degree of autonomy they once possessed. Existing communities are torn apart; the economy and the political arena cease to be the terrains of social control. The working class meanwhile ceases to be the central agency of revolution or social change, because protest is organized less around the workplace or the structure of the economy, more around resistance to the intrusion of the state into other areas of life. Some New Social Movement theorists argue that the labor movement now takes its place among a range of constituencies with equal status in struggles for social change. Others would argue that the labor movement has lost its place as an agent of social change.

Within the Marxist framework, the direct action and other movements of the seventies and eighties are inexplicable. Traditional Marxism has no explanation for movements that center on the defense and construction of identity (as in the gay and lesbian movements), the critique of personal life and gender (as in the women's movement), or the effort to realize a utopian vision of community (as in the direct action movement). Traditional Marxism reinforces the temptation to dismiss these movements as self-indulgent and irrelevant to social change—a temptation felt by many whose views were shaped by struggles of earlier eras. The unconventional qualities shared by many of the movements of the seventies and eighties are much more understandable in the context of an argument that the structure of capitalism and social control has taken new forms and that struggles over social control therefore take place over new issues, on other terrains than in the past.[17]

New Social Movement theory follows Gramsci's argument that ideology and culture have become important arenas of struggle. It explains why so many people have been drawn to struggles around identity and the defense or construction of community, why the feminist argument that "the personal is political" has so much resonance in the postwar period. It gives a new meaning to the role of symbolism, theater, and esthetics in political struggle. New Social Movement theory makes it easier to understand the significance of a political practice that goes beyond the accepted limits of the political, flouts convention, and has no interest in respectability. In an analysis of new social movements in

Italy, Alberto Melucci has argued that state control, having taken a new form, requires a new response. "When domination impinges upon daily life, on the rules of existing ways of life, opposition necessarily takes the form of marginality and of deviance."[18] In Italy the Communist Party and much of what has remained of the New Left joined in condemning the unconventional tactics of the new social movements. Melucci argues that by condemning movements that conduct political struggle outside the arena of accepted institutions, the older political movements have consigned themselves to the role of loyal opposition within the system.[19] The same argument could be made for the United States, although the remnants of the Old and New Lefts have had less power to deny the new movements' legitimacy. But in the United States as well as in Western Europe, the theory has allowed a number of scholars to argue for the importance of a range of new movements.[20]

Though New Social Movement theory has been helpful in legitimizing many of the movements of the postwar era, it has been a better guide to some aspects of those movements than others. It emphasizes the diffuse, fragmentary quality of many of the movements of the late twentieth century, their limited objectives, their defensive quality. The multiplicity of constituencies in the various movements and their concern that no one element come to dominate the rest make it easy to understand their reluctance to unify or even to construct a shared agenda. New Social Movement theory helps us understand why many people in the new movements are uneasy thinking about strategy, at least on the broad level of how it might be possible to transform society as a whole. But along with the particularistic, often defensive, quality of many of the new movements, there is also a utopianism that relies upon a shared vision, strong connections among the various movements, and an aspiration toward broad collective action. The aspiration toward new kind of universality is particularly salient in the direct action movement. New Social Movement theory does not understand this impulse nearly as well as it understands the impulse toward particularism.

The term "new social movements" encompasses organizations and popular mobilizations ranging from specific constituencies involved in defending the rights of particular communities to those organized around a broad social vision and seeking the support of anyone willing to act on its behalf. New Social Movement theory is best adapted to understanding the former. Neighborhood groups, organizations of racial and ethnic minorities, such specific groups as tenants and welfare recipients are likely to be concerned mainly with issues of immediate concern to their constituencies, even if they see themselves as part of a broader movement and share its vision of social change. At the other end of the scale, the peace and anti-intervention movements have no equivalent "natural" constituencies. They appeal to a broad sense of social responsibility. The movement against nuclear energy was supported by local communities with a direct, immediate interest in the issue, but it would have remained very weak if it had not also appealed to a larger constituency with a strong general commitment to ecological values.

New Social Movement theory's bias toward movements with particular constituencies and relatively narrow aims limits its ability to address the specific strengths and weaknesses of the direct action movement. The fact that the movement's appeal is due more to the strength of its vision than to any direct link with the daily concerns of existing communities gives it a certain fragility. A movement constructed almost entirely in the process of political action is readily dissolved. The labor movement of the thirties and the civil rights movement of the early sixties grew out of existing communities that were deeply politicized in the struggles of those periods; their roots in those communities gave them a great deal of resilience. The direct action movement has drawn its activists from a variety of communities that continue to exist independently of that movement. When activists remain part of or can easily rejoin their "root" communities it is easy for them to drift away from politics. On the other hand, the movement's relative independence from existing communities also gives it considerable freedom from existing groups or institutions; it is freer than many other movements to take risks, to behave outrageously, to construct a broad-ranging utopian vision. The direct action movement is certainly shaped by the impulse to construct community, which New Social Movement theory explains in terms of the political economy of late capitalism. But the need of communities to defend themselves against the intrusions of the state does little to explain either the strengths or the weaknesses of the direct action movement.

Another failing of New Social Movement theory, its lack of interest in the working class, limits its usefulness not only to the direct action movement but to the new social movements generally. Although it is true that in the postwar period, especially in the seventies and eighties, the working classes of the United States and Western Europe have not been central actors in movements for social change, this inaction does not justify a theory that abandons hope in the working class and looks elsewhere for social change (rather than to other sources in addition to the working class). On demographic grounds alone it is hard to believe that broad social change can take place, in either the United States or Western Europe, without substantial working-class involvement.[21] In fact, movements of people of color have drawn very largely from the working classes, as have neighborhood-based and urban movements. But many of the new social movements have been based on constituencies that are middle-class in current status or in origin, such as the environmental/ecology movements, the peace movement, and the direct action movement. The new social movements have not mobilized working-class people generally.

The Cultural Politics of the New Movements: The Question of Identity in the Postwar Era

In its attempts to explain a fragmented social reality that in many ways no longer fits traditional theoretical paradigms, New Social Movement theory overlaps with postmodernism, which encompasses a range of attempts to describe, defend, or in some way establish a stance in relation to, the loss of faith in absolute facts and universal values and the apparent instability of the connection between observed realities and the meanings assigned to them. The term "postmodernism" has mostly been connected to advocacy of these trends. The literary, artistic, and social critics who call themselves postmodernists celebrate fragmentation and the disappearance of universal values. For others, postmodernism has been anathema because it rejects accepted values and seems to undermine any effort to construct new ones. Postmodernist discourse attracts animosity also because it is conducted in obscure language that seems designed to exclude the uninitiated.

There are those who turn to postmodernism not in order to defend social fragmentation and the erosion of values but in order to describe and understand those phenomena as a first step toward dealing with them. Fredric Jameson's analysis of postmodernism intersects with Fordist developments within Marxism and thus indirectly with New Social Movement theory. He argues that postmodern culture can be understood as an expression of the extreme alienation of late capitalism. The process of commodification, Jameson writes, is rampant in all areas of life. Social control, which once operated primarily within political and economic spheres, has been extended to the cultural; the realm of culture, once relatively autonomous, has merged with the realm of political economy, and "cultural" struggles have become as important as any other.

Jameson argues that as long as capitalism was driven by the development of basic industry, social control was relatively simple and direct, designed to elicit hard work and discipline on the part of workers. Once basic industry had been constructed, consumption took its place as the driving force behind economic expansion. Mass culture emerged from the need for a motivated work force and cooperation from the population and was made possible by new levels of technological development. Ideology and culture gained importance as arenas of social control and struggle. High culture meanwhile retained enough autonomy to comment on social processes. Mass culture was distinct from critical or left culture, which challenged mass culture and the prevailing social system. Under the conditions of late capitalism, Jameson argues, commodification has extended so far, the tentacles of social control have so thoroughly invaded all areas of life, that an independent or rigorously critical stance is all but impossible. The boundaries among mass, high, and critical culture have blurred. Celebration and criticism of social reality are jumbled and there is no reliable independent basis for assertions of meaning or any clear distinctions between accommodation and resistance.[22]

Jameson's analysis can easily be translated into the terms of Fordism/post-Fordism. Jameson's argument suggests that the emergence of mass culture accompanied the shift from basic industry to production for consumption. This required Keynesianism as a strategy of growth and harmony between capital and labor to ensure stability. The Keynesian strategy of social control and the attendant capital-labor compromise were the bases of welfare state liberalism, that is, Fordism. As that strategy has broken down and liberalism has entered into crisis, Jameson argues, not only social order but systems of meaning have begun to unravel. Jameson has extended Fordist/post-Fordist analysis by looking at the connections between political economic and cultural levels of crisis. By placing cultural and social fragmentation in the context of late capitalism, Jameson implies the possibility of a transformative opposition, through efforts to create a new social system.

Jameson does not inquire what such a transformative politics might be. Ernesto Laclau and Chantal Mouffe, in *Hegemony and Socialist Strategy: Towards a Radical Democratic Politics,* begin to address this question by presenting a critique of the Marxist reliance on the working class and seeking a basis for a broader radical democratic movement.[23] Laclau and Mouffe use as their baseline a traditional Marxism consisting of economic determinism and historical teleology. According to their account, Marxism predicted the downfall of capitalism as a result of internal economic contradictions and assigned the working class, and it alone, the role of revolutionary agent in a predetermined transition to socialism. Laclau and Mouffe see Lenin as having implicitly broken with this approach by questioning whether all societies must pass through the same predetermined stages and arguing that the Russian working class might play a different role in revolution from that predicted by Marxist theory. The crisis brought on by World War One made a transition to socialism possible while capitalism was only in its early stages, but because the working class was small and relatively weak, Lenin argued, revolution required coalitions of workers and peasants. In the absence of democratic structures and the repressive capabilities of the tsarist state, Lenin maintained that a secretive, highly disciplined party was needed to lead the working class, which could in turn lead the peasants. In the course of revolution, the working class not only led the transition to socialism but also assumed two tasks earlier Marxist theory had assigned to the bourgeoisie: leading the struggle for democracy and bringing about industrialization.

Lenin developed his revised theory of revolution in the particular circumstances of Russian history; he did not claim to be revising Marxist theory. But, Laclau and Mouffe argue, Lenin's more flexible conception of the revolutionary process made room for an expanded understanding of the relationship between class and political action in Marxist theory as a whole and also raised the question of whether the working class might play a role in the establishment or expansion of democracy. They applaud Lenin for having described revolution as the result of particular circumstances and particular political actions rather than a foreordained playing out of contradictions inherent in capitalism, and they see that expanded role of the working class as a basis for linking struggles for socialism and for democracy. On the other hand, they criticize Lenin for continuing to believe that particular classes have innate interests and therefore determined, or essential, connections to particular historical tasks. They reject the view that the working class has a special role in bringing about socialism. They also criticize Lenin for introducing undemocratic processes into Marxism, for assigning the party a leading or tutelary role in relation to the working class and assigning the same role to the working class in relation to other forces participating in the revolution. Laclau and Mouffe accuse Marxist essentialism, including Lenin's belief that the working class has a special relationship to socialist revolution, of providing the basis for socialist authoritarianism.

Laclau and Mouffe criticize Marxism partly to attack an essentialism they object to on philosophical grounds, and partly out of commitment to a politics of egalitarianism or "radical democracy" in which the working class plays no special role. In effect, they are trying to find a theoretical basis for the politics of the new social movements, in particular the egalitarian current within those movements. They go further than perhaps anyone else toward outlining a theory for movements that have not themselves developed any clear theoretical orientation. Laclau and Mouffe's theory is worth looking at also because it accepts the terms of postmodernism, which, at least in their hands, has an affinity for anarchism. Postmodernism speaks to the fragmentation and dislocation that dominate the perspectives of many people drawn to the direct action and other movements in the same orbit. Its language resonates for them much more than traditional Marxism ever could.

Laclau and Mouffe rest their postmodernist politics substantially on Gramsci, whom they describe as having drawn upon and expanded the positive aspects of Lenin's break with traditional Marxism. Where Lenin regarded an alliance of the working class with other classes as a temporary necessity, directed toward particular objectives and in no way transforming the political identities of the classes involved, Gramsci used the concept of hegemony to describe a process of working-class leadership through which new political subjects would be constructed and the working class would be prominent but not the only force. He used the same concept to refer to the creation of a popular revolutionary ideology that would bring workers and others together around a shared perspective. Gramsci kept the working class at the center of his concept of hegemony; Laclau and Mouffe reject this aspect of his thought. They argue that it is not the working class but the new social movements that are the carriers of radical democracy. Gramsci used the concept of hegemony to refer to a contest for ideological and cultural leadership, which he argued was of crucial importance when popular compliance was required for the system to function and seizure of power was not possible. Laclau and Mouffe subtly shift the concept of hegemony to mean a process of political coalition rather than assertion of leadership within a coalition. In accordance with radical egalitarianism, they emphasize the construction of a consensus acceptable to all rather than a contest for ideological supremacy.

Many of the ideas put forward by New Social Movement theory are developed by Laclau and Mouffe in the context of recent philosophical discourse. They see a proliferation of political subjects and issues in the postwar period, part of a large historical trend away from simple or unified social structures toward multiplicity and complexity. Following Aglietta's account of the "extensive" or Fordist structure of postwar capitalism, organized around mass consumption and involving expanding and intrusive state bureaucracies, they put forward a Foucaultian analysis of the dispersion of sites of power. Social power is exercised, and resisted, at every level. Thus, they argue, the distinction between economic base and cultural or ideological superstructure breaks down, and there is no longer any privileged arena for political struggle.

New Social Movement theory, with the Fordist/post-Fordist perspective, helps account for the new constituencies that have been drawn to protest politics in the postwar era. Postmodernism helps account for their orientation toward a cultural politics and the variety of cultural strands that run through them. The style and spirit of the direct action movement especially overlap with that of postmodernism in many ways: the consensus process and the affinity group structure of the movement are congruent with postmodernism's emphasis on diversity, its vision of multiple rather than unitary sites of power. The fleeting, fragile quality of the movement appeals to the postmodernist fascination with the transitory and precarious nature of social life. The Pagans are particularly close to the postmodernist spirit, with their willingness to borrow elements from unrelated traditions to construct a worldview in which they only half believe. The postmodernist view of identity as multiple, fragmented, and shifting comes to life in a movement that brings together Pagans, Christians, and the nonreligious; anarchists and Marxists; that does not take these divisions very seriously and finds theater and symbolism more important than ideological debate.

Laclau and Mouffe's work is the beginning of a theory for the direct action movement and others for which egalitarianism is a high priority. By criticizing the authoritarianism implicit in Marxism they prepare for a theory of social change that is simultaneously revolutionary and democratic. But Laclau and Mouffe are ultimately less concerned with theorizing for or about the new social movements than with using these movements as a protagonist in a philosophical debate against what they regard as Marxist essentialism.

In the course of that debate, Laclau and Mouffe emphasize the qualities of the new social movements that fit their philosophical agenda. They do not acknowledge the search for universal values and for a politics based on them. The aspiration to universalism is a strong element in the utopianism many of these movements share and is particularly salient in the direct action movement. Laclau and Mouffe applaud fragmentation and particularity and argue against a unified project. If this bias were merely a peculiarity of Laclau and Mouffe's work, it would not be of great significance. Their views, however, express the politics implicit in the postmodernist perspective as a whole. Laclau and Mouffe go further than many postmodernists in denying the existence or at least the relevance to theory of objective reality. They argue that "everything is discourse. . . . all practices are discursive practices."[24] They insist that nothing lies outside the realm of the socially constructed, and they reject any search for a ground in laws of history or society. They criticize Marxism not only for holding a rigid conception of stages of social development but also for the attempt to locate any such stages and identify them with the interests of particular classes. Laclau and Mouffe reject also the Marxist view that classes have any identifiable interests, that there is any relationship between these interests and political practice.

In calling for an "open" or "unfixed" view of political process, Laclau and Mouffe call for a politics that renounces not only strategy but the pursuit of what Gramsci called a hegemonic project. By denying the existence of any ground outside the socially constructed, Laclau and Mouffe remove any basis for rational political analysis, prediction, or even preference. Even in their own work, they cannot sustain this view: when they come to elaborating what they see as the political implications, they put aside their agnosticism and present a teleology and agency of their own. They replace the materialist historical perspective—the idea that history revolves around political and economic stages of development—with an account of a centuries-long struggle for democracy and its extension, a process within which, they argue, the struggle for socialism is subsumed.

Laclau and Mouffe's identification of the Marxist tradition with a flat economism that leaves out human consciousness and agency is based on a very ungenerous reading of Marx and his followers. It is certainly possible to find this kind of economism within the tradition, but the strength of Marxism is that, at its best, it takes into account both human consciousness and action and the limits to action posed by social structure and technology. Moreover, having reduced Marxism to the mechanistic view that the contradictions of the capitalist system lead inevitably to its collapse, they substitute an equally mechanistic view that the idea of democracy leads inevitably to socialism.

Laclau and Mouffe's work, and the postmodernist perspective more generally, has very mixed implications for the direct action and other radical egalitarian movements. In the course of undermining perspectives that endorse hierarchies of various kinds (including traditional versions of Marxism) postmodernism has helped to open up an intellectual and cultural space within which egalitarianism can be valued. But the postmodernist perspective also reinforces some of the weaknesses of the direct action and other radical egalitarian movements. The insistence that there is no relationship between class position and politics, in particular between the working class and revolution, reinforces the tendency in the movement to remain content with existing constituencies, to allow the movement to be defined as one interest, one political subculture, among many.

Laclau and Mouffe's view that everything of interest is socially constructed reinforces the movement's avoidance of strategy by suggesting that there are no objective limits or structural frameworks to be taken into account in devising political action. Politics then consists of the construction and expression of a collective vision. There has been a strong tendency within the direct action movement to think that acting collectively and symbolically on a belief in a better world either is the same thing as strategy or makes strategy unnecessary. This kind of magical thinking leads people to believe that a large enough occupation will in itself close down a nuclear plant or arms facility and dooms them to disappointment and disillusionment.

Their extreme relativism leads Laclau and Mouffe to the view that all constituencies have equal claims, all perspectives equal legitimacy. The direct action movement has been plagued by its inability to resolve the tensions between a similar ideological pluralism and the need for political standards that would enable it to decide what is legitimate and what is not. If everyone's views are equally legitimate, what happens when a group or individual blocks the actions of the rest of the movement? The Clamshell Alliance was destroyed by just such a conflict. One group wanted to cut fences as part of a large occupation; others refused. The fence cutters promised to block any action in which they were not included. Those who opposed them had no legitimate ground for objection and thus resorted to subverting the consensus process. Other direct action organizations learned from this experience and have worked around the problems of consensus process. At least, no other mass direct action organization has suffered such extreme internal conflicts. But neither does the movement have an intellectual framework for addressing problems of this sort.

The most comprehensive answer to the extreme relativism of the postmodernist perspective is that of the German philosopher, Jürgen Habermas. Habermas is now the leading figure in the Frankfurt School, which came into existence in 1923 when an association of left intellectuals formed the Institute for Social Research. The School directed its efforts toward the development of Critical Theory, an open, undogmatic Marxism concerned with the analysis of ideology. In 1933, with Hitler's rise to power, the School was exiled. Many of its leading members pursued their work in the United States and remained even after the School was reestablished in Frankfurt in the early fifties. Habermas, who is several decades younger than the founding members of the School, has been associated with it in this latter phase. Critical Theory has had a long-standing influence in the left in the United States. Many of the activists of the sixties were drawn to the work of Herbert Marcuse, a founding member of the School, because of his vision of a radical cultural politics based on subjects other than the working class. The work of Murray Bookchin, which has been so important to the anarchist and ecofeminist tendencies in the United States, is rooted in the Frankfurt School and Critical Theory. But it is Jürgen Habermas whose work has most directly addressed the questions raised by the postmodernists.

Habermas is not as widely read among those in and close to the new social movements as Marcuse in the sixties or the French poststructuralists, or postmodernists, now. Nevertheless, his work is worth looking at because it addresses the question of whether universal values can be found and how they can be articulated. Habermas debates both the postmodernists and the neoconservatives, the former denying that there is any basis for deciding among alternative values, the latter claiming that the only choice is between traditional values and no values. The debate among postmodernists, neoconservatives, and Habermas about the possibility and content of values, or political rationality, uses the new social movements as its major point of reference. The postmodernists identify with the anarchist impulse in the new social movements; they tend to see those movements as exemplifying their perspective. The neoconservatives see postmodernism as a threat to civilization and the new social movements as its practical expression. Habermas sees the new social movements as containing an impulse toward a more rational society, and he criticizes both the postmodernists and the neoconservatives for in different ways denying this possibility.[25]

In the United States, at least, relatively few activists read Habermas or the postmodernists, and those who read the neoconservatives do so mostly to laugh at them. But this three-way debate about values and meaning is actually of great importance to the new social movements; it describes the context in which the stance of intellectuals toward politics is being fought out. In Western Europe and the United States intellectuals play a major role in shaping the political atmosphere: the prospects for social change are dampened when intellectuals are conservative, cautious, or cynical and enlivened when intellectuals are radical, optimistic, and engaged. It is thus worthwhile for activists to pay attention.

Habermas's thought is shaped by a Marxist commitment to a critical social theory, that is, to a philosophy and theory of society that is engaged in, and provides tools for, the struggle for human emancipation. Habermas believes that core moral and social values are universally felt and that historical development must articulate these values and construct societies in which they can be expressed. Habermas's search for a "communicative theory of action" involves the effort to understand how a set of values can be developed that will make rational consensus possible. He locates this process in the context of a capitalist society that has elevated certain aspects of rationality, especially economic and technical rationality, while suppressing and distorting its social and moral aspects. Habermas sees the struggle for socialism as necessary for the attainment of a more developed, balanced, and articulated rationality in which technical, moral, and expressive elements will be coordinated but autonomous, and in which none would dominate or distort the others.

Habermas argues that the quest for human emancipation requires pursuing rationality, not abandoning the possibility. Marx saw class society as the source of human alienation; he believed that transcending class society would mean the end of alienation. Habermas criticizes Marx for having failed to distinguish between capitalism and the process of rationalization it produced. Thus Marx could not see that negative aspects of rationalization, such as bureaucracy, could outlast capitalism. Max Weber had earlier pointed to the relationship between capitalism and rationalization, and in particular to the autonomous role of bureaucracy in a developed capitalist society. But where Weber saw rationality as having created the "iron cage" of modern civilization, Habermas sees the construction of rationality as an unfinished project, the pursuit of which can be the basis for a better society.

In the three-way debate with neoconservatives and postmodernists, Habermas disagrees with the postmodernists' denial that rationality is possible and at the same time with the neoconservatives' identification of rationality with traditional values and authorities. The neoconservatives, in turn, see themselves as embattled by a modern and postmodern spirit that threatens civilization and the values it rests upon. Many of the intellectuals now described as neoconservatives were once part of the left, or at least regard the reforms of the thirties as part of their heritage, but have rejected both the modernist faith in progress and the critical culture that developed in relation to it. Seeing themselves as engulfed by an "adversary culture," they believe that the new social movements undermine authority and social order and are supported by a left social criticism that dominates the universities and a media that attacks traditional values. The neoconservatives regard modernism as the source of this adversary culture. In this view postmodernism, or poststructuralism, with its relativism and its rejection of traditional authority, appears as a kind of advanced stage of the disease of modernism. The new social movements are seen as postmodernism on the streets—the threat of nihilistic anarchy.

In spite of the hostility between neoconservative and postmod-

ernist intellectuals, they share a pessimism about the possibility
that political action could lead to a better world. The postmodernists explicitly reject rationality and universal values. Though
the neoconservatives do not explicitly dismiss rationality, the only
basis they find for social order is a set of traditional values for
which they offer no rational basis other than tradition. The neoconservatives turned to patriotism, family, and religion when their
hopes for socialism collapsed some thirty or forty years ago. If
they were to lose their confidence in traditional values, the only
difference between them and the postmodernists would be their
preference for order and hierarchy and that of the postmodernists for transience, fragmentation, and in some cases equality.

One of the ironies of this debate is that the various forces the
neoconservatives see as having launched a highly successful joint
attack on Western civilization are in fact uneasy with one another; many of them think that the neoconservatives set the tone
for politics and culture. The social movements tend to be suspicious of intellectuals and especially of academics. Left intellectuals hardly see themselves as dominating the universities, and
most of them have only the most distant relationship to the new
social movements. Activists and intellectuals alike see the media
as providing powerful support for the status quo and themselves
as operating on the margins of a political and cultural terrain
controlled by conservatives. Perhaps one of the traits of late capitalist society is that everyone is convinced that someone else oc-
cupies the center. For those on the left, the question is where, in
those circumstances, to find leverage for change.

Habermas believes that there is hope in rational political action, but he does not put forward a theory that either accounts
for or can give direction to the new social movements. He tries
to find a basis for commonly accepted values in the concept of
"communicative rationality." He argues that there are universal
values that are understood intuitively. These values could be articulated and could become the basis for social decisions in an
"ideal speech situation" in which relations of dominance and subordination had been eliminated and all participants were equal.
This formalized vision of egalitarian social relations is considered
without reference to their political and economic context. It is
static and idealist; it portrays a society in which there are no con-

flicts or differences that cannot be resolved through rational discussion. In itself, Habermas's concept of an ideal speech situation does not explain why some might want an egalitarian society and others might not, or how one could be achieved.

The New Social Movements
and the Question of Strategy

The direct action movement and movements that it has been linked to flourished in the late 1970s and early 1980s. Through the late 1980s radical movements became increasingly diffuse and fragmented. Many activists find comfort in the observation that there is a lot going on on the left, many projects, many organizations. But this activity is not very visible, even to the left itself. The right is in power; it has succeeded not only in setting the terms of public discussion but also in winning broad public support. In order to put forward an effective challenge, the direct action and the other radical egalitarian movements need a strategy, and to formulate one they must look beyond New Social Movement theory, postmodernism, and Habermas's defense of rationality.

In the search for a strategy it is worth looking at discussions of left strategy among Western Europeans, especially in relation to Britain, where, as in the United States, the right holds power and the left is fragmented and disoriented. Stuart Hall, in *The Hard Road to Renewal: Thatcherism and the Crisis of the Left,* argues that the Thatcher government and the British right more generally have a hegemonic project, which he calls reactionary modernization.[26] The Thatcher government, Hall argues, wants to create a modern economy with a thriving corporate sector, more or less along the lines of the Silicon Valley. This goal requires dismantling the welfare state, inaugurating austerity, and blaming the resulting social chaos on declining morality in general and on the poor in particular. The Thatcher government has cultivated support for its policies through what Hall calls authoritarian populism, that is, the view that stability is threatened by crime and disorder at the bottom of society rather than greediness at the top and that repression is the proper response to it. In Gramscian terms, the British right has a hegemonic project, a coherent social vision, and a worldview and set of values that give it legitimacy. The left, clearly, does not.

One could make a similar argument for the United States. In the context of an uncertain economy and declining world power, the right appears to have the answers: it puts forward a clear and simple program and lays claim to traditional values. The right has been able to take advantage of widespread fear and insecurity in cultivating popular support for its program and its worldview. The appeal of the right lies in its willingness to put forward a hegemonic project: the restoration of American prosperity, international standing, and "traditional" values. The left responds that in a world with rapidly proliferating centers of economic and political power, the economic and political supremacy the United States enjoyed immediately after World War Two cannot be regained. Furthermore, the left points out, the world should not be dominated by one nation (or for that matter by two superpowers), and the economic boom of the fifties was based on military spending and the promotion of a wasteful consumerism—all of which may be true but does not address the fears and insecurities to which the right successfully appeals. It does not answer the question of what might be a "progressive" or democratic set of programs for an empire now clearly in decline. Nor is the postmodernist celebration of fragmentation an adequate response. In order to regain the initiative, the left needs to define its own hegemonic project.

The defensive position of the left is relatively recent. In the thirties, progressive forces took the initiative in the United States and in the Western European countries where fascism did not come to power. The project of the left/labor coalition of that time was the regulation of the economy and the construction of a welfare state. That moment of progressive initiative was based on the understanding, which remained intact for several decades, that the state bore a significant responsibility for the social and economic well-being of citizens. In the late seventies and the eighties this perspective was largely replaced by the belief that the state should encourage private enterprise. Why has the initiative passed to the right? Peter Glotz, a West German Social Democrat, has put forward what may be the beginnings of an answer, in an analysis of British society. Glotz argues that Britain is in the course of becoming a "two-thirds society" in which the leadership is willing to accept "the social decline . . . of the weakest third of society—the unemployed, the odd-jobbers, the elderly of the lower classes. . . . This means that the leadership is more or less consciously engaged in mobilizing the forces of individual ownership, including a 'workers' aristocracy,' in mobilizing core employees against marginal ones."[27]

Glotz suggests that, at least in advanced capitalist societies, the key to social change lies not so much in what working-class forces can do themselves as in their relation to other social forces, in particular the middle third of society that includes more privileged workers—the stably employed, professionals, and other sections of the middle class. The concept of the two-thirds society has also been used by American analysts to explain the conservative drift of American politics and culture. Barry Bluestone, Bennett Harrison, Michael Harrington, and others have argued that the crucial question is whether the middle third of society (which at one time consisted mainly of professionals and the self-employed but now includes sections of organized labor as well) identifies up or down, with the wealthy or with the poor.[28]

The New Deal, according to this analysis, was possible because large sections of the middle third of American society identified their interests with the right of workers to organize and the right of poor people generally to better conditions of life. This analysis suggests not that the middle third is the initiator of change but that it holds the swing vote, that the tone of political life is determined by the alliances this sector chooses to form. The driving force behind New Deal reform was the campaign to organize industrial workers. But it was the alliance between the labor movement and a newly created liberal middle-class majority that made the reforms of the New Deal possible. In the postwar decades the acceptance of Cold War politics undermined the progressive worldview of the thirties, but prosperity and a continuing bottom-middle alliance in favor of social spending were the basis for an expanding welfare state.

It is Glotz's middle third, or at least the portion of it made up by stably employed workers, that New Social Movement theory writes off when it dismisses the working class as a force for social change. The working class encompasses much of the bottom third, but this stratum is made up largely of people of color and single women and their children, who enter New Social Movement analysis through categories of race and gender. The debate about the working class is really about the upper levels of that class— the stably employed, including blue-collar, white-collar, professional, and lower-level managerial categories, especially the large numbers of white men in these categories. More broadly, the debate is over whether a movement for radical change needs to be majoritarian. The strategy implicit in New Social Movement theory (and much of current anarchist thinking) is to create a movement based on the bottom third, organized around issues of race, gender, and social dispossession (such as homelessness), and the culturally alienated among the middle third. But these groups are not a majority of American society or for that matter of Western European societies.

Gramsci argued that the creation of a hegemonic project involves the construction of a historic bloc. Glotz's analysis suggests the need for a historic bloc uniting the bottom and middle sectors of society around a shared commitment to egalitarian programs. Because of the diversity of the working class and the many issues that cut across classes, especially issues of race and gender, the aim is no longer to create an alliance between the working class and other sectors of society. But the working class will have to be part of any new historic bloc. It is hard to imagine how the bottom and middle thirds could be brought together if the upper sections of the working class were left out. Furthermore, the working class cuts across the bottom two-thirds of society. One of the tasks of the left is to help them see their interests in an economic restructuring of society, as well as in cultural issues that anarchist politics and New Social Movement theory emphasize, as common rather then competing.

The left's inclination to reject the working class as the basis for social change partly reflects the dramatic changes in the class structure of American society after World War Two. The traditional definition of the working class is no help at all in the effort to locate revolutionary agency. Expanding that definition to include the vast majority of the population destroys class boundaries and the power of traditional class analysis, which claimed a revolutionary role for the working class on the basis of its relationship to surplus value (a claim that is harder to sustain outside the sphere of material production).[29] Another reason that the left is uneasy about linking the working class to revolution is that the term "working class" conjures up organized labor and the white men who are its largest constituency. In the postwar period, especially the seventies and eighties, race and gender have largely replaced class as the organizing categories on the left, as progressive forces have become fragmented into a series of particular constituencies. The debate about the working class and revolution is not about the people on the bottom of that class, who are mostly women and people of color. The debate is about white men, especially heterosexual white men. There is in fact a "white male problem" in the late twentieth-century United States (and in Western Europe as well): in the identity politics that dominate the new social movements, white men have no voice except as members of groups that include white men, such as gays and some ethnic groups. Many white men have felt threatened by affirmative action and have reacted defensively to feminism and racial affirmation. But since most white men also suffer from the unequal distribution of wealth and power in capitalist society, there must be a place for them in any majoritarian movement for radical change.

Building such a movement requires a hegemonic project that is more than the array of particular constituencies and perspectives that now make up the opposition to the power of the right. This hegemonic project must involve a restructuring of society in the realms of both political economy and culture. The labor/liberal alliance of the thirties was organized primarily around economic justice and the redistribution of resources. In the late twentieth century, any parallel historic bloc will have to be organized around cultural as well as economic issues. In the thirties, Americans confronted economic depression. In the nineties and beyond we confront the danger of nuclear war, the unfolding repercussions of women's entry into the labor force, rapidly changing configurations of gender and personal life, and declining national prosperity and world power. There is still a need for economic restructuring, but the problems of the late twentieth century also require a profound transformation of values.

The decline of the United States in prosperity and world power raises difficult issues for the left. In the past, progressive politics have been linked to economic expansion. Radical consciousness has been most likely to spread at moments when there is hope that things can get better, that collective action can make a difference; an expanding economy, or the expectation that it will expand, is an important part of that hope. Prosperity has not in itself led to progressive politics (as the experience of the twenties and the fifties shows). But the progressive and socialist movements of the early twentieth century flourished in times of economic growth. The movements of the thirties attracted truly massive support only when the depression began to lift. The movements of the sixties grew out of the expansion of higher education in the fifties and sixties; the political counterculture required low living costs and easy access to resources and faded as the economy went into decline. One of the most difficult tasks of the left will be constructing a progressive alliance: persuading the middle third to identify its interests with the lower third in the context of declining resources, and persuading the bottom third that economic growth is not the answer. (The contraction of resources and power throws the term "progressive" itself into question, but so far there is no good substitute for it.)

In order to put forward a program, or series of programs, effectively to challenge those of the right, the direct action movement and movements for social change generally need a theoretical perspective on the social and historical terrain on which they move. If traditional Marxism is no longer adequate, what might replace it? Perhaps a first step is Gramsci's analysis of modern capitalism as a system in which culture and the question of legitimacy have become arenas in the contest for power. This analysis is expanded by the Fordist analysis of the crisis of state power and the transformation of forms of social control in the postwar era. It is further enriched by the argument, put forward by the New Social Movement theorists, that as the structure of society changes, issues once secondary to politics, such as community and the construction of identity, become salient, movements turn to new methods, and people organize themselves in terms of new categories (without necessarily abandoning the old ones). Gramsci's analysis can be extended also by postmodernism, especially the argument that the boundaries between mass and critical culture have all but disappeared, that the impulses to celebrate and to protest the status quo have become almost entirely intermingled. The basis for a protest movement is not stable but must be continually reconstructed, and sustaining such a movement may require a degree of attention not necessary in earlier periods. These threads of Gramscian analysis, New Social Movement theory, and postmodernism are compatible with the argument, made by some anarchists and radical pacifists, that the new society must be built within the shell of the old, that as prefigurative movements and institutions proliferate they may accrue power and create a basis for social transformation.

Traditional Marxism will probably not be replaced by any one theory. Nor, for that matter, will all of it necessarily be replaced: many aspects of the tradition remain valid and important. The amalgam of Gramscian analysis, New Social Movement theory, postmodernism, and anarchist and radical pacifist thought that I have presented is meant as a contribution to an ongoing discussion, not as a fixed or final theoretical perspective. Someone else might draw different threads from the perspectives I have discussed, or might draw on a different set of perspectives. The argument of this chapter is not that it is possible to discover any one correct theory with which to replace traditional Marxism, but that some theories are better guides than others and that the effort to construct more adequate theory is vital to the prospects for social change.

Conclusion

In this book I have tried to go beyond simply recounting the history of the nonviolent direct action movement in the late seventies and eighties to address some of the questions I believe that history raises. I have argued that in the late twentieth-century United States, cultural crisis has reached such proportions that the traditional language of the left is no longer adequate; that the appeal of the nonviolent direct action movement is in its efforts to find a language and a political practice that speak to this crisis. I have described the direct action movement as the most recent in a series of postwar attempts to find a new way of thinking about what revolution means and what a revolutionary movement should be like. I believe that the direct action movement has made significant contributions to a radical politics for the United States. A large proportion of activists, especially young activists, in the movements of the late eighties shared the direct action movement's rejection of traditional Marxism and its orientation toward a prefigurative and nonviolent politics. It is unlikely that any new movement will replicate the forms developed in the Clamshell, the Abalone, and LAG without major modifications, but it is probable that the philosophy and process developed in those organizations will influence large sections of whatever movements may appear in coming years.

Many people in the more conventional, electorally oriented section of the movements for social change have regarded the direct action movement and its prefigurative politics as eccentric, at best harmless, at times an embarrassment, certainly a distrac-

263

tion from "genuine" politics. But it is no longer possible to separate radical politics from cultural revolution; the cultural crisis
that has shaped the direct action movement is evident in too many
areas of American life. The search for a new political language
that it brought about has extended far beyond the movement itself. *Habits of the Heart: Individualism and Commitment in American
Life,* a recent study of where Americans look for meaning in their
lives and how they talk about it, finds that the language available
for discussing values is very impoverished. On the basis of interviews with Americans who might all be described as middle-class
but who are otherwise quite diverse, the authors of *Habits of the
Heart* argue that Americans know how to talk about their private
aspirations, but they have little if any language for talking about
the value of social commitment, even though many yearn for it
and some act upon it.[1]

Habits of the Heart traces two strands in American political and
social thought: an early Puritan and republican tradition that saw
the meaning of individual lives in terms of their contribution to
society and a countervailing approach that defined meaning in
terms of individual success in a competitive arena. The second
language, the authors argue, has overshadowed the first, until
Americans can scarcely articulate their own desires for community or their own experiences of meaning through action for the
common good. *Habits of the Heart* calls for a revival of the Bibli-
cally tinged civic republicanism of early America to restore a balance between individualism and community and a social basis for
meaning.

The problem with this recommendation is that the civic republicanism of the founders of the United States has not been a living language for a long time; and when it lived it was the language of the elite. The civic republicanism of the Revolutionary
era, like the Revolution itself, was concerned with political structures, not social ones, with public rather than private life. It put
forward goals of political equality and freedom but skirted the
issue of slavery and entirely ignored the subordination of women.
Early republicanism rejected the theocracy of the Puritans but
retained their preference for a hierarchical society and their view
of virtue as the subordination of individual interests to higher
ideals. It envisioned a society led by the well-bred and well-edu-

cated, and it confronted the democratic current within the revolution, which called for a broader sharing of power and perhaps even some steps toward greater economic equality, with a good deal of nervousness. Civic republicanism tended to see politics as involving the subordination of private, individual concerns to a conception of the public good that reflected the values of the elite.

In fact, of course, the civic republicanism of the Revolution opened the door to an expansion of democracy accompanied by a different political language. Jacksonian democracy tried to redefine the common good in a way compatible with the interests of capitalists and other middle-class groups in a competitive, commercial society. Since then, as the authors of *Habits of the Heart* point out, values based on competition and individual achievement have assumed a dominant position in American social and political discourse. A range of left and populist movements have echoed the early republican concern for community and the common good but have defined it quite differently from the leaders of the Revolution. These movements have tried to expand democracy to include social and economic as well as political rights and they have identified the common good with the interests of those at lower levels of society. For many of these movements, the transformation of culture, of how we think and talk about social relations and issues of meaning, has been at most a subsidiary concern. *Habits of the Heart* shows that such things have become more pressing in late twentieth-century America, and not only for movements of the left.

The direct action movement addresses these issues in terms that have a vitality that the tradition of civic republicanism lacks. By calling for cultural and personal transformation as well as economic and political change, the movement breaks down the boundary between the public and private realms. In a society where such distinctions have become largely irrelevant, the blurring of boundaries makes sense to many people. The utopianism of the direct action movement and its insistence on a radically egalitarian form of democracy likewise strike a chord, as do its emphasis on building community, its orientation toward spirituality, and its attempt to bring questions of meaning to the foreground of political action.

The direct action movement of the late seventies and early

eighties was not the first to question traditional Marxism and seek
an alternative. It built on the cultural radicalism of the sixties,
which was, however, not always tied to a positive social vision or
an attempt to live values, and which also lacked a coherent theoretical basis. Though anarchism and nonviolence never disappeared from the movement, by the late sixties the impulse to return to well worked out (if inappropriate) models of revolution
was too strong to withstand. Radicalism would probably have diminished in the early seventies in any event, as the war in Vietnam ended, the generation that had been the movement's main
constituency aged, and the economy declined. But a viable though
smaller movement could have remained as a framework for continued efforts toward social change. SDS and the sections of the
movement that thought along similar lines collapsed because they
stopped trying to find a new approach to politics and instead imposed Third World models on a society in which they made no
sense.

The direct action movement has resumed the effort to find a
politics of cultural revolution. It has trained a large number of
new activists, it has had moments of considerable public impact
and appeal, and at its high points it has been able to attract constituencies that were never drawn to more traditional left movements. But it has not been able to solve the problem of how to
build a movement that prefigures a better society and is at the
same time sustained and effective over time. All of the large organizations of the direct action movement I have traced have had
brilliant but brief trajectories, in which large and intoxicating
protests have been followed by organizational collapse. Movement activists do not want to see this pattern as a problem; the
movement as a whole has been allergic to discussion of strategy
and efforts to construct lasting organizations. But the record of
the direct action movement raises the question of whether a prefigurative, utopian politics can be the basis for a lasting movement and, if it can, what form that movement would take and
what direction it might follow.

This book represents a rethinking of my own political views. I
have described the movements of the sixties as containing two
currents, one consisting of various forms of Marxism and social
democracy, the other influenced by various forms of anarchism

and including many people who thought that the counterculture had something to offer radical politics. Like most intellectuals who entered the movement through the university, I was part of the first current. The roots of the nonviolent direct action movement of the seventies and eighties can largely be traced to the second. My involvement with and study of direct action has convinced me that the second side has a creative potential and an ability to speak to the issues that the more conventionally political wing of the movement lacked.

Though I believe that in many ways the direct action movement points in the right direction, I do not think that it has all or even most of the answers to the question of how to build a movement for radical change. It has a better sense than more traditional movements of the relationship between values and political practice, but it has been almost entirely at sea when the question is how to get from here to there—by what strategy or organization. In the sixties, strategy and organization were taken seriously by the Marxist and social democratic side of the movement. The direct action movement has inherited the anarchist tendency to disregard these questions. In order to have a large impact, a movement must be guided not just by conscience and imagination but also by an understanding of the constraints and possibilities of its historical moment; and it must pay serious attention to building lasting organizations.

Strategy has not, however, been entirely neglected in the direct action movement. Many of the peace activists involved in the formation of the Abalone Alliance saw it as a first step toward a movement for nonviolent revolution; they thought that their movement would proceed from nuclear energy to nuclear arms and then to an egalitarian and nonviolent society. These views corresponded to (and were in many cases influenced by) George Lakey's *Strategy for a Living Revolution*.[2] Lakey outlined a strategy of creating the new society in the shell of the old through prefigurative organizations that would live out the values of the new society, transforming the consciousness of participants and the culture of the existing society. As these organizations proliferated, Lakey argued, an alternative set of values would gradually prevail in large sections of society. The revolution might be accomplished by accretion; if it entailed a moment of decisive change, the organizations of the nonviolent movement would serve as its base.

Lakey was a leading activist in the Philadelphia-based Movement for a New Society (MNS), which was formed around the effort to propagate this strategy among movement activists, along with the specific techniques of nonviolent direct action and consensus decision making. MNS had a considerable influence on the political culture of the Clamshell Alliance, through its nonviolence trainings, and also on the Abalone, of which David Hartsough, an MNS member, was a founder and key activist. But it was mostly the MNS guidelines for conducting direct actions and making decisions by consensus that the Clamshell and Abalone activists absorbed. Though many activists shared the MNS orientation toward prefigurative politics and nonviolent revolution, the strategic perspective put forward in Lakey's book was never a focus of discussion. Many of the ideas introduced by MNS were compatible with the views of movement Quakers who were not part of MNS, and also with the broad anarchist counterculture from which the Clamshell and the Abalone emerged. The one distinctive MNS contribution, the power of the individual to block consensus, was rather rigidly retained long after MNS itself ceased to play an active role in these organizations. The semi-Gramscian MNS conception of strategy, on the other hand, which involved building and maintaining a network of counterorganizations and institutions, was swept aside in favor of a focus on mass direct actions, ultimately conducted for their own sake rather than to build organizations or even for their probable outcomes.

The direct action movement's lack of interest in strategy is related to its emphasis on building and maintaining alternative communities and its tendency to avoid issues that might be disruptive. Most movement activists assume that building alternative communities and pursuing radical politics are entirely complementary: many believe that radical politics consists of building alternative communities. In the frequent contests between claims of community and of politics, community usually wins out, partly because of the bias against conflict within the movement and the tendency to value achieving consensus above all. The large direct action organizations I have looked at sooner or later reached the limits of an exclusive focus on mass direct actions. The Clamshell and LAG continued to hold mass actions chiefly to maintain communities that had come to define themselves around that tactic. In LAG, the argument that more direct actions would not bring results was countered by the argument that the identity of the movement was at stake.

I have argued that in the late twentieth-century United States, protest politics must be utopian, in the sense that it must hold out a vision of a nonviolent and egalitarian society, and that it must build the new society within the shell of the old by creating a space within which these values can be realized as far as possible. But there is an assumption running through the direct action movement that constructing an egalitarian, nonviolent society requires abolishing power relations and doing away with conflict, especially in the movement. It is assumed that conflict means violence, that power means domination, and that all forms of hierarchy are bad. These assumptions run so deep that they are rarely if ever examined. But I think they are wrong. The movement's suspicion of power and conflict makes it difficult to make strategy and to build the kinds of organizations that can weather changes in issues or tactics.

The direct action movement rejects the idea that revolution means seizing power, substituting one set of rulers for another, and leaving the hierarchical structure of society intact. It is one thing to reject this model and to look toward a society in which there is no centralized state power; it is another thing to believe that power itself should be or can be abolished. Power is what human relations are made of. It is based on human interdependence. If human beings were entirely self-sufficient, capable of living outside the network of social bonds, it might be possible to eliminate power relations. But people need one another for productive activity, for reproduction, for care in childhood, old age, and illness, for the construction of culture and identity, for emotional life. Human interdependence and social power are two sides of the same coin; they are the glue that holds society together. Social power of course takes many forms. But working toward a better society means trying to create new forms of social power, not trying to eliminate it. If human interdependence means social power, it also means conflict. As long as people and social groups occupy different positions in relation to one another, they will

understand their needs differently; social difference means dis-
agreement and conflict—though not necessarily violence. Conflict
is not only a necessary part of social life but, as Marx argued, the
source of development and creativity. The task for the nonviolent
movement is not to abolish power and conflict but to find egalitarian forms of power and nonviolent means of conflict.

The consensus process has been the direct action movement's
illustration of what social relations should be like, in alternative
communities in the present and in the society of the future.
Sometimes the consensus process brings out the creative potential
of conflict. By requiring that everyone participate actively in decision making it brings differences to the surface that might otherwise remain unexpressed and provides an arena for persuasion
and understanding. When the consensus process works well, it
strengthens bonds within the movement; during large actions it
can contribute to an atmosphere of intoxicating solidarity. Consensus process does, however, increase the pressure to achieve
unanimity in relatively short order. It can work well in organizations with specific immediate aims; but it may not be the best
model for a movement that hopes to sustain itself over time, grow,
and change. I do not argue that the consensus process should be
rejected or propose any particular modifications; these decisions
are probably best arrived at in the process of political activity itself. But an organizational model that has difficulty tolerating
conflict is likely to produce a fragile movement. Consensus is certainly not sufficient as a vision of a future society, which would
necessarily be far more diverse, and far more conflict-ridden, than
the direct action movement.

Though many people in the direct action movement, especially
the Christian activists, regard Gandhi as a major influence, the
conceptions of nonviolent direct action that prevail in the movement have been different from Gandhi's, particularly on questions of conflict and consensus and on the related issue of moral
elitism, the right of the movement to claim possession of the truth.
Gandhi's concept of satyagraha involved acting upon values that
would form the basis for a good society but was not utopian in
quite the same sense as the direct action movement's. Many people in the direct action movement envision nonviolence as if it
were a trip to an imagined land in which harmony prevails.

For Gandhi nonviolence was a way of interrupting a cycle of

violence, a conscious and principled strategy for arriving at a resolution of conflict that would be an advance over the initial positions of all parties. Nonviolence, for Gandhi, meant acting on one's
beliefs, perhaps risking one's life for them, but at the same time
remaining open to changing one's position if persuaded that another view was closer to the truth.[3] Many of the organizations of
the direct action movement, especially those with strong Quaker
influence, have admonished participants to remain "open, friendly
and respectful" to adversaries. But the Gandhian view goes beyond this. It understands nonviolence as a way of advancing toward
a never fully attainable truth, and conflict as the field within which
such advances can be made. This view is not necessarily contrary
to the use of consensus process, but it implies a perspective significantly different from that which has governed the direct action movement. The early civil rights movement was closer to
Gandhi's view of the relationship between nonviolence and conflict. The organizations I have looked at have functioned in a
more privileged arena, more remote from violence, which perhaps explains their tendency to imagine that the aim of politics is
to transcend conflict.

The question of hierarchy, and its relation to an egalitarian
movement and society, is also considerably more complex than
the direct action movement often takes it to be. The absolute
equality to which the movement aspires can never exist, and attempts to achieve it easily take on repressive overtones. No large
organization can function unless some people make sure that it
does. Preferably these people should not be self-appointed but
should be responsible to the rest of the organization. The failure
to acknowledge leadership, or to train new leaders to replace those
who need to reduce their involvement, has created problems for
each of the large direct action organizations. In each case an initial belief that the movement was and should be leaderless eventually gave way to a recognition among some activists of the need
for some form of leadership, but in no case soon enough to be
put into practice. Absolute equality is unrealistic, not only as a
basis for movement practice now, but also as a model of a future
society. In any society people will have a range of skills, capaci-
ties, and needs. To deny those inequalities would be to flatten
social relations and in the extreme to make society unworkable.

Michael Walzer, in *Spheres of Justice: A Defense of Pluralism and*

Equality, addresses the problems posed by a model based on absolute, or "simple," equality. He argues that it is legitimate and necessary for differences of power and status to exist in particular arenas of life: teachers may legitimately hold more power than students in the educational system; people with greater training and expertise in particular professions may legitimately have more say than others in certain kinds of professional decisions. What is unjust is for status in such hierarchies to carry over to social status, to determine access to social goods and power to influence decision making on the level of society as a whole. This analysis does not address the fundamental inequalities of class, gender, race, which as long as they exist cannot be isolated to particular realms but pervade society as a whole. But the concept of "complex equality" may be useful in thinking about how a movement could adhere to egalitarian values and at the same time function effectively, or what a viable egalitarian society might look like.[4]

Greater acceptance of conflict and of certain kinds of hierarchical structures (such as an accountable leadership) might give the movement more resilience and a more realistic and persuasive vision of a future society, but they do not solve the problem of strategy. In the narrowest sense, strategy is a conception of how to reach a particular goal: how to shut down a plant or a research laboratory or, on a broader scale, undermine the nuclear industry or end the arms race. The direct action movement has been more concerned with applying the method of direct action to these problems than with assessing whether the means will accomplish the ends. Because these objectives are moments in the process of building a nonviolent and egalitarian movement and society as much as ends in themselves, some neglect of strategy on this level may be appropriate (though it also has its price, in the form of widespread disappointment when immediate goals are not achieved).

I am more concerned with the movement's failure to develop, or even to imagine, a strategy in the broader Gramscian sense of an understanding of the movement's direction that is linked to a hegemonic project—a conception of the middle-range aims of the movement, longer-term than the closing of a particular plant but short of achieving a nonviolent, egalitarian society. A conception of this sort would include different tasks for different movements or constituencies; it would not require the direct action movement to do everything, or always to provide leadership. But it would give the movement some basis for assessing the importance of particular issues or campaigns and for deciding what organizations to work with and what constituencies to appeal to. Aims such as socialism or a stateless, decentralized society can anchor a movement's values and provide guidance on a very broad level. But a hegemonic project is more immediate. It rests on an understanding of current conflicts. It proposes a reorganization of society and a corresponding set of values that address these conflicts and at the same time take society further in the direction in which the movement would like to see it go.

Often the hegemonic project of a particular movement becomes clear only in retrospect. Communist Party members in the 1930s sincerely believed in a socialist society, but the hegemonic project of their movement was the organization of the industrial working class and its incorporation into American political life on as nearly equal terms with other social groups as possible. The hegemonic project of a movement may be broader than its immediate focus. By the latter part of the sixties, when they grew to mass proportions, the focus of contemporary movements was ending the war in Vietnam; their hegemonic project was cultural revolution.

Cultural revolution is still on the agenda, and it is the project of the direct action movement. Its achievement, however, seems considerably more distant now than in the sixties. Twenty-five years ago, even without dismantling corporate capitalism, it seemed possible to reduce the inequalities of gender and race (and in fact these structures were changed to some degree, though not in all ways for the better). Some movement values took hold in large areas of American society (though by the mid-seventies they were being twisted in the service of consumerism). Whatever the failures of the sixties in the light of the experience of later decades, there seemed to be room in American society to begin the process of social transformation the movements of the time aspired to. It would be hard to say the same for the direct action movement two decades later. Though American society still calls fundamental transformation of social relations and valu 1990s the obstacles to such a transformation have bec more apparent.

Though it may never be possible for a movement t

project with the clarity of hindsight, it is still important to make the effort, to try to think about objectives and ways of approaching them in terms that are large but nevertheless grounded in the reality of the present society. An analysis of this sort requires not only clarity about the social change desired but also an understanding of the fundamental tensions in the society and the aims of other social forces in relation to them. Stuart Hall's analysis of contemporary Britain as a stunted and declining world power, and of the hegemonic project of the British right as a repressive form of modernization, helps to explain the right's attack on the welfare state. It also provides a framework for thinking on the left, a first step toward formulating a progressive response to the problems of a stagnant system.

The question is what a similar analysis would be like for the United States. The British right, Hall argues, hopes to solve its problems by taking the United States as a model, constructing a modernized, high-technology economy while polarizing the class structure, improving the situation of those at the top while making conditions harsher for those at the bottom. The United States has problems too: a fragile and lopsided economy, deteriorating conditions for a large proportion of the population, declining political and economic power internationally. But the American right has no external model to look to; it may not have as clear a sense of direction as its British counterpart.

Listening to the rhetoric of the Reagan administration, one would have thought that its intent, and presumably that of the American right as a whole, was to reestablish the position the United States had held in the early years of the Cold War as the leading force in the world, with the accompanying prosperity. But the actions of the Reagan administration often did not match its words; though the military was greatly expanded, little was done to challenge the influence of the Soviet Union or, for that matter, to extend the power of the United States in any situations that looked dangerous. Perhaps the rhetoric was mainly for public consumption; it may be that the right, at least the right in power (as opposed to the popular right), does not have anything that could be called a social vision but merely hopes to protect the wealth and privileges of the upper class, especially against the Third World and poor people, mostly people of color, at home.

In a society rapidly becoming more racially and culturally diverse, in a world in which the familiar bipolar structure of power seems to be on the verge of collapse, the right may simply have adopted a fortress mentality.

In a sense it does not matter too much whether the American right genuinely aspires to restore the United States to its earlier position of power (and to the traditional values and social relations associated with that moment) or subscribes to that vision in order to maintain public support while actually intending only to preserve the power and privileges of its own class. The concept of democracy has become the framework within which issues of social and political direction are being fought out, and the right is compelled to defend its policies in that context. In the past the American right has often been relatively unconcerned with the question of democracy. The New Deal coalition constructed in the thirties was based on an association of the left with popular forces and the conception of democracy; in the postwar period, while that coalition lasted the right was associated with the defense of wealth and privilege. By the late seventies popular right-wing movements began to give the right a claim to the concept of democracy, and by the mid-eighties the Reagan administration was making extensive use of the opportunity, presenting itself as the genuine force for democracy at home and democratic change in the world.

Many movements for social change have challenged that claim by protesting the politics of the right: its support for the Nicaraguan Contras and for antidemocratic forces throughout the Third World, cuts in domestic social programs, policies in the schools and elsewhere that reinforce a unitary concept of American culture and deprive minority cultures of legitimacy. The definition of democracy has not wholly defaulted to the right: Central American solidarity groups, for instance, have insisted that democracy must include human rights and social reform as well as elections. But the question of what democracy means has not been a focus of discussion on the left. The vision of armed revolution has largely been abandoned but has not been replaced with any clear alternative. There is still a lingering association between democracy and liberalism, a sense that democracy is fundamentally bourgeois and therefore ultimately the property of the right.

Though the direct action movement has not directly engaged in a debate with the right about what democracy means, it has the basis for doing so, because its concept of democracy is a clear alternative to that of the right and because it sees genuine, radical democracy and revolution as synonymous. For the right, democracy means, fundamentally, electoral and constitutional processes through which the sway of capitalism and the current organization of power can be maintained, in the United States and throughout the world. This concept of democracy is linked to the preservation of the status quo. The direct action movement's concept of democracy, which involves everyone's expressing his or her views in all areas of society, may be closer to what most Americans think democracy should be.

Debate about what democracy means is not strategy. But understanding prefigurative politics and utopian democracy as part of a much broader contest could help to give the direct action movement, and other movements with similar values, a framework for their political practice. This perspective might reinforce a point made by Lakey and others, that although massive nonviolent direct action can be an important tactic, it is the process of building democratic and revolutionary organizations and institutions as an alternative basis for power (as well as for alternative social relations and values) that is crucial to social transformation. The direct action movement's claim to represent a better and more democratic society, expressed in organizations that revolve around direct actions and dissolve when they end, remains ephemeral. It needs to be worked out in organizations and institutions that hold together even when movement activity is low. The contest over what democracy means and the effort to put a different conception of it into practice needs to be extended also into the institutions of mainstream society where most people have their lives and identities. As long as prefigurative politics is restricted to groups that stand carefully apart from the Democratic party, trade unions, mainstream churches, and other such organizations, the movement will probably continue to consist largely of marginal or exceptional constituencies, those who are willing to join a movement simply because they share its ideas and commitments. Most movements are formed more organically; people join them in the context of their existing communities, out of the daily concerns of their lives.

Even if some of the ideas of the direct action movement were to be brought to efforts for social change in the existing institutions of society, the movement itself, or even some further-evolved version of the movement, will almost certainly stand outside those institutions as an alternative to them. The tension between efficacy and moral witness, or what I have called the politics of experience, is more or less a constant in American protest movements. Both sides of this tension are necessary, and as long as neither side of the movement claims to represent the only correct approach or tries to eliminate the other, each can be strengthened by the other's presence. The direct action movement, or some descendant of it, can usefully play the role of insisting upon the importance of the vision while other movements pay more attention to winning immediate victories.

Richard Flacks, in *Making History: The Radical Tradition in American Life*,[5] presents a framework for understanding why an American protest movement might avoid taking on the issue of political power directly and turn its energies instead toward constructing an alternate culture through which to influence the way Americans live and think about society. Flacks argues that in the United States the left has faced extraordinary obstacles to achieving its traditional goals, such as uniting the working class and infusing it with socialist consciousness, or taking power and transforming the political economy. Deep racial, ethnic, and religious divisions in the working class have impeded unity; a stubborn tradition of privatism and individualism has stood in the way of collective consciousness and action. The American left has been unable to provide the kinds of material gains that in other countries have bound the working class and other constituencies to the left and has thus, for the most part, been a failure on the terrain of politics.

But if the American left has been a political failure, Flacks argues, at its high points it has been a cultural success. In the early twentieth century, in the thirties, and in the sixties, movements of the left were able to form deep connections with particular communities. The left became a university in the values of democratic community and social commitment not only for activists but for large sections of the population. At its moments of strength, the left has provided the ideological and cultural basis for sustained democratic activism, and it has enabled the oppressed, disadvantaged, and excluded to identify with one another and to press for change. The left, Flacks writes, "has provided a continuing 'adversarial' thread in our culture that has counterbalanced themes that promote conformity to the logics of capitalism and the nation-state." Although the diversity of American society and the grip of individualism on American culture have prevented the left from becoming a powerful political force, other currents within the American tradition, such as the stubborn commitment to individual morality, have helped it to shape the thinking of many people outside the organizations and communities identified with the left. "Americans," Flacks writes, "are at least as likely to admire those who obey their conscience as those who obey the State, and more than a little disposed to question rather than accept the wisdom of those at the top."[6]

This analysis helps to explain the attraction and the influence of a movement that focuses on building an alternative, exemplary community and transforming culture rather than directly confronting state power or trying to reorganize the political economy. This analysis does not answer the question of how a politics of cultural radicalism can intersect with the struggles for political and institutional change that are also an indispensable part of the effort to move toward a better society. Though I have tried to suggest some broad directions, I have not suggested a strategy for the direct action movement or whatever related movements for cultural revolution may next appear. Answers to these questions are more likely to emerge in the context of political activity than to be given by any one historian or social theorist, however sympathetic to the movement and its aims.

Notes

Introduction

1. Interview with Osha Neumann, January 28, 1990.
2. Interview with Robbie Osman, January 29, 1990.
3. Ernesto Laclau and Chantal Mouffe, *Hegemony and Socialist Strategy: Toward a Radical Democratic Politics* (London: Verso, 1985).

Chapter 1

1. For a discussion of the oscillation between class politics and cultural revolution in the history of the American left, see Paul Buhle, *Marxism in the United States: Remapping the History of the American Left* (London: Verso, 1987).

2. Much of the literature on the history of the Communist Party stresses its failings, especially those of its early years in the twenties and early thirties. James Weinstein, *The Decline of Socialism in America, 1912–1925* (New York: Monthly Review Press, 1967), argues that the American Communist Party was founded on an ill-advised attempt to impose a foreign experience and ideology on the United States, that this error played a large role in the destruction of what had been a vital socialist movement, and that Soviet influence over the Party made it inescapably sectarian. Lewis Coser and Irving Howe, *The American Communist Party: A Critical History, 1919–1957* (Boston: Beacon, 1957), portrays the Party as the carrier of an "alien" ideology, not only in its early days but throughout its history. The Party's foreign ties and its sectarianism are also stressed by Theodore Draper in *The Roots of American Communism* (New York: Viking, 1957) and in *American Communism and Soviet Russia* (New York: Viking, 1960). Some more recent historians of the American Communist Party take a more positive view of its history or of segments of that history. Roger

Keeran, *The Communist Party and the Auto Workers' Unions* (Blooming-ton: Indiana University Press, 1980), defends the Party's history as a whole; he stresses the importance especially of the Party's organiza-tion of industrial unions in its early period. James Green, in his ar-ticle "Working Class Militancy in the Depression" (*Radical America* 6 [November–December 1972]: 1–35), disputes the portrayal of the Party's trade union work during the Third Period as sectarian. For a sympathetic portrayal of the Party's work organizing the unem-ployed, see Roy Rosenzweig, "Organizing the Unemployed: The Early Years of the Great Depression, 1929–1935" (*Radical America* 10 [July–August 1976]: 36–60). Frances Fox Piven and Richard A. Cloward, in *Poor People's Movements: Why They Succeed, How They Fail* (New York: Random House, 1977), portray the unemployed movement of the early thirties as spontaneous, rather than as the result of the inter-vention of the Party or any other organization—an interpretation they extend to the wave of strikes that took place in 1934. During the years when Third Period policies held sway (roughly 1928 to 1935), the most important contributions of the Party to the Ameri-can left may have been its recognition of the importance of race and the effort it devoted to fighting racism and attracting blacks. At its 1928 convention, the Party adopted a position of "self-determination for the Black Belt." Believing that the largely black-populated belt that cut across several states of the deep South constituted a largely independent economy and culture, the Party, prodded by the Soviet Union, identified American blacks as a "national minority" with the right to autonomy, if it wanted it. The problem with this position was that it became less true over time: southern blacks were migrat-ing north in large numbers and taking a greater part in the national economy and culture. Nevertheless, the Communists paid a con-certed attention to racism that contrasted sharply with the deplor-able record of most of the white American left. The Party's work among blacks in the thirties is discussed, sympathetically, in Mark Naison's *Communists in Harlem During the Depression* (Urbana: University of Il-linois Press, 1983). See also Mark Naison, "Harlem Communists and the Politics of Black Protest," *Marxist Perspectives* 1 (Fall 1978): 20–50.

3. The New Left, looking back later on the Popular Front, was sharply critical of the Party for showing so little interest in revolu-tion. James Weinstein, in *Ambiguous Legacy: The Left in American Pol-itics* (New York: Franklin Watts, 1975), argues that although Party members privately believed in socialism, the cause of socialism was not served by the Party's failure to advocate it publicly, except as an occasional afterthought, and that both the lack of an open defense

of socialism and the fact that many Communists kept their membership in the Party secret left the Party vulnerable to attack in the
McCarthy period. Al Richmond, in the chapter "Notes on the Thirties and Revolution" in his autobiography, *Long View from the Left:
Memoires of an American Revolutionary* (Boston: Houghton-Mifflin,
1972), 220–249, argues that it had become clear by the mid-thirties
that socialism was not on the agenda and that Communists would
have been excluded from many arenas had they been open about
their Party membership. The New Left criticism of Communists for
having concealed their membership in the Party during the thirties
and forties was made in retrospect; through this period left and right
groupings vied for power in the Party, but over different issues. In
1944 Earl Browder, leader of the Party through the thirties and ar-
chitect of the Popular Front policy, presided over the Party's formal
dissolution and its transformation into the Communist Political Association. The Popular Front had been based on the view that socialist revolution could be put off to the future while the fight against
fascism abroad and democratic reform at home were pursued by the
working class and its allies. The dissolution of the Communist Party
reflected a more extreme extension of this view. Browder argued
that the forces of democracy had prevailed, revolution was no longer
on the agenda, and that the existence of a Communist Party would
be an obstacle to establishing class harmony. A year later, in response to international criticism (in the form of an article by Jacques
Duclos, leader of the Communist Party of France), the Communist
Political Association was disbanded, the Communist Party reestablished, and Browder expelled. The discrediting of Browder and the
right-wing position that he represented opened the way for William
Z. Foster, Browder's longtime rival from the left within the Party.
As Browder's successor, Foster revived an approach that stressed class
struggle and foresaw the impending victory of one side or the other,
socialism or fascism. Some historians sympathetic to the overall aims
of the Party have deplored its return to left sectarianism, without
endorsing Browder's abnegation of class struggle. Peggy Dennis, in
her memoir *The Autobiography of an American Communist: A Personal
View of a Political Life, 1925–1975* (Westport, Conn.: Lawrence Hill,
1977), defends the role of her late husband, Gene Dennis, in opposing Foster's return to a conventional left politics. A similar argument
is made by Joseph Starobin in *American Communism in Crisis, 1943–
1957* (Cambridge, Mass.: Harvard University Press, 1972) and by
Maurice Isserman in *Which Side Were You On: The American Communist Party During the Second World War* (Middletown, Conn.: Wesleyan

University Press, 1982). Both see the Popular Front as the Party's best period precisely because its politics were closer to social democracy than to socialist revolution; both argue that such politics are the most promising basis for a broad-based American left and regret the Party's return to a more left stance after the expulsion of Browder in 1945. Maurice Isserman, in the chapter "The Collapse of the Communist Party" (*If I Had a Hammer: The Death of the Old Left and the Birth of the New* [New York: Basic, 1987], 12–14), points to the tensions created by the fact that the Party simultaneously provided a proletarian internationalist vision and a route to Americanization and membership in the American middle class.

4. The split that took place in the American left in the late forties and early fifties was extraordinarily and often bitterly emotional, because the issue of whether or not one was a legitimate American collided with questions of loyalty toward or betrayal of the left. Many in the group that began its trajectory toward neoconservatism at that time continue to be driven to justify their choice by demonstrating the authoritarian roots of popular movements, or at least popular movements of the left, and discovering a right-wing definition of democracy. The attempt to identify Populism with McCarthyism, which pervaded writing about both movements in the fifties and early sixties, identified both as anti-intellectual and shaped by a spirit of resentment, on analogy with fascism, and offered a dim view of all popular movements. Many of the neoconservative inheritors of that tradition have at least partially revised their views in the 1980s, with the emergence of conservative and anti-Communist popular movements in the United States and elsewhere; but their effort to construct a right-wing definition of democracy, which helped the Reagan administration legitimize its policies in the Third World, refers back to the debates of the late forties and the argument that one can be simultaneously anti-Communist and democratic. An excellent account of the postwar split in the American left is Mary McAuliffe's *Crisis on the Left: Cold War Politics and American Liberals, 1947–1954* (Amherst: University of Massachusetts Press, 1975). See also Norman D. Markowitz, *The Rise and Fall of the People's Century: Henry A. Wallace and American Liberalism, 1941–1948* (New York: Free Press, 1973).

5. My understanding of the history of the American left as rooted in two different cultures is drawn from Mari Jo Buhle's account of the American women's movement in the early twentieth century, *Women and American Socialism, 1870–1920* (Urbana: University of Illinois Press, 1981), and from Paul Buhle's history of American radi-

calism as a whole, *Marxism in the United States: Remapping the History of the American Left* (London: Verso, 1987).

6. For accounts of the political culture the IWW created on the basis of its largely footloose working-class constituency, see Melvin Dubofsky, *We Shall Be All: A History of the I.W.W.* (Chicago: Quadrangle, 1969), and Rosalyn Baxandall, ed., *Words on Fire: The Life and Writings of Elizabeth Gurley Flynn* (New Brunswick, N.J.: Rutgers University Press, 1987).

7. The Women's Trade Union League (WTUL) provides an interesting study in the tensions between immigrant and native-born cultures and the difficulties of integrating feminist and working-class perspectives. The women of the WTUL were committed to both socialism and feminism but torn by the conflicting pressures and demands of the largely immigrant labor movement and the largely native-born middle- and upper-middle-class women's movement. For accounts of this experience see Alice Kessler-Harris, "Organizing the Unorganizable: Three Jewish Women and Their Union," *Labor History* 17, no. 1 (Winter 1976); Robin Miller Jacoby, "The Women's Trade Union League and American Feminism," in *Class, Sex, and the Woman Worker,* ed. Milton Cantor and Bruce Laurie (Westport, Conn.: Greenwood, 1977), 203–224; and Nancy Shrom Dye, "Creating a Feminist Alliance: Sisterhood and Class Conflict in the New York Women's Trade Union League, 1903–1914," in *Class, Sex, and the Woman Worker,* 225–245.

8. See Joan V. Bondurant, *Conquest of Violence: The Gandhian Philosophy of Conflict* (Berkeley and Los Angeles: University of California Press, 1965), esp. chap. 7, "The Gandhian Dialectic and Political Theory."

9. C. Seshachari, *Gandhi and the American Scene: An Intellectual History and Inquiry* (Bombay: Nachiketa, 1969), esp. chap. 6, "Gandhi and Pacifism: A Dream and Its Distortions."

10. For a general history of the postwar peace movement in the United States, see Lawrence S. Wittner, *Rebels Against War: The American Peace Movement, 1933–1983* (Philadelphia: Temple University Press, 1984). For an account of radical pacifism in the fifties, see Isserman, "Radical Pacifism: The Americanization of Gandhi," in *If I Had a Hammer.* For a detailed account of the history of the CNVA, see Neil H. Katz, "Radical Pacifism and the Contemporary American Peace Movement: The Committee for Nonviolent Action, 1957–1967" (Ph.D. dissertation, University of Maryland, 1974). If one figure was central in the radical pacifist movement of the forties and fifties, it was A. J. Muste; see Jo Ann Ooiman Robinson, *Abraham Went Out:*

A Biography of A. J. Muste (Philadelphia: Temple University Press, 1981), and "A. J. Muste and Ways to Peace," in *Peace Movements in America,* ed. Charles Chatfield (New York: Schocken, 1973). The best primary source for the history of radical pacifism in the forties and fifties is the journal *Liberation,* edited and published in New York by Dave Dellinger, Roy Finch, A. J. Muste, and Bayard Rustin, leaders of that movement. On the effort to create intentional communities, see Staughton Lynd, "The Individual Was Made for Community," and Dave Dellinger, "The Community Was Made for Man," both in *Liberation* 1, no. 11 (February 1957). See also David R. Newton, "The Macedonia Community," *Politics* (Winter 1948), 27–30. For first-person accounts of the connections between radical pacifism and the early civil rights movement, see *We Are All Part of One Another: A Barbara Deming Reader,* ed. Jane Meyerding (Philadelphia: New Society Publishers, 1984), esp. "The Early Sixties"; and Bayard Rustin, *Down the Line: The Collected Writings of Bayard Rustin* (Chicago: Quadrangle, 1971). On the conflict between the radical pacifists and the leadership of Sane over the question of Communist participation in the peace movement, see A. J. Muste, "The Crisis in Sane," *Liberation* 5, nos. 5–6 (July–August 1960): 10–13; "The Crisis in Sane: Act II," *Liberation* 5, no. 9 (October 1960); and the exchange between Muste and Norman Cousins in *Liberation* 5, no. 10 (December 1960).

11. For an account of the various expressions of dissident politics that nevertheless managed to flourish in the late fifties and early sixties see Isserman, *If I Had a Hammer.* Most histories of the 1960s emphasize the newness of the New Left and neglect the connections between the remaining Old Left organizations and communities and the emergence of a new movement. An unpublished manuscript by Ilene Rose Feinman, "Out of the Sandbox: SLATE and the Emergence of a New Left," provides a perceptive account of these connections in the San Francisco Bay Area.

12. For accounts of the mutual antagonism between the Students for a Democratic Society (SDS) and its social democratic parent organization, the League for Industrial Democracy, see Kirkpatrick Sale, *SDS* (New York: Random House, 1973), and James Miller, *"Democracy Is in the Streets": From Port Huron to the Siege of Chicago* (New York: Simon & Schuster, 1987). For a sample of social democratic suspicions of the New Left, see Irving Howe, "New Styles in 'Leftism,' " in *The Radical Imagination* (New York: New American Library, 1967), 64–89. See also Michael Harrington's regrets about his role in this process in "Between Generations," *Socialist Review* 93/94 (May–August 1987): 152–158. The antagonism between the Communist

Party and SDS has been written about less because there were no organizational ties at stake, but it was no less strong. For a sample of the debate between the Old Left and the New over the merits of Communist history, see James Weinstein, "The Left, Old and New," *Socialist Review* 10 (July–August 1972): 7–60; Max Gordon, "The Communist Party of the Nineteen-Thirties and the New Left," James Weinstein's response, and Max Gordon's reply, *Socialist Review* 27 (January–March 1976): 11–66. See also Peggy Dennis, "On Learning from History," a response to James Weinstein's *Ambiguous Legacy: The Left in American Politics*, in *Socialist Review* 29 (July–September 1977): 125–143.

13. For a discussion of the impact of the war and the subsequent process of modernization on race relations in the South, see Piven and Cloward, "The Civil Rights Movement," in *Poor People's Movements*, 182–202.

14. For a good survey of the changes in the place of women in American society in the postwar era, see William H. Chafe, *The American Woman: Her Changing Social, Economic, and Political Roles, 1920–1970* (New York: Oxford University Press, 1972). Betty Friedan's *Feminine Mystique* (New York: Norton, 1967) details the gap between the prevailing standards of femininity and the actual conditions experienced by middle- and upper-middle-class white women.

15. In *The Feminine Mystique*, Betty Friedan described the dissatisfaction of many women, especially young middle- and upper-middle-class women, with the prospect of lives like their mothers', largely confined to the domestic sphere. The uneasiness young men of the same class felt about following in their fathers' footsteps has been less discussed but was no less important as a source of radicalism in the sixties. The appeal of Paul Goodman's *Growing up Absurd: The Problem of Youth in the Organized System* (New York: Random House, 1956) reflected the widespread desire to find different paths. Kenneth Keniston, *Young Radicals: Notes on Committed Youth* (New York: Harcourt, Brace & World, 1968), studies participants in the 1967 Vietnam Summer Project and describes their ambivalence about accepted notions of success and their reluctance to enter the "establishment." Richard Flacks, *Making History: The Radical Tradition in American Life* (New York: Columbia University Press, 1988), traces the cultural radicalism of the sixties to the social and cultural contradictions of the postwar era; see "The Postwar Charter" (53–57), "The Erosion of the Postwar Charter" (58–63), and "The Revival of Activism in the Sixties" (160–168).

16. The transformation of race relations in twentieth-century

America is traced in Harold Baron's essay "The Demand for Black Labor: Historical Notes on the Political Economy of Racism," *Radical America* 5, no. 2 (March–April, 1971), and in Michael Omi and Howard Winant, *Racial Formation in the United States: From the 1960s to the 1980s* (New York: Routledge & Kegan Paul, 1986). See also Robert Allen, *Black Awakening in Capitalist America: An Analytic History* (Garden City, N.Y.: Doubleday, 1969). Baron traces the incorporation of blacks into the national economy as a result of economic expansion. Omi and Winant, writing about racial minorities in the United States generally, argue that because it includes both second-class status based on race and incorporation, the experience of these groups cannot be understood on either an "immigrant" model, which expects any group entering American society at the bottom to rise and be integrated into it, or an "internal colonialism" model that sees nonwhite groups as semi-autonomous. They argue for the concept of a "racial state." In the realm of economics, a parallel concept is put forward by David M. Gordon, Richard Edwards, and Michael Reich, in *Segmented Work, Divided Workers: The Historical Transformation of Labor in the United States* (New York: Cambridge University Press, 1982). In the postwar years especially, economic incorporation without corresponding social and political integration highlighted racial inequities and led to increased protest.

17. Bernard Brodie, an early analyst of nuclear strategy, recognized that the existence of nuclear weapons meant that the conventional goal of winning wars must be abandoned in favor of avoiding them and also undermined the view that more military capability led to more political power. Fred Kaplan, *The Wizards of Armageddon* (New York: Simon & Schuster, 1983; 30–32) shows the resilience of strategic thinking to such ideas and the continuing influence of conventional military assumptions. Gregg Herken, in *The Atomic Bomb in the Cold War, 1945–1950* (New York: Vintage, 1982), looks at the Truman administration's confidence in the bomb's ability to confer political power.

18. Nuclear strategy is modeled on war in Western Europe, where most analysts agree nuclear war is unlikely to start. Mary Kaldor points to the fantastic quality of strategic nuclear thinking in her article "The Imaginary War," in *Prospectus for a Habitable Planet*, ed. Dan Smith and E. P. Thompson (Harmondsworth: Penguin, 1987).

19. For indications of the growing appeal of pacifist thinking among at least some sections of the American population, see Paul Loeb, *Hope in Hard Times: America's Peace Movement and the Reagan Era* (Lexington, Mass.: Lexington Books, 1987).

20. See Paul Buhle, "Jews and American Communism: The Cultural Question," *Radical History Review* 23 (Spring 1980): 9–33.

21. Challenges to male dominance were never an important part of the Party's political program, but the fact that Leninist theory recognized the danger of "male chauvinism" meant that there was room for criticisms of what would later be called sexism in the internal life of the Party. For discussion of this aspect of the history of the Communist Party, see Ellen Kay Trimberger, "Women in the Old and New Left: The Evolution of a Politics of Personal Life," *Feminist Studies* 5, no. 3 (Fall 1979): 432–461; and the response by Peggy Dennis in the same issue. See also Baxandall, ed., *Words on Fire*. The Party's failure to make a systematic critique of traditional modes of exercising power left its leadership open to abuses of power much like those that routinely appear in conventional politics. At moments during the Popular Front period the Party's leadership was willing to betray its constituency and its own integrity in order to protect its alliance with the leadership of the CIO. The leadership intervened, for example, in the UAW elections of 1939 on behalf of a corrupt centrist candidate, preventing the election of the candidate of the union's left caucus, and actively supported the resolution put forward at the 1947 CIO convention that equated communism and fascism and rejected both. For a discussion of the Party's accomplishments and the internal contradictions that led to its decline, see Flacks, "How the CP Nurtured—and Destroyed—Grassroots Activism," *Making History*, 143–160.

22. Paul Potter, *A Name for Ourselves* (Boston: Little, Brown, 1971), 52.

23. Richard Flacks, "Some Problems, Issues, Proposals," in *The New Radicals: A Report with Documents,* ed. Paul Jacobs and Saul Landau (New York: Vintage, 1966), 163–164.

24. Much of the literature on the movements of the sixties describes how rapidly they were radicalized and the relationship between their turn to revolutionary politics and their demise in the late sixties and early seventies. Clayborne Carson, *In Struggle: SNCC and the Black Awakening of the 1960s* (Cambridge, Mass.: Harvard University Press, 1980), explains SNCC's turn toward Black Power sympathetically, but points out the political cost. See also James Foreman, *The Making of Black Revolutionaries* (New York: Macmillan, 1972). Sara Evans, in *Personal Politics: The Roots of Women's Liberation in the Civil Rights Movement and the New Left* (New York: Vintage, 1980), describes a different and ultimately more lasting process of radicalization. Several books about SDS view the shift from the ide-

alism of the early years to the revolutionary anger of the later years as unfortunate: Nigel Young, in *An Infantile Disorder? The Crisis and Decline of the New Left* (Boulder, Colo.: Westview, 1977), argues that the movement's effectiveness was undermined by its abandonment of pacifism and its growing attraction to violence, at least in its rhetoric; Miller, in *"Democracy Is in the Streets,"* argues that the vagueness of the early New Left concept of participatory democracy left SDS open to a late takeover by Marxist-Leninist sects, whose influence in the late sixties led to its downfall. Todd Gitlin, in *The Sixties: Years of Hope, Days of Rage* (New York: Bantam, 1987), gives a somewhat more sympathetic account of the process of radicalization but believes that the revolutionary posture of the antiwar movement by the late sixties doomed it to marginality and irrelevance. Wini Breines, in *Community and Organization in the New Left, 1962–1968* (New York: Praeger, 1982), provides a much more positive view of the late sixties, pointing to the flowering of feminism and grass roots organizing. Jane J. Mansbridge's *Beyond Adversary Democracy* (New York: Basic, 1980) is not a history of the New Left but an account of its political theory and a comparison of its conception of democracy with the conventional liberal conception. Mansbridge contributes indirectly to the discussion of the New Left's rejection of liberalism by providing a perceptive and sympathetic account of the radical conception of democracy that was widespread in the movement by the late sixties.

25. Paul Potter, "The Incredible War," in *The New Left: A Documentary History,* ed. Massimo Teodori (Indianapolis: Bobbs-Merrill, 1969), 246–248.

26. Carl Oglesby, "Trapped in the System," in *New Left,* 182–188.

27. Potter, *A Name for Ourselves,* 101.

28. This process is tellingly described by Elinor Langer in her account of her own experience in the movement, "Notes for the Next Time: A Memoir of the 1960s," *Working Papers* (Fall 1973): 48–81.

29. The breakup of SDS is described throughout the literature on the New Left; see Sale, *SDS,* for a detailed account; for analyses see Gitlin, *Sixties,* and Miller, *"Democracy Is in the Streets."* For an account of the antiwar movement that stresses sources other than SDS, see Nancy Zaroulis and Gerald Sullivan, *Who Spoke Up? American Protest Against the War in Vietnam, 1963–1975* (Garden City, N.Y.: Doubleday, 1984).

30. The Berrigans, for instance, were widely admired for conducting raids on Selective Service and FBI offices and publically burning files; in some cases these actions resulted in long jail sentences. For an account of the role of nonviolent protest in the anti-

war movement, see Robert Cooney and Helen Michalowski, eds., *The Power of the People: Active Nonviolence in the United States* (Culver City, Calif.: Peace Press, 1977): 182–209.

31. For an account of the flowering of radical culture in the late sixties, see Breines, *Community and Organization*.

32. See the discussion in note 24, above.

33. Flacks, "Some Problems, Issues, Proposals," 163.

34. Judith Hole and Ellen Levine, *Rebirth of Feminism* (New York: Quadrangle, 1971), describes the development of the radical wing of feminism in the mid- to late sixties, coming largely out of SNCC, SDS, and the antiwar movement.

35. Osha Neumann, unpublished manuscript.

36. The roots of the antinuclear movement in the countercultural left and in its flight to the countryside are described in a pamphlet published by a collective in the Jamaica Plains neighborhood of Boston that was part of that movement. *Strange Victories: The Anti-Nuclear Movement in the U.S. and Europe* (Boston: Midnight Notes Collective, 1979) argues that the movement must acknowledge its particular historical and class base in order to break out of its cultural isolation.

37. The attempt to develop a Gramscian politics for the American left was expressed in "The Making of Socialist Consciousness," *Socialist Revolution* 1, no. 1 (January–February 1970): 3–11, and no. 2 (March–April 1970): 7–32; and in a critique of the New Left and the antiwar movement by John Judis, "The Triumph of Bourgeois Hegemony in the Face of Nothing That Challenges It," *Socialist Revolution* 1, no. 2 (March–April 1970): 107–125. A closely related theoretical and political orientation was expressed by Karl Klare in "The Critique of Everyday Life, the New Left, and the Unrecognizable Marxism," in *The Unknown Dimension: European Marxism Since Lenin,* ed. Dick Howard and Karl E. Klare (New York: Basic, 1971).

38. The Gramscian/feminist analysis that led the editors of *Socialist Revolution* to support the effort to build such a movement was put forward in "The New American Movement: A Way to Overcome the Errors of the Past," *Socialist Revolution,* no. 7, vol. 2, no. 1 (January–February 1971): 31–68.

Chapter 2

1. Little has been written about the antinuclear movement of the late seventies, and most of what has appeared is descriptive rather than analytical. See Marty Jezer, "Who's on First? What's on Second?

A Grassroots Political Perspective on the Anti-Nuclear Movement,"
WIN, October 12, 1978, 5–12; Stephen Vogel, "The Limits of Protest: A Critique of the Anti-Nuclear Movement," *Socialist Review* 54
(November–December 1980): 125–134; and Jim O'Brien, "Environmentalism as a Mass Movement: Historical Notes," *Radical America*
17, nos. 1, 2 (May–June 1983): 7–27. The June 16–23, 1977, issue
of *WIN,* entitled "Seabrook 2," was devoted to the Clamshell Alliance
and similar organizing efforts around the country; see in particular
Murray Rosenblith, "Surrounded by Acres of Clams," 4–10, and Marty
Jezer, "Learning from the Past to Meet the Future," 17–23.

2. Interview with Anna Gyorgy, January 26, 1985.

3. Interview with Cathy Wolff, August 25, 1985.

4. Interview with Cindy Leerer, August 25, 1985.

5. For an account of the Wyhl occupation and other European
antinuclear actions, see Anna Gyorgy and friends, *No Nukes: Everyone's Guide to Nuclear Power* (Boston: South End Press, 1979), 347.

6. Interview with Sam Lovejoy, January 26, 1985. See the account
in Gyorgy, *No Nukes,* 393–402; and also the film *Lovejoy's Nuclear
War,* distributed by Green Mountain Films.

7. Interview with Sam Lovejoy.

8. Ibid.

9. Interview with Guy Chichester, August 24, 1985.

10. Interview with Elizabeth Boardman, June 8, 1985.

11. Interview with Guy Chichester.

12. These and quoted remarks in next two paragraphs from an
interview with Meg Simonds, November 13, 1984.

13. Interview with Elizabeth Boardman.

14. Interview with Richard Bell, June 7, 1985.

15. My account of this debate is drawn from interviews with many
former Clams, including Harvey Halpern, who was a leader of the
hard Clam group (August 25, 1985); Richard Bell, a leader of
the opposition within Boston Clams (June 7, 1985); Anna Gyorgy
and Sam Lovejoy (January 26, 1985), who were members of Montague Farm; and seacoast activists Cathy Wolff (August 25, 1985)
and Sharon Tracy (August 24, 1985). Former Clams disagree sharply
among themselves about why the organization was destroyed. The
interpretation that I give here, and elsewhere in this chapter, is my
own.

16. *Seabrook '78: A Handbook for the Occupation/Restoration Beginning June 24,* Clamshell Alliance, 1978, 9.

17. *Seabrook '78,* 14.

18. Interview with Harvey Halpern.

19. Interview with Richard Bell.

20. Ibid.

21. Interview with Murray Bookchin, May 26, 1986.

22. Interview with Cathy Wolff.

23. Interview with Aikos Barton, January 17, 1986.

24. "Goal of Clamshell: Stopping Nukes and Creating a Better World" (mimeographed paper in Anna Gyorgy's archives).

25. *Seabrook '78,* 10.

26. Interview with Anna Gyorgy.

27. Interview with Aikos Barton.

28. Interview with Crystal Gray, October 3, 1985.

29. Interview with Richard Bell.

30. Interview with Cathy Wolff.

31. Interview with Richard Bell.

32. Marty Jezer discusses this problem in his article "Learning from the Past." The limited nature of the Clamshell constituency is also the subject of a pamphlet produced by a Clamshell group, "Strange Victories: The Anti-Nuclear Movement in the U.S. and Europe" (Boston: Midnight Notes Collective, 1979). The pamphlet argues (as I do here) that the social base of the antinuclear movement was mainly the middle-class youth counterculture, transplanted from the cities to the countryside, strongest in northern New England and California. The pamphlet points to the difficulties in maintaining a coalition between this group and local inhabitants uneasy about nuclear plants in their backyards, and the political cost to the Clamshell of its restricted constituency.

33. Jezer, "Learning from the Past," 21.

Chapter 3

1. Interviews with Liz Walker, September 19, 1983, and October 5, 1984, and David Hartsough, November 8, 1984.

2. For a brief history of the Abalone Alliance, see Mark Evanoff, "Once upon an Earthquake Fault," *It's About Times,* November–mid-December 1980. *It's About Times,* the Abalone newspaper, is the best source on the development of the Abalone. My account is based on interviews with Mark Evanoff (October 28, 1984), Raye Fleming (April 21, 1987), Susan Lawrence (October 24, 1984), Tommy Reynaldo (January 31, 1987), Marcy Darnovsky (February 14, 1987), Steven Leeds (November 1, 1984), Joyce Howarton (April 21, 1987), and Susan Swift (October 20, 1984), among others.

3. See the October–November 1981 issue of *It's About Times,* which was devoted to reporting the blockade.

4. Interview with Raye Fleming.

5. Interview with Sandy Silver, April 21, 1987.

6. Interview with Scott Kennedy, February 21, 1987.

7. Interview with Tommy Reynaldo.

8. My account of the development of the anarcha-feminist current within the Abalone is based on interviews and discussions with Noël Sturgeon (October 31, 1984), Crystal Gray (October 3, 1985), and Jackrabbit (February 17, 1987).

9. Interview with Jackrabbit.

10. Ibid.

11. Ibid.

12. Interview with Noël Sturgeon.

13. Ibid.

14. Interview with Jackie Cabasso, February 27, 1987.

15. Interview with Jackrabbit.

16. Interview with Jackie Cabasso.

17. Interview with Noël Sturgeon.

18. Interview with Charlotte Davis, February 22, 1987.

19. Interview with Jackie Cabasso.

20. Interview with Joyce Howarton.

21. Ibid.

22. Interview with Mark Evanoff.

23. Interview with Susan Lawrence.

24. Interview with Joyce Howarton.

25. Marcy Darnovsky, "Direct Action as Living Theater in the Movement Against Nuclear Power" (unpublished paper, University of California, Santa Cruz, 1989).

Chapter 4

1. LAG had roots in the radical pacifist wing of the peace movement as well as in the direct action wing of the antinuclear movement; there is more literature on the former than the latter. See Robert Cooney and Helen Michalowski, eds., *The Power of the People: Active Nonviolence in the United States* (Culver City, Calif.: Peace Press, 1977), for the history of the nonviolent movement through the Vietnam war. Charles Chatfield, *For Peace and Justice: Pacifism in America, 1914–1941* (Knoxville: University of Tennessee Press, 1971), is a detailed account of the early peace movement. The postwar period is discussed in Carl Wittner, *Rebels Against War: The American Peace Movement, 1941–1960* (Philadelphia: Temple University Press, 1969). More recent history is discussed in Paul Boyer, "From Activism to

Apathy: The American People and Nuclear Weapons, 1963–1980," *Journal of American History* 70, no. 4 (March 1984): 821–844, and in Paul Rogat Loeb, *Hope in Hard Times: America's Peace Movement and the Reagan Era* (Lexington, Mass.: Lexington Books, 1987). But there is little discussion of the direct action wing of the peace movement in the recent period.

2. For the following account I relied on interviews with Ken Nightingale (September 5, 1983), Tamara Thompson and Arlene Feng (March 26, 1984), Patrick Diehl (October 28, 1983), Robbie Osman (September 28, 1983), and Osha Neumann (November 4, 1983).

3. For an account of this blockade by two participants, see Jackie Cabasso and Susan Moon, *Risking Peace: Why We Sat in the Road* (Berkeley, Calif.: Open Books, 1985).

4. Interview with Terry Messman, November 23, 1983.

5. Ibid.

6. Interview with Pamela Osgood, October 17, 1983.

7. Interview with Erica Fox, August 5, 1984.

8. Interview with Starhawk, September 26, 1983.

9. Ibid.

10. Ibid.

11. Starhawk's proposal for a feminist model of leadership was presented in "The Leadership Workshops," *Reclaiming Newsletter* 15 (Summer 1984), and was further developed in her book *Truth or Dare: Encounters with Power, Authority, and Mystery* (San Francisco: Harper & Row, 1987), 276.

12. Interview with Patrick Diehl.

13. Interview with Ken Nightingale.

14. In November 1982 the *LAG Rag* published a letter from Bob Rivera of the Overthrow Cluster, outlining objections held by many in the Cluster to the pledge not to damage property. A pamphlet by Howard Ryan, "Blocking Progress: Consensus Decision-Making in the Anti-Nuclear Movement" (Berkeley, Calif.: Overthrow Cluster of the Livermore Action Group, 1983), contained a sharp critique of the consensus process. The Cluster, in an introductory note, described the piece as "a starting point for dialogue."

15. Interview with Anna Graves and Steven Sutcher, June 14, 1984.

16. *San Francisco Examiner,* Tuesday, January 31, 1984; *Oakland Tribune,* Wednesday, February 1, 1984; *Direct Action,* March 1984.

17. Interview with Doris Bowles, October 18, 1984.

18. Ibid.

19. Interview with Pat Daane, November 14, 1984.

20. Ibid.

21. Interview with Joan McIntyre, October 29, 1984.
22. Interview with Robbie Osman, January 29, 1990.
23. Interview with Osha Neumann, February 6, 1990.

Chapter 5

1. For descriptions of the Women's Pentagon Actions, see Susan Pines, "Women's Pentagon Action," *WRL News* (War Resister's League), January–February 1981; and Lynn Johnson, "Weaving a Web of Life: Women's Pentagon Action 1981," *WIN*, January 15, 1982.

2. See Starhawk, *Dreaming the Dark: Magic, Sex and Politics* (Boston: Beacon, 1982), 168–169.

3. For an account of the Seneca Peace Camp, see Lois Hayes, "Separatism and Disobedience: The Seneca Peace Encampment," *Radical America* 17, no. 4 (July–August 1983): 55–64. *We Are Ordinary Women: A Chronicle of the Puget Sound Women's Peace Camp*, by participants of the Puget Sound Women's Peace Camp (Seattle: Seal Press, 1985), includes personal accounts of a smaller but in many ways similar camp, also held in 1983.

4. Murray Bookchin, *Post-Scarcity Anarchism* (Berkeley: Ramparts Press, 1971).

5. Peggy Kornegger, "Anarchism: The Feminist Connection," in *Anarchism and Feminism: Three Essays '75–'80* (Brisbane: Brickburner Press, 1981), 11–12.

6. Carol Ehrlich, *Socialism, Anarchism and Feminism* (London: Black Bear, September 1978), 5.

7. Kytha Kurin, "Anarcha-Feminism: Why the Hyphen?" in *Anarchism and Feminism: Three Essays '75–'80* (Brisbane: Brickburner Press, 1981), 25–36.

8. Jo Freeman (writing as Joreen), "The Tyranny of Structurelessness," reprinted in *Radical Feminism,* ed. Anne Koedt, Ellen Levine, and Anita Rapone (New York: Quadrangle, 1973), 285.

9. Ehrlich, "Socialism, Anarchism and Feminism," 14. See also Cathy Levine, *The Tyranny of Tyranny* (London: Dark Star Distribution Service, no date).

10. Margaret Murray, *The Witch Cult in Western Europe* (Oxford: Oxford University Press, 1921); Margot Adler, *Drawing Down the Moon: Witches, Druids, Goddess-Worshippers, and Other Pagans in America Today* (Boston: Beacon, 1979).

11. Interview with Margot Adler, July 4, 1987. This estimate is based on a survey conducted by the Covenant of the Goddess.

12. Ibid.

13. Ibid.

14. Charlene Spretnak, ed., *The Politics of Women's Spirituality: Essays on the Rise of Spiritual Power Within the Women's Movement* (New York: Anchor, 1982); Merlin Stone, *When God Was a Woman* (New York: Harcourt Brace Jovanovich, 1976); Riane Eisler, *The Chalice and the Blade: Our History, Our Future* (San Francisco: Harper & Row, 1987).

15. Bronislaw Malinowski, *The Sexual Life of Savages in North-Western Melanesia: An Endographic Account of Courtship, Marriage and Family Life Among the Natives of the Trobriand Islands* (London: Routledge & Kegan Paul, 1952).

16. Annette Weiner, *Women of Value, Men of Renown: New Perspectives in Trobriand Exchange* (Austin: University of Texas Press, 1976).

17. Robert Briffault and Bronislaw Malinowski, *Marriage, Past and Present: A Debate Between Robert Briffault and Bronislaw Malinowski* (Boston: Porter Sargent, 1956).

18. Starhawk pointed out to me that in a society that denies the power of women, stories about a matriarchal past and Goddess worship can be psychologically beneficial to men as well as women. Nancy Chodorow once made a related point in a discussion with me, suggesting that belief in a Golden Age of matriarchy is intuitively appealing because it resonates with the individual histories of the vast majority of people, who as infants experienced a degree of closeness with their mothers that they never attained afterward with any person.

19. This view is put forward in the essays on "kinship" and "tribal society" in *A Dictionary of Marxist Thought*, ed. Tom Bottomore (London: Blackwell, 1983). On the relationship between hierarchies of class and of gender, see Christine Ward Gailey, "Evolutionary Perspectives on Gender Hierarchy," in *Analyzing Gender: A Handbook of Social Science Research*, ed. Beth B. Hess and Myra Marx Ferree (Newbury Park, Calif.: Sage, 1987); Eleanor Leacock and Mona Etienne, eds., *Women and Colonization* (New York: Praeger, 1980); Christine Ward Gailey, *Kinship to Kingship: Gender Hierarchy and State Formation in the Tongan Islands* (Austin: University of Texas Press, 1987); Karen Sacks, *Sisters and Wives: The Past and Future of Sexual Equality* (Westport, Conn.: Greenwood, 1929); Eleanor Leacock, *Myths of Male Dominance* (New York: Monthly Review Press, 1981); Ruby Rohrlich, "Women in Transition: Crete and Sumer," in *Becoming Visible: Women in European Society*, ed. Renate Bridenthal and Claudia Koonz (Boston: Houghton Mifflin, 1977); and Sherry Ortner, "The

Virgin and the State," *Feminist Studies* 4, no. 3 (October 1978): 19–36.

20. Françoise d'Eaubonne, *La Feminisme ou la mort* (Paris: P. Horay, 1974).

21. Susan Griffin, *Woman and Nature: The Roaring Inside Her* (New York: Harper & Row, 1978); Carolyn Merchant, *The Death of Nature: Women, Ecology and the Scientific Revolution: A Feminist Reappraisal of the Scientific Revolution* (New York: Harper & Row, 1980); Spretnak, ed., *Politics of Women's Spirituality;* Mary Daly, *Gyn/Ecology: The Meta-ethics of Radical Feminism* (Boston: Beacon, 1978); *Heresies: A Feminist Journal of Art and Politics,* February 1983; Adler, *Drawing Down the Moon;* Starhawk, *Dreaming the Dark.*

22. Max Horkheimer, *The Eclipse of Reason* (New York: Oxford University Press, 1947).

23. Ynestra King, "Feminism and the Revolt of Nature," *Heresies,* February 1983, 15.

24. Interview with Susan Cavin, September 3, 1987.

25. Interview with Ynestra King, July 6, 1987.

26. Starhawk, *Dreaming the Dark,* 180.

27. Interview with Charlotte Davis, February 22, 1987.

28. Interview with Nina Swain, July 5, 1987.

29. Interview with Houdini, October 22, 1984.

30. Interview with Ynestra King, April 1, 1987.

31. Several months after the 1982 action, Anna Kissed (also known as Robin Banks) of the Solar affinity group and the Feminist Cluster wrote a letter to the *LAG Rag* (at that time the name of the LAG newspaper, later *Direct Action*). The letter, printed in the November 1982 issue, attacked Christianity, "heterosexism," patriarchy, classism, and racism as structures that oppress women and seemed to call for female separatism. It provoked a number of letters in response, mostly from people who argued against blanket condemnation of religion, heterosexuality, or men. Several letters alluded to the Bible-burning incident in jail. In the January 1983 issue of *Direct Action* a letter from the Solar affinity group pointed out that Anna Kissed had expressed her own views and not any consensus of either Solar or the Feminist Cluster. The letter also said that many women in the cluster "had come to believe that there are actions to take in small tightly bonded groups and actions to take in coalitions. When we do work in coalitions we want to do so respectfully and in a spirit of solidarity."

32. Interview with Kate Hoffman, May 21, 1987.

33. Interview with Margot Adler.
34. Interview with Kate Hoffman.

Chapter 6

1. The best account of the history of religious pacifism in the United States is Lawrence S. Wittner, *Rebels Against War: The American Peace Movement, 1933–1983* (Philadelphia: Temple University Press, 1984), which includes an extensive account of the importance of religious pacifism in reviving the peace movement in the fifties in chapters 8 and 9.

2. Ibid., 257; also from my own recollections, as a member of the high school branch of Students for a Sane Nuclear Policy.

3. On the practice of nonviolent direct action in the early civil rights movement and the turn away from nonviolence in the mid-sixties, see Clayborne Carson, *In Struggle: SNCC and the Black Awakening of the 1960s* (Cambridge, Mass.: Harvard University Press, 1981).

4. The best source on MNS is their own newsletter, variously called *Dandelion Wine, Dandelion,* and *Wine,* and published by the Life Center, Philadelphia. My discussion of MNS and its role in the direct action movement is also drawn from several interviews with Fred Cook in San Francisco, in 1983 and 1984, and an interview with George Lakey in Philadelphia, February 8, 1985.

5. Interviews with Philip Berrigan, Ellen Grady, and Suzanne Schmidt, members of Jonah House, January 30, 1985.

6. The following account of the Pacific Life Community/Ground Zero is from an interview with Jim and Shelley Douglass, June 17, 1987.

7. For the White Train campaign, see Jim Douglass, "Tracking the White Train: People of Faith Resist the Rolling Threat," *Sojourners,* February 1984, 12–16, and the accounts of local actions in the same issue by Don Mosley (Comer, Georgia), Mary Harren (Wichita, Kansas), Clare Hanrahan (Memphis, Tennessee), Mary Dell Miles (Birmingham, Alabama), and Archbishop Raymond Hunthausen and Bishop Levy Methiesen (Amarillo, Texas).

8. My account of the history of Witness for Peace is based on interviews with David Sweet, April 14, 1987, and Ron Stief, May 6, 1987.

9. My discussion of trends within the Sanctuary movement is based on interviews with Gus Schultz, March 17, 1987, and Marilyn Chilcote, March 16, 1987. For an account of the movement from the

perspective of the Chicago group, see Rennie Golden and Michael McConnell, *Sanctuary: The New Underground Railroad* (Maryknoll, N.Y.: Orbis Books, 1987).

10. Interview with Ken Butigan, March 18, 1987.

11. Interview with Jim Rice, April 30, 1987.

12. Interview with Ron Stief.

13. Interview with David Cooper, April 13, 1987.

14. Robert McAfee Brown, *Theology in a New Key: Responding to Liberation Themes* (Philadelphia: Westminster Press, 1978) and *Unexpected News: Reading the Bible with Third World Eyes* (Philadelphia: Westminster Press, 1984).

15. Interview with Marilyn Chilcote.

16. Interview with Ron Stief.

17. Interview with Terry Messman, February 15, 1987.

18. Interview with Ken Butigan.

19. Interview with Philip Berrigan.

20. Interview with Carolyn Scarr, February 14, 1987.

21. Interview with Lee Williamson, February 26, 1987.

22. Interview with Ken Butigan.

23. Interview with Darla Rucker, February 3, 1987.

24. Interviews with Sherry Beville, March 10, 1987, and Frank Beville, March 4, 1987.

25. Interview with Will and Jane Lotter, March 23, 1987.

Chapter 7

1. For a classic statement of the pluralist view of American history, see Louis Hartz, *The Liberal Tradition in America: An Interpretation of American Political Thought Since the Revolution* (New York: Harcourt, Brace, 1955). Robert E. Brown, in *Middle Class Democracy and the Revolution in Massachusetts, 1691–1790* (Ithaca, N.Y.: Cornell University Press, 1955), finds a basis for pluralism in the economic and political structure of colonial New England. The liberal disenchantment with popular movements was expressed by Seymour Martin Lipset and Earl Raab, *The Politics of Unreason: Right Wing Extremism in America, 1790–1970* (New York: Harper & Row, 1973); Richard Hofstadter, *The Paranoid Style in American Politics and Other Essays* (New York: Knopf, 1965); Daniel Bell, *The End of Ideology: On the Exhaustion of Political Ideas in the Fifties* (Glencoe, Ill.: Free Press, 1960); Peter Viereck, *Shame and Glory of the Intellectuals: Babbitt, Jr., Versus the Rediscovery of Values* (Westport, Conn.: Greenwood, 1965); and Daniel Bell, ed., *The New American Right* (New York: Criterion, 1955),

in articles by Bell, Richard Hofstadter, David Riesman, Nathan Glazer, Peter Viereck, Talcott Parsons, Seymour Martin Lipset, and others.

2. This argument rested on the assumption that McCarthyism was best understood as a popular, antielitist movement, similar to the populist movement of the late nineteenth century. A large number of articles explored this theme in the fifties and early sixties. Richard Hofstadter's *Age of Reform: From Bryan to FDR* (New York: Vintage, 1951), included a serious and well-researched account of the populist movement, demonstrating that populism did contain strains of hostility to the cities, anti-Semitism, and anti-intellectualism; but Hofstadter did not explicitly link populism to McCarthyism. Where this connection was made, it was asserted rather than explored and there was no serious study of McCarthyism. Michael P. Rogin, on the basis of detailed studies of both movements, has argued in *The Intellectuals and McCarthy: The Radical Specter* (Cambridge, Mass.: MIT Press, 1967) that although both were strong in the Midwest, they were based on different constituencies; that whereas populism expressed the demands of poor farmers, McCarthyism was promoted by the elites of small and medium-size cities. Rogin also argues that whereas populism was a radical movement that challenged a privileged elite from the outside, McCarthyism was tacitly supported by the elite and collapsed only when elite interests, especially the media, withdrew their support. This critique of the pluralist view of McCarthyism was not an element of the debate during the fifties; in academic and other liberal intellectual circles, McCarthyism was widely seen as an example of what can go wrong when the irrational passions fostered by popular movements enter the political process, tamper with established processes, and challenge legitimate leadership.

3. See, for instance, Charles Tilly, *From Mobilization to Revolution* (Reading, Mass.: Addison Wesley, 1978).

4. William Gamson, *The Strategy of Social Protest* (Homewood, Ill.: Dorsey, 1975). Mancur Olson, Jr., *The Logic of Collective Action* (Cambridge, Mass.: Harvard University Press, 1965), first stated the view that rational choice was the basis for collective action. Other important statements of Resource Mobilization theory include John D. McCarthy and Mayer N. Zald, "Resource Mobilization and Social Movements: A Partial Theory," *American Journal of Sociology* 82 (May 1977): 1212–1241, and John D. McCarthy and Mayer N. Zald, *The Trends of Social Movements in America: Professionalization and Resource Mobilization* (Morristown, N.J.: General Learning Press, 1971).

5. An exception to this is Doug McAdam, *Political Process and the*

Development of Black Insurgency, 1930–1970 (Chicago: University of Chicago Press, 1982), which recognizes the importance of the transformation of consciousness in the development of the civil rights movement.

6. I am indebted to Noël Sturgeon in my understanding of the strengths and weaknesses of Resource Mobilization theory.

7. See Antonio Gramsci, "Americanism and Fordism," in *Selections from the Prison Notebooks of Antonio Gramsci,* ed. and trans., Quentin Hoare and Geoffrey Nowell Smith (New York: International, 1971).

8. See Gregory Calvert and Carol Nieman, "Socialist Consciousness and the New Left," *Guardian,* August 24, August 31, and September 7, 1968. The debate about the definition of the working class and its relation to social change is reviewed in Donald Hodges, "Old and New Working Classes," *Radical America* 5, no. 1 (January–February 1971): 11–32.

9. For the debate on housework and the status of women in Marxist theory, see Margaret Benston, "The Political Economy of Women's Liberation," *Monthly Review* 21, no. 4 (September 1969): 13–27. Mariarosa Calla Costa and Selma James, *The Power of Women and the Subversion of the Community* (Bristol: Falling Wall Press, 1975); Wally Seccombe, "The Housewife and Her Labour Under Capitalism," *New Left Review* 83 (January–February 1973): 3–24; Margaret Coulson, Branka Magas, and Hilary Wainwright, "The Housewife and Her Labour Under Capitalism—a Critique," *New Left Review* 89 (January–February 1975): 59–72; and Jean Gardiner, "Women's Domestic Labour," *New Left Review* 89 (January–February 1975): 47–58.

10. Alain Touraine, *The Post-Industrial Society: Tomorrow's Social History: Conflict and Culture in the Programmed Society* (New York: Random House, 1971).

11. André Gorz, *A New Strategy for Labor: A Radical Proposal* (Boston: Beacon, 1967).

12. Serge Mallet, *Essays on the New Working Class* (St. Louis: Telos Press, 1975).

13. Michel Aglietta, *A Theory of Capitalist Regulation: The U.S. Experience* (London: Verso, 1979), and "Phases of U.S. Capitalist Expansion," *New Left Review* 110 (1978). See also Mike Davis, " 'Fordism' in Crisis: A Review of Michel Aglietta's 'Regulation et crisis: L'experience des Etats-Unis,' " *Review* 2 (1978), and discussion of the political economy and politics of "late imperialist America" in the latter half of Mike Davis, *Prisoners of the American Dream* (London: Verso, 1981). Signs of impending economic crisis in the sixties are

discussed in Thomas Weisskopf, "The Current Economic Crisis in Historical Perspective," *Socialist Review* no. 57, vol. 11, no. 3 (May–June 1981): 9–54; and Arthur MacEwan, "International Economic Crisis and the Limits of Macropolicy," *Socialist Review* no. 59, vol. 11, no. 5 (November–December 1981): 13–138.

14. Samuel Bowles, David M. Gordon, and Thomas E. Weisskopf, *Beyond the Wasteland: A Democratic Alternative to Economic Decline* (New York: Anchor, 1983). See also Samuel Bowles and Herbert Gintis, *Democracy and Capitalism: Property, Community, and the Contradictions of Modern Social Thought* (New York: Basic, 1986).

15. For statements of New Social Movement theory, see Joachim Hirsch, "The Fordist Security State and the New Social Movements," *Kapitalistate,* nos. 10–11 (1983), 75–87; Alberto Melucci, "The New Social Movements: A Theoretical Approach," *Social Science Information* 19, no. 12 (1980); and Roland Roth, of the Department of Political Science, Free University of Berlin, "Fordism and New Social Movements" (conference paper, 1985). See also Joachim Hirsch, "The Apparatus of the State, the Reproduction of Capital, and Urban Conflicts," in *Urbanization and Urban Planning in Capitalist Society,* ed. Michael Dear and Allen Scott (New York: Methuen, 1981).

16. See Hirsch, "The Fordist Security State."

17. The idea of "a politics of daily life" was explored earlier by Karl E. Klare in "The Critique of Everyday Life, the New Left, and the Unrecognizable Marxism," in *The Unknown Dimension: European Marxism Since Lenin,* ed. Dick Howard and Karl E. Klare (New York: Basic, 1972). The idea of the construction of collective identity as an arena of political struggle has been explored by Michael Omi and Howard Winant, *Racial Formation in the United States from the 1960s to the 1980s* (New York: Routledge & Kegan Paul, 1986), and by Jeffrey Escoffier, "Sexual Revolution and the Politics of Gay Identity," *Socialist Review,* nos. 82/83, vol. 15, nos. 4–5 (July–October 1985): 119–153.

18. Alberto Melucci, "New Movements, Terrorism, and the Political System: Reflections on the Italian Case," *Socialist Review,* no. 56, vol. 11, no. 2 (March–April 1981): 97–136.

19. Alberto Melucci, "The Symbolic Challenge of Contemporary Movements," *Social Research* 52, no. 4 (Winter 1985): 789–816.

20. Carl Boggs, *Social Movements and Political Power: Emerging Forms of Radicalism in the West* (Philadelphia: Temple University Press, 1986) looks at the new movements in the United States and Western Europe from the perspective of new social movement theory. Noël Sturgeon's work on the political theory of the new movements is also

informed by this approach. There have also been efforts to extend Fordist and new social movement analysis to an understanding of the global economy and of movements in areas of the Third World. See Alan Lipietz, *Mirages and Miracles: The Crises of Global Fordism* (London: Verso, 1987); and André Gunder Frank and Marta Fuentes, "Nine Theses on Social Movements," *Economic and Political Weekly*, August 29, 1987, 1503–1510.

21. For evidence on the role of working-class support in achieving reform, see Thomas Byrne Edsall, *The New Politics of Inequality* (New York: Norton, 1984).

22. Fredric Jameson, "Postmodernism, or The Cultural Logic of Capitalism," *New Left Review* 146 (July/August 1984): 53–93. Jameson's use of the term "late capitalism" is influenced by the work of Ernest Mandel. The terms "Fordism" and "post-Fordism" refer to very much the same thing. Others prefer the term "postindustrialism." Although Alain Touraine initiated the use of that term, it has been adopted by the neoconservatives; Daniel Bell, for instance, relied on it in *The End of Ideology*. In general the term "late capitalism" is code for some degree of identification with Marxism; "Fordism" and "post-Fordism" for sympathy with the left, if not with Marxism per se; and "postindustrialism" for a neoconservative perspective.

23. Ernesto Laclau and Chantal Mouffe, *Hegemony and Socialist Strategy: Toward a Radical Democratic Politics* (London: Verso, 1985).

24. Ibid., 107.

25. For Habermas's critiques of the postmodernists and the neoconservatives, see Jürgen Habermas, *Autonomy and Solidarity: Interviews*, ed. Peter Dewes (London: Verso, 1986). See also Jürgen Habermas, "Neoconservative Culture Criticism in the United States and West Germany: An Intellectual Movement in Two Political Cultures"; Martin Jay, "Habermas and Postmodernism"; and Richard Rorty, "Habermas and Lyotard on Postmodernity," in *Habermas and Modernity*, ed. Richard J. Bernstein (Cambridge, Mass.: MIT Press, 1985).

26. Stuart Hall, *The Hard Road to Renewal: Thatcherism and the Crisis of the Left* (London: Verso, 1988), esp. Part 1, "The New Challenge of the Right."

27. Peter Glotz, "Forward to Europe: A Declaration for a New European Left," *Dissent*, Summer 1986, 335.

28. The idea that politics are being shaped by polarization between two sectors of the working population is employed by Stuart Hall, "The British Left After Thatcher," *Socialist Review* 92 (March–April 1987), and Bennett Harrison and Barry Bluestone in the con-

clusion to *The Great U-Turn: Corporate Restructuring and the Polarization of America* (New York: Basic, 1988). See also Michael Harrington, *The Next Left: The History of a Future* (New York: Holt, Rhinehart, 1987). This concept was pointed out to me (and to many others now using it) by Jim Schoch.

29. See Adam Przeworski, *Capitalism and Social Democracy* (Cambridge: Cambridge University Press, 1985).

Conclusion

1. Robert N. Bellah, Richard Madsden, William M. Sullivan, Ann Swidler, and Steven M. Tipton, *Habits of the Heart: Individualism and Commitment in American Life* (Berkeley and Los Angeles: University of California Press, 1985).

2. George Lakey, *Strategy for a Living Revolution* (New York: Grossman, 1973).

3. Joan V. Bondurant, *Conquest of Violence: The Ghandian Philosophy of Conflict* (Berkeley and Los Angeles: University of California Press, 1965).

4. Michael Walzer, *Spheres of Justice: A Defense of Pluralism and Equality* (New York: Basic, 1983).

5. Richard Flacks, *Making History: The Radical Tradition in American Life* (New York: Columbia University Press, 1988).

6. Ibid., 188–190.

Sources

This is a list of the sources I have drawn on in my account of nonviolent direct action in the United States in the 1970s and 1980s. I have not attempted an exhaustive list of sources for the philosophy of nonviolence or even for the history of nonviolent direct action generally, which would include the history of the civil rights movement of the 1960s. Nor have I listed sources for the other movements that have shaped the direct action movement (anarchism, feminism, civil rights, the New Left) except when they bear directly on the direct action movement itself.

My main source for this book has been interviews with activists. I have also drawn on written materials from the movement, including handbooks for particular actions, movement newspapers and newsletters, minutes of meetings, position papers, pamphlets, handouts, letters between activists, participants' written accounts of actions, and other such materials. Many activists generously allowed me to borrow their files; some lent me particularly extensive collections. I am especially grateful to Anna Gyorgy for giving me access to her records of the Clamshell Alliance; to Marcy Darnovsky for lending me her collection of *It's About Times,* which she edited; to Fred Cook for his collection of Movement for a New Society materials; and to Guy Chichester and Cathy Wolff for materials on the Clamshell Alliance. When the LAG office closed the staff offered to move their six filing cabinets of materials to my house. I regretfully turned down the offer.

It is difficult to give standard references for much of this material; little of it was published by mainstream presses, and most of it was not published by any press at all. The materials listed here are not likely to be available in any library; they can be found in the

305

basements and attics of movement activists. The books, pamphlets, and articles listed under "descriptions of actions" are the most like standard sources. The articles are in magazines that can be found in libraries; the books were published by presses (though many were movement presses that no longer exist). The handbooks are the best guides to the direct action movement. They were the movement's most important printed educational resources: they are collections of pieces about the movement's philosophy, structure, and approach to politics. Most of the handbooks were compiled by collectives, photocopied, and distributed by movement offices and affinity groups. They do not have conventional publishers, and their dates and places of publication can in general be inferred only from the action for which they were produced. Some give the address of an office from which they could be obtained; in most cases these offices no longer exist. All but a very few position papers were circulated as photocopies of the author's typescript. The minutes I have seen from movement meetings were also photocopies. What this all means is that the nonviolent direct action movement does not have archives that are readily available to the public.

Primary Sources

Interviews with Activists

Abalone Alliance staff (Rachel, Geoff, Brook), October 22, 1984, San Francisco

Margot Adler, July 4, 1987, Amherst, Mass.

Nancy Alach, May 21, 1987, Cambridge, Mass.

Andrea Ayvazian, July 1987, Amherst, Mass.

Aikos Barton, January 17, 1986, Santa Cruz, Calif.

Amy Bauer, August 8, 1987, New York

Richard Bell, June 7, 1985, Cambridge, Mass.

Philip Berrigan, January 30, 1985, Baltimore

Frank Beville, March 4, 1987, San Leandro, Calif.

Sherry Beville, March 10, 1987, San Leandro, Calif.

Elizabeth Boardman, June 8, 1985, Acton, Mass.

Murray Bookchin, May 26, 1986, Burlington, Vt.

Laura Booth, May 21, 1987, Cambridge, Mass.

Doris Bowles, October 18, 1984, Berkeley, Calif.

Jerene Broadway, March 3, 1987, San Francisco

Carol Brown, December 12, 1989, Berkeley, Calif.

Jeff Brummer, June 9, 1985, Brookline, Mass.

Stewart Burns, October 10, 1983, Santa Cruz, Calif.
Ken Butigan, February 13 and March 18, 1987, Oakland, Calif.
Jackie Cabasso, February 27 and March 3, 1987, Oakland, Calif.
Larry Casalino, June 28, 1989, Berkeley, Calif.
Susan Cavin, September 3, 1987, New York
Bob Chastain, April 13, 1987, Berkeley, Calif.
Guy Chichester, August 24, 1985, Rye, N.H.
Marilyn Chilcote, March 16, 1987, Berkeley, Calif.
Dick Clark, February 22, 1987, San Francisco
Fred Cook, November 17 and December 5, 1983; January 11, 1984, San Francisco
David Cooper, April 13, 1987, Berkeley, Calif.
Nancy Culver, April 22, 1987, San Luis Obispo, Calif.
Pat Daane, November 14, 1984, Piedmont, Calif.
Marcy Darnovsky, February 14, 1987, Berkeley, Calif.
Charlotte Davis, February 22, 1987, San Francisco
Patrick Diehl, October 28, 1983, Berkeley, Calif.
Jim Douglass, June 17, 1987, Poulsbo, Wash.
Shelley Douglass, June 17, 1987, Poulsbo, Wash.
Mark Evanoff, October 28, 1984, San Francisco
Arlene Feng, March 26, 1984, Oakland, Calif.
Raye Fleming, April 21, 1987, San Luis Obispo, Calif.
Erica Fox, August 5, 1984, Berkeley, Calif.
Ellen Grady, January 30, 1985, Baltimore
Anna Graves, June 14, 1984, Berkeley, Calif.
Crystal Gray, October 3, 1985, Santa Cruz, Calif.
Anna Gyorgy, January 26, 1985, Turner Falls, Mass.
Barbara Haber, October 16, 1984, Berkeley, Calif.
Harvey Halpern, August 25, 1985, Cambridge, Mass.
David Hartsough, November 8, 1984, San Francisco
Chaya Heller, July 5, 1987, Amherst, Mass.
Martha Henderson, November 18, 1984, Berkeley, Calif.
Kate Hoffman, May 21, 1987, Cambridge, Mass.
Joyce Howarton, April 21, 1987, San Luis Obispo, Calif.
Houdini, October 22, 1984, San Francisco
Jackrabbit, February 17, 1987, San Francisco
Shelley Kellman, May 22, 1987, Brookline, Mass.
Scott Kennedy, February 21, 1987, Santa Cruz, Calif.
Ynestra King, April 1 and September 8, 1987, New York; July 6, 1987, Amherst, Mass.
Peter Klotz-Chamberlain, February 12, 1987, Santa Cruz, Calif.
Steve Ladd, November 10, 1984, Oakland, Calif.

George Lakey, February 8, 1985, Philadelphia
Susan Lawrence, October 24, 1984, Berkeley, Calif.
Steven Leeds, November 1, 1984, San Francisco
Cindy Leerer, August 25, 1985, Portsmouth, N.H.
Barbara Levy, November 3, 1984, San Francisco
Andrew Lichterman, February 26, 1987, Oakland, Calif.
Jane Lotter, March 23, 1987, Davis, Calif.
Will Lotter, March 23, 1987, Davis, Calif.
Sam Lovejoy, January 26, 1985, Montague, Mass.
Pam McAllister, August 8, 1987, New York
Joan McIntyre, October 29, 1984, Berkeley, Calif.
Karen Malpede, July 5, 1987, Amherst, Mass.
Terry Messman, November 23, 1983; February 15 and March 17, 1987, Berkeley, Calif.
Catherine Morris, March 28, 1987, Los Angeles
Bill Moyer, March 1987, San Francisco
Osha Neumann, November 4, 1983; January 28 and February 6, 1990, Berkeley, Calif.
Ken Nightingale, September 5, 1985, Berkeley, Calif.
Bill O'Donnell, February 15, 1987, Berkeley, Calif.
Pamela Osgood, October 17, 1983, Berkeley, Calif.
Robbie Osman, September 28, 1983; January 29, 1990, Berkeley, Calif.
Grace Paley, July 5, 1987, Amherst, Mass.
Eve Ann Pearson, October 27, 1984, Walnut Creek, Calif.
Tommy Reynaldo, January 31, 1987, San Francisco
Jim Rice, April 30, 1987, Washington, D.C.
Vicki Rovere, August 8, 1987, New York
Darla Rucker, November 9, 1983, Berkeley, Calif.; February 3 and 23, 1987, Oakland, Calif.
Howard Ryan, October 9, 1984, Oakland, Calif.
Carolyn Scarr, February 14, 1987, Berkeley, Calif.
Suzanne Schmidt, January 30, 1985, Baltimore
Gus Schultz, March 17, 1987, Berkeley, Calif.
Cynthia Sharp, November 1984, Berkeley, Calif.
Sandy Silver, April 21, 1987, San Luis Obispo, Calif.
Meg Simonds, November 13, 1984; November 2, 1985, Bolinas, Calif.
Ann Snitow, August 8, 1987, New York
Norman Solomon, February 23, 1985, Nyack, N.Y.
Starhawk, September 26, 1983, Berkeley, Calif.; March 27, 1987, San Francisco
Ron Stief, May 6, 1987, Berkeley, Calif.
Doddi Stone, March 24, 1987, Berkeley, Calif.

Noël Sturgeon, October 31, 1984, Santa Cruz, Calif.
Steven Sutcher, June 14, 1984, Berkeley, Calif.
Nina Swaim, July 5, 1987, Norwich, Vt.; telephone interview
David Sweet, April 14, 1987, Santa Cruz, Calif.
Susan Swift, October 20, 1984, Berkeley, Calif.
Diane Thomas, July 1984, Berkeley, Calif.
Tamara Thompson, March 26, 1984, Oakland, Calif.
Tom Tiller, June 1984, Berkeley, Calif.
Brian Tokar, April 23, 1987, Berkeley, Calif.
Sharon Tracy, August 24, 1985, Portsmouth, N.H.
Ginna Vogt, July 6, 1987, Amherst, Mass.
Kate Walker, June 9, 1987, Brookline, Mass.
Liz Walker, September 19, 1983; October 5, 1984, San Francisco
Diana Wear, May 3, 1987, Berkeley, Calif.
Lee Williamson, February 26, 1987, San Francisco
Cathy Wolff, August 25, 1985, Portsmouth, N.H.

*Newspapers, Newsletters, and Journals
of the Direct Action Movement*

Against the Grain: Black Rose. Anarchist newspaper. Stanford, Calif., 1979.

Aurora: Feminist Newspaper for the Stanford Community. 1979.

Clamshell Alliance News. Published by the Clamshell Alliance. Portsmouth, N.H., 1977–1979.

Comment: New Perspectives in Libertarian Thought. Edited by Murray Bookchin, Hoboken, N.J.

The Dandelion: Newsletter of the Movement for a New Society. At times called *Dandelion Wine* and *Wine.* Philadelphia, approximately 1972–1980.

Direct Action. Newspaper published by the Livermore Action Group. Berkeley, Calif., approximately 1981–1984.

Ground Zero. Center for Nonviolent Action. Poulsbo, Wash.

It's About Times: Abalone Alliance Newspaper. San Francisco, January 1979–March/April 1985.

No Nukes Left! A Political Journal for the Anti-Nuclear Movement. Amherst, Mass., 1980.

Reclaiming Newsletter. Published by Reclaiming: A Center for Feminist Spirituality and Counseling, San Francisco.

Handbooks

We Can Stop the Seabrook Nuclear Plant: Occupier's Handbook. Join Us, April 30. Clamshell Alliance, April 30, 1977.

Moyer, William. *A Nonviolent Action Manual: How to Organize Nonvi-*

olent Demonstrations and Campaigns. Philadelphia: New Society Press, 1977.

Seabrook '78: A Handbook for the Occupation/Restoration Beginning June 24. Portsmouth, N.H.: Clamshell Alliance, 1978.

Handbook for the Land and Sea Blockade of the Seabrook Reactor Pressure Vessel. Clamshell Alliance, 1979.

Let's Shut Down Seabrook! Handbook for the Oct. 6, 1979, Direct Action Occupation. Cambridge, Mass.: Clams for Direct Action at Seabrook, 1979.

Up Against the Wall Street Journal: 50th Anniversary of the Stock Market Crash of 1929. Training Handbook, the Wall Street Action, Oct. 29, 1979. New York and Seabrook, N.H.: The Manhattan Project (with the assistance of the Clamshell Alliance and the War Resister's League), 1979. The Manhattan Project was a project of the Clamshell Alliance.

It Won't Be Built! Seabrook, May 24, 1980 Occupation/Blockade Handbook. Cambridge, Mass.: Clams for Direct Action at Seabrook, 1980.

Direct Action Handbook: Blockade Diablo Canyon, 1979–80. San Francisco: American Friends Service Committee, for Abalone Alliance, 1980.

Diablo Canyon Blockade/Encampment Book. Santa Cruz: Waller Press, 1981.

Livermore Weapons Lab Blockade/Demonstration Handbook, June 21, 1982. Berkeley, Calif.: Livermore Action Group, 1982.

International Day of Nuclear Disarmament June 1983 Action Handbook. Berkeley, Calif.: Livermore Action Group, 1983.

San Francisco Hall of Shame Handbook. Berkeley, Calif.: Livermore Action Group, February 16, 1983.

The Vandenberg Action: A Handbook for Nonviolent Direct Action. Berkeley, Calif.: Livermore Action Group, 1983.

Women's Encampment for a Future of Peace and Justice: Resource Handbook. Summer 1983, Seneca Army Depot. Handbook Committee of the Women's Encampment for a Future of Peace and Justice, 1983.

Stop the Bomb! Site 300 Occupation. A Handbook for Site 300 Nonviolent Direct Actions, Dec. 3–7, 1984, April 1985. San Francisco: Site 300 Working Group, 1984.

Action Handbook: Nevada Test Site, May 8–10, 1987. Prepared by Noël Sturgeon and Sara Shapiro. Santa Cruz, 1987.

Minutes and Other Internal Materials

Clamshell Alliance Coordinating Committee. Minutes, April 1977–June 1978.

Direct Action Occupations: The Orange Proposal. Clams for Democracy Statement. A pamphlet produced and distributed by the Hard Rain affinity group of the Clamshell Alliance, Somerville, Mass., 1979.

"Goal of Clamshell: Stopping Nukes and Creating a Better World." No date. Mimeographed paper in Anna Gyorgy's archives.

O/RTF (Occupation/Restoration Task Force, Clamshell Alliance). Minutes, January 1978.

"On Process and Policy: A Position Paper by the Spruce Mountain Affinity Group of the Green Mountain Alliance, Plainfield, Vermont." 1978. Spruce Mountain was also an affinity group of the Clamshell Alliance.

Ryan, Howard. "Blocking Progress: Consensus Decision-Making in the Anti-Nuclear Movement." Overthrow Cluster of the Livermore Action Group, Berkeley, Calif., 1983.

"Strange Victories: The Anti-Nuclear Movement in the U.S. and Europe." Midnight Notes Collective, affinity group of the Clamshell Alliance, Boston, 1979.

Vandenberg Coalition. Minutes, 1983.

Descriptions of Actions

Allport, Catherine G. *We Are the Web: The Women's Encampment for a Future of Peace and Justice, Romulus, New York, 1983.* New York: Artemis Project, 1984. A collection of photographs of the encampment.

Cabasso, Jackie, and Susan Moon. *Risking Peace: Why We Sat in the Road.* Berkeley, Calif.: Open Books, 1985.

"The Diablo Blockade." *It's About Times,* October–November 1981.

Johnson, Lynn. "Weaving a Web of Life: Women's Pentagon Action, 1981." *WIN,* January 15, 1982.

1981 Diablo Canyon Blockade: An Illustrated Anthology of Articles, Essays, Poems and Personal Experiences. Santa Cruz, Calif.: Diablo Writing Project, 1983.

Pines, Susan. "Women's Pentagon Action." *WRL News [War Resister's League],* January–February 1981.

Rosenblith, Murray. "Surrounded by Acres of Clams." *WIN* 13, nos. 21–22 (July 16–23, 1977): 4–10.

"Seabrook 2." *WIN* 13, nos. 21–22 (July 16–23, 1977). Articles about the 1977 Seabrook occupation.

We Are Ordinary Women: A Chronicle of the Puget Sound Women's Peace Camp. By participants of the Puget Sound Women's Peace Camp. Seattle: Seal Press, 1985.

Books, Articles, and Pamphlets

Adler, Margot. *Drawing Down the Moon: Witches, Druids, Goddess-Worshippers and Other Pagans in America Today.* Boston: Beacon, 1979.

Anarchism and Feminism: Three Essays '75–'80. Peggy Kornegger, "Anarchism, the Feminist Connection," 1–19. Zero Collective, "Anarcha/Feminism," 20–24. Kytha Kurin, "Anarcha-Feminism: Why the Hyphen?" 25–36. Brisbane: Brickburner Press, 1981.

Anarcho-Feminism: Two Statements. Black Bear Pamphlet no. 1. "Who We Are: An Anarcho-Feminist Manifesto," 1–2. "Blood of the Flower: An Anarcho-Feminist Statement," 3–5. Both by Red Rosia and Black Maria, Black Rose Anarcho-Feminists. No date.

Black Rose 1, no. 3 (Fall 1979). See esp. Rudy Perkins, "Breaking with Libertarian Dogma: Lessons from the Anti-Nuclear Struggle," 8–24; and Chris Hables Gray, "The New Libertarians," 29–39.

Daly, Mary. *Gyn/Ecology: The Metaphysics of Radical Feminism.* Boston: Beacon, 1982.

Ehrlich, Carol. *Socialism, Anarchism and Feminism.* London: Black Bear, September 1978.

Evanoff, Mark. "Once upon an Earthquake Fault." *It's About Times,* November–mid-December 1980.

Gyorgy, Anna, and friends. *No Nukes: Everyone's Guide to Nuclear Power.* Boston: South End, 1979.

Jezer, Marty. "Learning from the Past to Meet the Future." *WIN,* June 16–23, 1977, 17–23.

Kennedy, Scott. "Civil Disobedience and Legal Strategy." *WIN,* June 28, 1979, 5–15.

King, Ynestra. "Feminism and the Revolt of Nature." *Heresies: A Feminist Journal of Art and Politics,* February 1983, 11–15.

Lakey, George. *Strategy for a Living Revolution.* New York: Grossman, 1973.

Levine, Cathy. *The Tyranny of Tyranny.* London: Dark Star Distribution Service, no date. Originally published in *Black Rose,* no. 1.

Murray, Margaret. *The Witch Cult in Western Europe.* Oxford: Oxford University Press, 1921.

Reweaving the Web of Life: Feminism and Nonviolence. Edited by Pam McAllister. Philadelphia: New Society Publishers, 1982.

Sheehan, Joanne. "The Changing Nature of CD Trainings." *Nonviolent Activist: Magazine of the War Resister's League* (March 1986): 3–10.

Sojourners, February 1984. Accounts of the White Train campaign, esp. Jim Douglass, "Tracking the White Train: People of Faith Resist the Rolling Threat."

Charlene Spretnak, ed. *The Politics of Women's Spirituality: Essays on the Rise of Spiritual Power Within the Feminist Movement.* New York: Anchor, 1982.

Starhawk. *Dreaming the Dark: Magic, Sex and Politics.* Boston: Beacon, 1982.

————. *The Spiral Dance: A Rebirth of the Ancient Religion of the Great Goddess.* San Francisco: Harper & Row, 1979.

————. *Truth or Dare: Encounters with Power, Authority, and Mystery.* San Francisco: Harper & Row, 1987.

An Account from the Other Side

Daubert, Victoria L., and Sue Ellen Moran. *A Rand Note: Origins, Goals, and Tactics of the U.S. Anti-Nuclear Protest Movement.* Prepared for the Sandia National Laboratories. Santa Monica, Calif.: Rand Corporation, March 1985.

Secondary Sources

Boggs, Carl. *Social Movements and Political Power: Emerging Forms of Radicalism in the West.* Philadelphia: Temple University Press, 1986.

Bondurant, Joan V. *Conquest of Violence: The Gandhian Philosophy of Conflict.* Berkeley and Los Angeles: University of California Press, 1967.

Boyer, Paul. "From Activism to Apathy: The American People and Nuclear Weapons, 1963–1980." *Journal of American History* 70, no. 4 (March 1984): 821–844.

Brenner, Johanna. "Beyond Essentialism: Feminist Theory and Strategy in the Peace Movement." In *Reshaping the US Left: Popular Struggles in the 1980s,* edited by Mike Davis and Michael Sprinker. London: Verso, 1988. 93–113.

Chatfield, Charles. *For Peace and Justice: Pacifism in America, 1914–1941.* Knoxville: University of Tennessee Press, 1971.

Cooney, Robert, and Helen Michalowski, eds. *The Power of the People: Active Nonviolence in the United States.* Culver City, Calif.: Peace Press, 1977.

Darnovsky, Marcy. "Direct Action as Living Theater in the Movement Against Nuclear Power." Unpublished paper, University of California, Santa Cruz, 1989.

Epstein, Barbara. "The Politics of Prefigurative Community: The Nonviolent Direct Action Movement." In *Reshaping the US Left: Popular Struggles in the 1980s,* edited by Mike Davis and Michael Sprinker. London: Verso, 1988. 63–92.

Fitzsimmons, Margaret, and Robert Gottlieb. "A New Environmental Politics." In *Reshaping the US Left: Popular Struggles in the 1980s,* edited by Mike Davis and Michael Sprinker. London: Verso, 1988. 114–131.

Golden, Rennie, and Michael McConnell. *Sanctuary: The New Underground Railroad.* Maryknoll, N.Y.: Orbis Books, 1987.

Hayes, Lois. "Separatism and Disobedience: The Seneca Women's Peace Encampment." *Radical America* 17, no. 4 (July–August 1983): 55–64.

Isserman, Maurice. *If I Had a Hammer: The Death of the Old Left and the Birth of the New Left.* New York: Basic, 1987.

Jezer, Marty. "Who's on First? What's on Second? A Grassroots Political Perspective on the Anti-Nuclear Movement." *WIN,* October 12, 1978, 5–12.

Kirkpatrick, R. George. "Feminist Witchcraft and Pagan Peace Protest: Sociology of Religious Counter-Cultures and Social Movement Intersections." Paper read at the meeting of the American Sociological Association, San Antonio, Texas, August 24, 1984.

Katz, Neil H. "Radical Pacifism and the Contemporary American Peace Movement: The Committee for Nonviolent Action, 1957–1967." Ph.D. dissertation, University of Maryland, 1974.

Loeb, Paul Rogat. *Hope in Hard Times: America's Peace Movement and the Reagan Era.* Lexington, Mass.: Lexington Books, 1987.

Loffland, John, Mary Anna Colwell, and Victoria Johnson. *Peace-Seeking: The American Peace Movement in the Eighties.* Rutgers, N.J.: Rutgers University Press, 1991.

Mayer, Margit, ed. *The New Social Movements in Western Europe and the United States.* London: Unwin & Hyman, 1991.

Meyerding, Jane, ed. *We Are All Part of One Another: A Barbara Deming Reader.* Philadelphia: New Society Publishers, 1984.

O'Brien, Jim. "Environmentalism as a Mass Movement: Historical Notes." *Radical America* 17, nos. 1–2 (May–June 1983): 7–27.

Robinson, Jo Ann Ooiman. *Abraham Went Out: A Biography of A. J. Muste.* Philadelphia: Temple University Press, 1981.

Sesachari, C. *Gandhi and the American Scene: An Intellectual History and Inquiry.* Bombay: Nachiketa, 1969.

Sturgeon, Noël. "Opposition in Action: The U.S. Nonviolent Direct Action Movement." Unpublished paper, University of California, Santa Cruz, 1989.

Trinkl, John. "Struggles for Disarmament in the USA." In *Reshaping the US Left: Popular Struggles in the 1980s,* edited by Mike Davis and Michael Sprinker. London: Verso, 1988. 51–62.

Wittner, Lawrence S. *Rebels Against War: The American Peace Movement, 1933–1983.* Philadelphia: Temple University Press, 1984.

Index

Abalone Alliance, 7, 98–99; consensus process in, 93, 101–2; contribution to nonviolent direct action movement, 93; decline of, 104–6, 117–24; growing pains of, 101–2; modeled on the Clamshell, 11, 92; "new Abalones," 106, 108; "old Abalones," 106, 107, 115; origin of name, 97. *See also* Diablo, actions against; Diablo Blockade (1981)

Abzug, Bella, 164

Activism: reasons for decline of, 46–47; socioeconomic factors in, 146–47

Act Up, 183

Adler, Margot, 170, 172, 175, 176, 189–90

Affinity groups, 3, 9, 66, 67; attractive to feminists and Christians, 188; autonomy of in LAG, 126; membership in a requirement, 65, 131; prior use of, 66, 98; villages or clusters of, 3, 65, 130

Agape Community, 202–3

Aglietta, Michel, 237, 247

AIDS-related protests, 166, 183

Alliance for Survival, 101

American Federation of Labor (AFL), 25

American Friends Service Committee (AFSC). *See* Quakers

Anarcha-feminism: in Abalone, 95–96, 108–13; critique of dominance, 168; roots and ideology of, 167–70. *See also* Black Rose; Hard Rain; Militancy; Paganism; Witchcraft

Anarchism: conflict with militant political strategy, 93; impulse toward in nonviolent direct action movement, 6, 17, 69, 252, 269; role of in LAG, 138, 139–41

Anarchist/utopian democracy, 117–24

Antielitism, 94, 115

Anti-intervention movement, 13, 154; emphasis on human rights, 275. *See also* Pledge of Resistance; Sanctuary movement; Witness for Peace

Antinuclear Civil Disobedience Community (ACDC): in Diablo blockade, 110–11

Antinuclear movement: emergence of, 82–83. *See also* Abalone Alliance; Christian nonviolent direct actions; Clamshell Alliance; Livermore Action Group (LAG)

Antiwar movement, 4–5, 11, 14, 36

Atlantic Life Community, 201

Atomic Energy Commission (AEC), 96

Authoritarianism: in movements, 44, 141

Authoritarian populism, 255

Backcountry actions, 110–11, 113, 132

Balloons for peace, 163

Bangor Trident Base: train vigils against, 201–3

Bardemaeus, 220–21

Bay Area Rapid Transit (BART): action on, 143–44

Bell, Dick, 74, 88–89

Berkeley City Council, 144

Berrigan, Philip, 134, 200

Beville, Sherry, 221–22

Bible burning, 186–87

Black Panthers, 44

Black Power, 198

317

Compositor: Maple-Vail Book Manufacturing Group
     Text: 10½/13 Baskerville
  Display: Baskerville
  Printer: Maple-Vail Book Manufacturing Group
   Binder: Maple-Vail Book Manufacturing Group